REVOLUTIONARY SPIRIT

The **Institute of Southeast Asian Studies (ISEAS)** was established as an autonomous organization in 1968. It is a regional centre dedicated to the study of socio-political, security and economic trends and developments in Southeast Asia and its wider geostrategic and economic environment. The Institute's research programmes are the Regional Economic Studies (RES, including ASEAN and APEC), Regional Strategic and Political Studies (RSPS), and Regional Social and Cultural Studies (RSCS).

ISEAS Publishing, an established academic press, has issued more than 2,000 books and journals. It is the largest scholarly publisher of research about Southeast Asia from within the region. ISEAS Publishing works with many other academic and trade publishers and distributors to disseminate important research and analyses from and about Southeast Asia to the rest of the world.

REVOLUTIONARY SPIRIT
JOSE RIZAL IN SOUTHEAST ASIA

JOHN NERY

WITH A FOREWORD BY F. SIONIL JOSE
MAGSAYSAY AWARDEE FOR LITERATURE, JOURNALISM AND COMMUNICATION ARTS

INSTITUTE OF SOUTHEAST ASIAN STUDIES
Singapore

First published in Singapore in 2011 by ISEAS Publishing
Institute of Southeast Asian Studies
30 Heng Mui Keng Terrace
Pasir Panjang
Singapore 119614

E-mail: publish@iseas.edu.sg
Website: <http://bookshop.iseas.edu.sg>

All rights reserved. No part of this publication may be reproduced, stored in a retrieval system, or transmitted in any form or by any means, electronic, mechanical, photocopying, recording or otherwise, without the prior permission of the Institute of Southeast Asian Studies.

© 2011 Institute of Southeast Asian Studies, Singapore

The responsibility for facts and opinions in this publication rests exclusively with the author and his interpretations do not necessarily reflect the views or the policy of the publisher or its supporters. E-mail the author at: joserizal150@gmail.com.

ISEAS Library Cataloguing-in-Publication Data

Nery, John.
Revolutionary spirit : Jose Rizal in Southeast Asia.
1. Rizal, Jose, 1861–1896—Criticism and interpretation.
2. Philippines—History—1812–1898.
3. Nationalism—Philippines—History.
4. Nationalism—Southeast Asia—History.
I. Title.
DS675.8 R5N45   2011

ISBN 978-981-4345-05-7 (soft cover)
ISBN 978-981-4345-07-1 (hard cover)
ISBN 978-981-4345-06-4 (e-book, PDF)

Cover art: "Blot and Splatter" by Bixie Reyes, Manila
Typeset by Superskill Graphics Pte Ltd, Singapore
Printed in Singapore by Markono Print Media Pte Ltd

*For my father and mother
their eightieth*

What [the indio] lacks in the first place is liberty to allow expansion for his adventurous spirit and good examples, beautiful prospects for the future. It is necessary that his spirit, although it may be dismayed and cowed by the elements and the fearful manifestations of their mighty forces, store up energy, seek lofty purposes, in order to struggle against the obstacles in the midst of unfavourable natural conditions. In order that he may progress, it is necessary that a revolutionary spirit, so to speak, should stir in his veins, since progress necessarily requires change, implies the overthrow of the past and there deified by the present, the victory of new ideas over old and accepted ones.

Rizal in *La Solidaridad,* 15 September 1890
(Guadalupe Fores-Ganzon translation)

Contents

Foreword
by
F. Sionil Jose
xi

Message
xv

Preface
xvii

Acknowledgements
xxi

INTRODUCTION
The Uses of Error
A Rizal Chronology
1

1

TURNING POINTS
46

2

"THE VERY SOUL OF THIS REBELLION"
69

3
DOCTOR RIZAL
87

4
"*HALFBLOED*"
103

5
"NO MARX OR LENIN"
122

6
UNDER THE SOUTHERN SUN
143

7
THE HOPE OF MILLIONS IN ASIA
161

8
"HIS NAME IS SWEET IN OUR MEMORY"
172

9
THE MYTH BUSTERS
190

10
"A GREAT HISTORICAL EXPERIMENT"
213

Epilogue
231

Appendices
A: A Man of Letters
B: Falling for the American Trap
C: "Colour and Scent, Light and Sound"
235

References
257

Index
271

Foreword

On the 150th birth anniversary of Rizal, the publication of this stringently researched study enables us to relate with more conviction our pride in having a novelist lay down the firmest and most durable foundation of the Filipino nation. With the journalist's eagle eye, John Nery traces that influence which Rizal wields in Southeast Asia to this very day, when the enduring vestiges of colonialism are still so much a determinant of our future. Rizal did this with his pen as well as with his life; as the American literary scholar Roland Greene said, "he was the first post-colonial writer".

Nery's search confirms the prescience, the brilliance and profundity of Rizal's thinking as also expressed in his letters and articles. For instance, and this has not been clearly understood by many of those who studied his life, though seemingly opposed to revolution Rizal among the early Filipinos who railed against Spanish colonialism was in fact one of its first and staunchest believers.

But it is his novels, his literary creations which gave Rizal his marmoreal reputation; it is to Rizal's credit that he elected to use the literary art. He could just have published those manifestos, those inciting articles as did his colleagues in the Propaganda Movement. But he chose literature to magnify and broadcast his deepest feelings, his dreams for his unhappy country. He saw that literature — the noblest of the arts — would prevail long after the fact, that it is literature that renders history alive.

So many scholars miss this significant distinction; like so many illiterate Filipino leaders, they do not regard novelists and their fictions as the truest building blocks in the foundation of a nation. All too often, when they exalt Rizal, they forget it is the committed writers who are his real heirs.

Nery discusses yet another novelist who influenced Rizal. In 1860, Eduard Douwes Dekker (pen name: Multatuli), who had served in the Dutch East Indies (now Indonesia), published *Max Havelaar, Or the Coffee Auctions of a Dutch Trading Company,* in Amsterdam. Rizal wrote to his friend Ferdinand Blumentritt how he envied Multatuli whose novel was "so viciously anti-colonial — but was so beautiful". Two generations later, in that very same setting of Multatuli's fiction, two Indonesians — the Founding Father of Indonesia, Sukarno, and that country's foremost novelist, Pramoedya Ananta Toer — also read Rizal.

All too often, writers are judged and admired only for their work. Their peccadilloes, their sins are glossed over by the very fact that their being writers can wipe away their moral lapses. This should not be; writers should also be judged by how they act out their values. If this measure were applied to Rizal, there is no doubt that his resonance and his glitter would even be wider and brighter. As a person, he brimmed with goodwill, compassion and virtue though he was always critical of the vices of his colleagues and countrymen. Unfortunately, such influence did not instruct his foremost Indonesian admirers. Sukarno and his ally Pramoedya oppressed their political critics when both were at the height of their power. Pramoedya burned the books of the writers he didn't like and withheld jobs from them. Likewise, in the Philippines, Ferdinand Marcos and some of the writers who pandered to him extolled Rizal in their speeches but did not follow his humane example as they, too, oppressed writers who criticized them.

Rizal envisioned a just society after the revolution — not the authoritarian regimes that followed, particularly in Southeast Asia. Understand this sequence after the upheaval — chaos first, then iron order, and the darkest night during which Rizal was martyred before that dawn.

The controversies surrounding Rizal's last days in prison continue to this very day. Some think he turned his back on the very ideas he espoused. Nery repeats how Rizal wanted to go to Cuba to work, not on the side of the Cubans who were waging their revolution against Spain, but for the Spaniards. He also recounts Rizal's least known evasions at his trial, the contrary manifesto which he wrote denying the revolution. Indeed, although his biographer Austin Coates said that Rizal did not retract Masonry as claimed by the Jesuits, I can even believe that he did. Poor man — he tried desperately to save himself.

Remember, he returned to the Philippines to pursue the dreams he knew wouldn't be realized if he lingered in Europe. He could have stayed there or elsewhere and would have fared handsomely because he was a doctor and already had an excellent practice in Hong Kong. But patriotism is selfless; no patriot is ever safe or comfortable — he transcends the ego, he gives himself freely, affectionately to the earth — the nation — which sustains him. Rizal couldn't undo his own heroism; by writing those two novels where he expressed his truest feelings, he sealed his fate.

Rizal is read not just in Southeast Asia but, I am sure, more widely in Spanish South America. His *Last Farewell* is included in so many anthologies of Spanish poetry, it is memorized by so many.

In his own country, he should have the most and lasting impact. Every town plaza is adorned by his monument, each main street bears his name. And the Rizal industry continues to thrive, churning out so many books and myriad forms of hossana. But like the rice we eat, Filipinos have made him a mundane habit.

Sure, Rizal is one Indio who is now read universally, translated as he is in so many languages. This knowledge is comforting to Filipinos, a form of national narcotic even. But let us now nurture in our very bones those beliefs that Rizal — the Malay paragon — lived and died for.

F. Sionil Jose

Message

19 June 2011 is the 150th anniversary of Jose Rizal's birth. Rizal was a patriot, poet, novelist, scholar and artist. Through his writings, he galvanized the Filipino people into a nation that resisted continued colonization by Spain, although he himself emphasized the difficult tasks of preparation and education, the essential conditions, as he saw them, for personal freedom and national independence. It is because of this that he has been called "the first Filipino".

However, Rizal's influence went beyond the Philippine archipelago. It radiated to other parts of Southeast Asia, inspiring their peoples on the possibilities of hoping and struggling for freedom and independence. Thus, he has also been called "the pride of the Malay race".

It is for this reason that the Institute of Southeast Asian Studies decided to commission and publish this book on Rizal, one not so much on Rizal as a person or his place in the Philippines' history, but on his role on the larger stage of Southeast Asia, at a time when the countries of the region were struggling both against their colonizers and to define themselves as nations.

In this endeavour, ISEAS has asked John Nery to write on Rizal from the point of view of his influence on the rise of nationalism and the movement for independence in Southeast Asia. John is a young Filipino journalist and, therefore, can be depended upon to regard Rizal with a fresh eye and share with us his "take" on Rizal's impact on Southeast Asia in a style that both regales and illumines.

K. Kesavapany
Director
Institute of Southeast Asian Studies
Singapore

Preface

In 1986, when Goenawan Mohamad, the prominent Indonesian journalist, was prompted by the post-election turmoil in the Philippines in the last days of Ferdinand Marcos to write an essay on Jose Rizal, he drew a portrait of a conflicted, upper-class thinker, an "anxious Rizal [who] was not the type who would usually go on to become a hero" (Goenawan 2005: 192). A quarter of a century later, when Carlos Celdran, an enterprising social activist, wanted to protest the Catholic Church's position on the ongoing reproductive health debate in the Philippines, he simply went up the steps to the altar at the Manila Cathedral and held up a sign with a single word, a name, on it: "Damaso". He was referencing a corrupt friar from Rizal's first novel, the *Noli Me Tangere*.

I find that the relative silence, even silent agreement, with which Goenawan's sketch will be received by college-educated Filipinos even today, and the enormous uproar that immediately greeted Celdran's protest, effectively define the parameters of this study into Rizal's influence in Southeast Asia. The philosophical Goenawan subscribes to the common mistake of an indecisive Rizal, perhaps undeserving of his pre-eminence but certainly relevant to public discourse in Southeast Asia. The political Celdran proves that, all along, Rizal remains a powerful source of potential subversion.

I could not have known it at the start, but the research into Rizal became an object lesson on the many uses of error. It is possible to gain a clear vantage point of Rizal and the revolutionary spirit with which he infused the struggle to create a Filipino nation in the late nineteenth century, and by which his example invigorated Indonesian nationalism and Malaysian scholarship, regional political discourse and world literature, in the twentieth — but it is a view overgrown with many obstructions, not all of them deliberately sown. I have used the Introduction to try and clear a path through the bramble.

This approach, I must admit, is congenial to me. It reflects the deepest instinct of my op-ed journalism, which is to engage another point of view. What a pleasant surprise during the research, then, to gain a better insight into it through Syed Hussein Alatas, the trailblazing Malaysian intellectual. Something he wrote pointed me in the direction of the Spanish philosopher Ortega y Gasset, who once proposed that: "all thought represents *thought against*, whether so indicated verbally or not. Our creative thought is always shaped in opposition to some other thought, which we believe erroneous, fallacious, and needful of correction." (Ortega y Gasset 1967: 74; emphasis his).

That Rizal retains both continuing relevance and political promise I never doubted; I think of Rizal as a revolutionary spirit with an essentially religious (i.e., Catholic) sensibility who strove to create a secular, national community — and who had some impact on the region he learned to call his own. (I have no doubt, too, that the use of his farewell poem during the Indonesian revolution would have gratified him; he had been deeply moved, to both thought and action, by Multatuli's novel of the crisis in Java in the mid-nineteenth century.)

These, then, are the book's parameters. The sequence I followed is, more or less, chronological. The first three chapters are an attempt to recover a more accurate sense of Rizal: to see him as he is, and then as the Spaniards and the revolutionaries at that turning point in Philippine history saw him. The last seven trace Rizal's influence outside the Philippines: in the Dutch East Indies of Ernest Francois Eugene Douwes Dekker, in the exile's world of Tan Malaka (shaped in part by a politicising labour sector in Manila), in the last year of Japanese-occupied Java, in the first flush of Indonesian independence, in the history-bending sweep of Sukarno's rhetoric, in the pioneering and consequential studies of Syed Hussein Alatas, not least in the consuming historical fiction of Pramoedya Ananta Toer. The appendices revisit certain points raised in the preceding discussion, and place them in some relief.

As anyone can readily see, this survey is hardly comprehensive. I did not discuss the millenarian aspects of Rizal's image (for which Reynaldo Ileto's *Pasyon and Revolution* remains the standard text), or the American sponsorship of a Rizal cult of hero worship (Floro Quibuyen's *A Nation Aborted* is the indispensable reference), or even the question of Rizal's re-conversion to Catholicism (for which the relevant books are too many to list, and which for the record I believe did not happen *and* is actually irrelevant to Rizal's achievement). I did not discuss the Japanese appropriation of Rizal (although this policy can be discerned in the numerous stories the censors allowed to run in occupied Indonesia), or the possible connection with Burmese or Vietnamese nationalists, or his impact on the East Timorese struggle for independence.

The book is only meant as a primer, a point of departure. It collects all previously known references to the subject, and adds a few of its own. If it can provoke renewed debate on Rizal, or encourage new research into other aspects of Rizal's influence in Southeast Asia, or advance the discussion on the civic virtues Rizal championed or outline the contours of the ethical community he proposed, then it would have played a modest part in commemorating Rizal's 150th birthday.

In the course of the work, I have accumulated many debts of gratitude. I happily recognize them in the following extended Acknowledgements page. Allow me, on this page, only to give first thanks to five persons (and two institutions) who helped me the most, and who at the same time exemplify the kind of generosity I received over the course of the work: Ambassador K. Kesavapany, Ambassador Rodolfo Severino, and Singapore's iconic Institute of Southeast Asian Studies for tasking me with the challenging, deeply fulfilling assignment; Sandy Prieto-Romualdez and Jorge Aruta of the *Philippine Daily Inquirer* for granting me time off to write and for actively supporting both the research and the writing; and *Pak* Rosihan Anwar of Jakarta, without whom this book, or indeed the Rizal story in Southeast Asia, would have taken a different course.

To Rizal, then: patriot, polymath, and post-colonial poster child.

Acknowledgements

I have benefited greatly from the goodwill of journalists and the generosity of scholars — and from one particular accident of history.

My interest in Rizal dates back to 1977, when my graduation happened to coincide with the centenary of *his* graduation; it was a milestone the school we both went to celebrated with relish. My interest was renewed over the years, when I reread the Leon Ma. Guerrero version of the *Noli Me Tangere* and his Rizal biography in the mid-1980s; when I read the Soledad Locsin translation about ten years later; when I read the Harold Augenbraum translation for Penguin Books as well as Benedict Anderson's *Imagined Communities* another decade or so after.

My interest has only deepened since I started writing opinion for the *Philippine Daily Inquirer*, in 2001. Because the Philippines does not make sense without reference to Rizal, I thought it was incumbent on me to read as much of Rizal as I could: his substantial correspondence, his essays, and as many translations of his novels as I could find. (For the reader who wants a faithful if sometimes awkwardly rendered version of the Spanish, I recommend Jovita Ventura Castro's translations of both the *Noli* and the *El Filibusterismo*.)

I read the standard biographies too: Guerrero's *The First Filipino*, Rafael Palma's *The Pride of the Malay Race*, Quirino's *The Great Malayan*; Austin Coates' *Rizal: Philippine Patriot and Martyr*, Frank Laubach's *Man and Martyr*, Austin Craig's *Lineage, Life and Labours*; and big chunks of Wenceslao Retana's *Vida y Escritos* — with the help of Elizabeth Medina's selections and through the tedious use of a line-by-line, dictionary-enabled, Google-powered translation.

(My 12 units of Spanish in college should have sufficed to see me safely through, if I had been paying attention.)

Despite the repeated readings, however, none of this was enough to write a book on Rizal's influence in Southeast Asia with. I needed, I learned soon enough, to depend on the work of journalists and scholars.

My overall sense of Rizal was shaped in large measure by John Schumacher, SJ. Some of the best writing on both Rizal and the Philippine revolution can be found in his books, especially *The Propaganda Movement*, the definitive chronicle of the Filipino political campaign in Spain; *The Making of a Nation*, essays that track the emergence of Filipino nationalism in the nineteenth century; and *Revolutionary Clergy*, the still-underappreciated account of the role Filipino priests played in the nationalist awakening. (It is an account that helps explain something I had myself seen up close and been inspired by: the dissident role the clergy performed during the dark days of the Marcos dictatorship.)

I do not agree with all of Father Jack's conclusions, of course, nor would he expect me or any other reader to. But it is a source of continuing amazement to me to find almost every major question I phrase already answered in his work. Even in those points where his research has already been superseded, such as the question of the meaning of "Rd. L. M." and the nature of that secret organization, he readily acknowledges the historiological rigour of other scholars — in this case, Leoncio Lopez-Rizal, the source of the definition now preferred by historians and polemicists alike. His emails are both prompt and thoughtful, and always written with a view to being useful. I cannot thank him enough.

Benedict Anderson, whom I met only once, and only fleetingly, has almost single-handedly been responsible for igniting the current, renewed interest of academics around the world in Rizal and his pioneering work. His explorations in *Imagined Communities* are deservedly influential, and his startling yet deeply satisfying discovery of Rizal as exemplary — nothing less than the illustration of "homogenous empty time", for instance — has pushed Rizal studies on to newer, perhaps even higher, ground. Partial proof of this influence can be found, I think, with the use of Googlelabs' newfangled N-Grams, which shows a new surge in Rizal references in the universe of English books after *Imagined Communities* saw print.

Anderson's work has provoked exciting new questions about Rizal (his *Under Three Flags*, for example, worries the connection between the Propagandists in Spain and the international anarchist moment) or suggested new lines of inquiry (as we can trace, for instance, in Vicente Rafael's classic-in-the-making, *Contracting Colonialism*). As a political journalist working in the opinion pages, I have serious questions about Anderson's notion of "official nationalism", among other concepts, but there is no doubt in my mind that the fertility of that corner of the academic grove where Rizal is studied today is due in large part to Anderson's experiments in cultivation. I gratefully recognize my debt to him.

F. Sionil Jose was an iconic writer long before I went to college, when I eagerly consumed his Rosales novels. It is a privilege for me to be able to call him "*Manong* Frankie" now, as many others do. His many responsibilities, as novelist, journalist, publisher (and bookstore owner!), can be read as an essay in continuation — of nothing less than Rizal's work. He has certainly continued to introduce discomfiting questions into the public discourse, and his use of fiction as the main means for exploring the limits and possibilities of Philippine society recalls Rizal's own strategy. He has published key works (including the first edition of Father Schumacher's *Propaganda Movement*), and for a long time edited *Solidarity*, an Asia-wide journal of ideas. I thank him for his time, his graciousness, and especially for the conversations bristling with ideas and the Foreword with which he honours this book.

Without Rosihan Anwar, this book would have taken a different turn. He proved to be the ideal host, strict about parcelling his day between his many commitments, but totally generous at the appointed time. In two interviews and three phone calls, he deployed his famous memory ("People tell me you have a great memory," I said once. "It's a myth," the 88-year-old veteran journalist replied) to remember as much as he could of the circumstances in which he wrote his translation of "Mi Ultimo Adios" in 1944 and the context in which that translation became not only possible but necessary. It was a pleasure to listen to him in his crisp English, and a greater pleasure to hear him run through his translation, line by line, and rethink it in English. My debt to *Pak* Rosihan is profound; I thank him most sincerely.

Aside from my four formative sources, so to speak, many others also helped.

Of the other eminences who went out of their way to lend me a hand, I am most grateful to the prodigious Anthony Reid — a gentle, generous presence — who spent the better part of a morning walking me through my ideas and suggesting points of further inquiry; Norman Owen, who encouraged me with warm words, ran through a long list of names and references to start me off, and offered sage advice I took to heart; Merle Ricklefs, who pointed out the Bootsma book, written in Dutch, and taught me how to negotiate the language barrier, and who also offered a corrective to the "exoticising" tendencies of some culture-oriented political scientists or historians writing about Indonesia; Jim Richardson, who generously set me straight on the Katipunan's true demographics; Bernhard Dahm, who pointed me in the right direction, and who drew the context in which the attempts of both Sukarno and Rizal to appropriate "elements" of "their respective cultural backgrounds" could be understood; and John Ingleson, who welcomed the project and wrote something that struck me in particular as a forceful and necessary reminder: "We have so often written about colonial nationalism in 'national' terms neglecting the fact that most of the key leaders were well aware on what was going on elsewhere in Asia (and Europe for that matter)."

I have learned much from the work of Reynaldo Ileto, whose *Pasyon and Revolution*, while certainly not immune to criticism, dramatically changed the way Philippine history is conceived. I have also greatly benefited from the work and work-related wisdom of Resil Mojares, who gave important suggestions as to both approach and reading list, and whose supple writing is a continuing inspiration; Floro Quibuyen, who offered specific, most useful advice; Rommel Curaming, who among many other favours helped me gain a foothold on the slippery terrain of comparative Indonesian and Philippine history; and especially my friend Patricio "Jojo" Abinales, from whom I drew both practical insight (starting from the proposal stage) and sustained support.

Through Rommel, I was privileged to attend a rousing conference on contemporary classics in Southeast Asian studies, which he organized with Syed Muhd Khairudin Aljunied, an assistant professor at National University of Singapore. It was a revealing look at the academic way of proceeding. At that conference, I was introduced to the exciting new work of Joseph Scalice, heard Ramon Guillermo's many pointed interventions, and saw the erudite Michael Montesano in action. I also witnessed Tony Reid's masterly summary of the discussion and his inspired "extraction" of publishable material from the forum.

(The scholars I followed or consulted inspired me, and I held myself to scholarly standards, but I am primarily a journalist, and this book is therefore more journalism than scholarship. I used the author-date citation method because it was the most practical way to handle references, allowing me to limit the number of endnotes to only 70. I also like the fact that it can quickly show up a writer's weaknesses, source-wise — mine not excluded.)

I conducted several interviews which helped give shape to the book. Aside from the two Rosihan sessions in Jakarta, I also interviewed Max Lane, the English translator of the Buru Quartet, in Singapore. I cannot overestimate his assistance in helping me gain a better understanding of the work ("When I read *Bumi Manusia* there was this fantastic, very vivid, alive explanation of where Indonesia actually came from, and in that story was an explanation of why humanist and radical values were so difficult to eradicate"), and of Pramoedya Ananta Toer himself ("His attitude was, translation was a completely separate thing." He didn't reread his novels, but "10 to 15 years later" after the first two translations in English came out, he "read the second one in English." He said: "Even re-reading it in English, I cried." "It was something he said in passing").

Three other important interviews were also held in Singapore: with Alan Chong and Farish A. Noor, both of the S. Rajaratnam School of International Studies at Nanyang Technological University; and with Syed Farid Alatas, like his iconic father before him the head of Malay Studies at the National University of Singapore. The talks were both to-the-point and wide-ranging, and extremely useful. (Professor Alatas, too, was kind enough to share copies of his pioneering studies on Rizal, including a still-unpublished manuscript.)

I conducted a lengthy and deeply thought-provoking interview with Shaharuddin bin Maaruf in Kuala Lumpur. The author of the unjustly neglected *Concept of a Hero in Malay Society*, Shaharuddin proved to be both a genial host and a radical thinker. I hope conference organizers thinking of commemorating Rizal's 150th birth anniversary by inviting academic superstars such as Farish Noor and Farid Alatas will make room for him too.

I owe a special thanks to Maitrii Victoriano Aung Thwin, who wrote a longish letter suggesting a different direction for the project; Chandra Muzaffar and Bambang Sulistomo, who were kind enough to answer me by email; and Mark Frost, who gave me a grounding in port polities, from the vantage point of Hong Kong, without a doubt one of the greatest in existence.

I must also thank the engineers at Google Translate. (Seriously.) To them I owe in part the experience of reading workable translations off my trusty cellphone while browsing through the Indonesian national library in Salemba (which is not only cosily airconditioned but outfitted with wifi on every floor). But I have a real debt of obligation to the few who helped me with the translations, especially Hartono Budi SJ for most of the Indonesian and Alain Borghijs for the Dutch. The eminent Otto van den Muijzenberg graciously offered to do some translating too, but because of my schedule I was not able to seize the opportunity. The translations from Tagalog, incidentally, are mine, as are the few unattributed passages in Spanish and a couple of phrases in Indonesian.

I was able to access many old newspapers as well as hard-to-find old books online; I've included those I've found most useful in the References list. It's hard to pick a favourite, but if I had to recommend only one source I would begin with the University of Michigan's archive on the United States and its Territories, especially the collection optimistically dated "1870–1925: The Age of Imperialism".

The greater part of the research, however, took place inside libraries; I was the happy beneficiary of the assistance of helpful staff. At the Ateneo de Manila's aptly named Rizal Library, I found much of what I needed on Rizal (and a surprising amount on Indonesia). At the University of the Philippines Main Library, I found an otherwise difficult-to-obtain selection of Sukarno's speeches. At the magnificent National Library of Singapore, I was able to track down old Malay and English newspapers published on the island, as well as key volumes on Indonesian history. At the Perpustakaan Nasional Salemba, in Jakarta, I found the frayed pages of *Asia Raya* and *Bakti* that I was looking for, among other publications, as well as the impressively minimalist *Het Tijdschrift*, Ernest Francois Eugene Douwes Dekker's nearly century-old journal that would not look out of place in today's newsmagazine stands. I am especially grateful to Ms Atikah on the seventh floor, Ms Anglila Shinta Putranti and Ms Endang Sumarsih on the eighth, and Mr Nasrul on the fifth, for their service-with-a-smile. The library at the Institute of Southeast Asian Studies must be one of Singapore's best-kept secrets. I spent countless hours on the nearly always almost-empty third floor, for which privilege I wish to thank Ms Ch'ng Kim See, the head of the library, as well as Susan Low and Gandhimathy Durairaj.

In ISEAS, I especially wish to thank the unflappable Triena Ong, Head of ISEAS Publishing, and her dedicated staff for their careful, painstaking work on the book; Mark Iñigo Tallara, formerly with the ASEAN Studies Centre and now with ISEAS Publishing, for his unfailing assistance; and the remarkable Mrs Y. L. Lee, who manages ISEAS affairs with both verve and dispatch.

The assistance of Indonesian journalists has been invaluable. Elok Dyah Messwati of *Kompas*, who wrote a profile on Rosihan, helped me arrange my first interview with him. Frans Padak Demon of the Voice of America in Jakarta led me to possibly the most famous Indonesian alive named after Rizal, the prominent playwright Jose Rizal Manua. A conversation with Harry Bhaskara, formerly of the *Jakarta Post*, during a bus ride in Hong Kong on the way to a conference, helped firm up some leads. Samiaji Bintang, then on study leave in Manila, also sent me a tip. (And Chi-Jia Tschang, a friend from Hong Kong, directed me to her contacts in Indonesia.)

I have relied heavily on the supportive environment of the *Philippine Daily Inquirer*, where I've found a nurturing home in the last ten years. I received the warm encouragement and sustained support of company president Sandy Prieto Romualdez and opinion editor Jorge Aruta (who even subbed for me on certain days, an arrangement that meant I was inadvertently delegating upwards!). Editor in chief Letty Jimenez Magsanoc and the executive committee made a two-month book-writing leave official. Even the newspaper's own research library, under Miner Generalao, proved very useful.

Not least, I was also able to use my column in the opinion page to test certain ideas. Thus, columns on Rizal's influence on Indonesian nationalists appeared on 14 September 2010 ("Aquino and the troublemaker"), 21 September ("Aquino and the evangelist"), and 28 September ("Aquino and the mouthpiece"). A column on the pernicious influence of the great Spanish philosopher Miguel de

Unamuno came out on 19 October ("One who got it all wrong"). A column on the Tagalog correspondence of the three leading Propagandists appeared in two parts, on 28 December 2010 ("A Tagalog conspiracy") and 4 January 2011 ("Rizal's open secrets"). A column on Hermenegildo Cruz's *Kartilyang Makabayan* saw print on 11 January ("Patriot's primer"). Another two-part column, this time on the mistaken reading of the influential Filipino historian Renato Constantino, ran several months earlier; a revised version can be found in Appendix B.

On Facebook, that final frontier, I have drawn encouragement from the support of friends who have kept partial track of the progress of the book, including Coco Alcuaz, Marvin Beduya, Frank Navarrete, and Ted Sta. Ana in Metro Manila; Almond Aguila in Edmonton; Gigi Santos in Los Angeles; Chandler Ramas in Miami; and Tapi Balce in Sydney.

To three friends, I am especially indebted: Tony de Castro, SJ, who introduced me to Father Schumacher and jump-started my research with judicious links; Maricor Baytion of the Ateneo de Manila University Press, who remained an endless source of grace and encouragement all throughout the project; and Howie Severino, who alerted me to the project in the first place. I still keep his text message — which begins "Wd u be interested in writing Rizal book?" — in my phone's inbox.

Friends and family helped immeasurably. Rolly and Mabee Unas offered the hospitality of their home in Singapore, again and again; Tim Gabuna allowed me to live in the Ateneo de Manila Residence Halls in the first five, most difficult weeks of writing; my sister Cristy Abasolo tracked down a few more books in Singapore; Gejo Jimenez boosted morale tirelessly, while keeping other book projects tantalizingly in view; Bixie Reyes helped me visualize the manuscript as a book to hold in one's hands; above all, my wife Paz and children Carmela Isabel, Maria Teresa, and Juan Diego cheered me on, learned to put up with my absences, forced me to take the occasional break, and created the space for me to write. To them I am grateful beyond words.

It was Ambassador Rodolfo Severino of the ASEAN Studies Centre in ISEAS, former secretary-general of the Association of Southeast Asian Nations (ASEAN), who thought of marking Rizal's 150th birth anniversary with a book on the Philippine national hero's impact on Southeast Asian nationalism, and Ambassador K. Kesavapany, Director of the Institute of Southeast Asian Studies (ISEAS) who pushed the project with enthusiasm. I am deeply grateful to them both for pursuing the project, and eventually involving me in it. The work, in large part, was kept honest by Professor Owen's sage advice. It seems to me appropriate to end this series of acknowledgments by recalling it. While Rizal's impact in Southeast Asia is real, he wrote, it is easy to exaggerate. "But still he stands, along with Dr Sun Yat-sen and a few others, as one of the Asians capable of inspiring others. Documenting this, and trying to put it in perspective (not too big, not too small) will be your challenge."

I have tried to measure up to this test; needless to say, all shortcomings are mine.

Introduction

THE USES OF ERROR

I

It may be best to begin with an instructive error. In "The First Filipino," an essay in the *London Review of Books* occasioned by a new translation of *Noli Me Tangere*, the preeminent scholar Benedict Anderson references Jose Rizal's encounter with the demon of double-consciousness (Anderson 1998: 229), "which made it impossible ever after to experience Berlin without at once thinking of Manila, or Manila without thinking of Berlin. Here indeed is the origin of nationalism, which lives by making comparisons."

And then the error:

> It was this spectre that, after some frustrating years writing for *La Solidaridad*, the organ of the small group of committed "natives" fighting in the metropole for political reform, led him to write *Noli Me Tangere*, the first of the two great novels for which Rizal will always be remembered. He finished it in Berlin just before midnight on 21 February 1887 — eight months after Gladstone's first Home Rule Bill was defeated, and eight years before *Almayer's Folly* was published. He was twenty-six.

In fact, the *Noli*, as it is familiarly, even affectionately known in the Philippines, was published two years before the first number of *La Solidaridad* (the *Soli* in current speak, but just plain *Sol* to Rizal in his time) came off the press. It was primarily because of the *Noli*, and the fame or notoriety that quickly surrounded its author, that Rizal became the lead attraction of the main fortnightly newspaper of the

Propaganda — the campaign in Spain to publicize the need for urgent reform of the Philippine colony. There were others who dared publish their names in full, like the Austrian scholar Ferdinand Blumentritt, or wrote just as well or even better, like the gifted polemicist Marcelo del Pilar — but it was Rizal the daring novelist who attracted the most attention, at least in the two years he wrote for the newspaper.

What explains the error? Anderson may have conflated Rizal's first sojourn in Europe, from 1882 to 1887, with his second, which ran from 1888 to 1891. (Rizal returned to Europe a third time, in 1896, but almost literally only for a day.)

During his first stay in Europe, Rizal studied for his licentiate in philosophy and in medicine in Madrid, assumed a leadership role in the Filipino community in Spain, apprenticed at a famous ophthalmological clinic in Paris and then in another one in Heidelberg, and wrote his first novel in the bleakest conditions: he had meagre funds, went on forced fasting, endured a forbidding winter. The second time he found himself in Europe, he spent a year of research at the British Library in London, copying Antonio de Morga's early seventeenth century history of the Philippines by hand and then annotating it; contributed many articles to the *Soli*, including two historic essays; and wrote his second novel *El Filibusterismo* (better known in the Philippines, inevitably, as the *Fili*).

Anderson's review does not advert to this second stay, and it isn't hard to imagine why. Rizal's formative experiences in Europe seem all of a piece, in the exact same way that Rizal's life seems almost scripted: They fall into the familiar pattern of a hero's narrative. A precocious childhood and a brilliant youth, then a time of struggle and difficult achievement, ending finally in an all-consuming blaze of glory. It is the basic three-act structure of the cineplex movie or the stage play. But while Rizal's gift of presentiment was acute (his accounts of some of his premonitory dreams are almost clinical in their precision), and throughout his short life he was shadowed by a sense of destiny (one of his pseudonyms was *Laong Laan*, a name often translated as "Ever Prepared" but perhaps better rendered as "Preordained"), in fact life never merely unfolded for him. He had to will himself into becoming Rizal.

The year or so he spent between the two European sojourns was decisive. Despite the grave risk, he still insisted on returning — because he knew, to appropriate a vivid phrase made current a hundred years after his birth, that was where the action was. The half-year he spent home, after the temerity of writing the *Noli*, was joyous but also often tense, his every move fraught with implication. A young lieutenant of the Civil Guard was even assigned to his personal detail. And yet, writing a few years later, he described that idyll as ideal.

> *Yaong limang buan itinira ko roon ay isang halimbawang buhay, isang librong magaling na di lalo sa Noli Me Tangere. Ang parang na paglalabanan ay ang Filipinas: doon tayo dapat magtatagpo.*
> [Rizal 1933: 250]

> Those five months I lived there are a living example, a book much better than *Noli Me Tangere*. The field of battle is the Philippines: that's where we should meet.

The most likely date for this letter, of which only a fragment is extant, is October 1891, toward the end of his second European spell. It was not the first time he spoke of the Philippines, or the last, as the arena of engagement. In July 1889, for instance, in a long letter in Tagalog to del Pilar (Rizal 1931: 208–11), he asked for many copies of *Sol* (he was then in Paris), in order to send them to the Philippines. "*Doon dapat itong basahin* — There is where it should be read." He welcomed the news of an accomplished new Filipino student[1] on his way to Madrid, wishing him the best. "*Dapat lamang bumalik sa Filipinas* — Only, he should return to the Philippines." And he gave other suggestions for smuggling the newspaper into the country, through the assistance of Filipino seamen[2] and other means. "*Huag nating limutin na doon tayo dapat mag tanim kung ibig nating pumitas ñg buñga* — Let us not forget that it is there where we should sow [the seeds] if we want to pick the fruits."

He left the Philippines a second time only when the spectre of consequence threatened to turn solid, and in order, he said, not to shorten his parents' lives (*"di ko ibig paikliin ang buhay ng aking mga magulang"*). But by the time he wrote of the field of battle, he was already preparing to return to the Philippines, via Hong Kong. Denied a corner of the true battlefield the first time around, he was determined on his second return to pitch his tent regardless of the consequences. He knew the risks involved: Before leaving for Manila in June 1892, he left two letters, one for his family and another "*A Los Filipinos,*" with Lourenco Pereira Marques, a Portuguese doctor he had befriended in Hong Kong. They were to be opened, he said, only after his death.

When Rizal arrived in Marseilles on 12 June 1882, to take the train to Barcelona, he was very much the earnest student, the tireless tourist. He had landed in Europe a week shy of his twenty-first birthday. (He actually disembarked the following day, but had spent an hour in Naples the day before. "Greetings to you, O Napoli!," he had written in his diary.) When he returned to the great continent in June 1888, arriving at the port of Liverpool after an eventful detour through Japan and an unremarkable one through the United States, he was much more the reluctant traveller, more critical of Europe (of his compatriots abroad too), and impatiently devising schemes of returning to the battlefield.

The difference, in part, can be traced back to that ideal time, from 5 August 1887 to 3 February 1888, when Rizal found himself back in the Philippines, living the *Noli*. (And it led directly, on his return to Europe, to the forging of his most consequential alliances, with del Pilar and Mariano Ponce.)

We can understand the conflation of the two periods in Europe, then, as a fairly common error, something we can excuse under the label of "European influence," but it is part of a larger mistake: Call it the inevitability trap. The sweeping arc of Rizal's biography creates its own momentum, gives even his difficult decisions the air of the inevitable. While his letters written from various parts of Europe in 1887, after the *Noli* had gone to press, have a bittersweet quality to them — he was only too keenly conscious that the freedoms he took for granted in Europe did not exist in the Philippines — he all the same longed to go home. When he had to leave the Philippines again, he at first breathed a sigh of relief — "At last I can write you freely," he wrote his great friend Blumentritt from Hong Kong — but he could not hide his despair: "They forced me to leave my country" (Rizal 1963c: 161).

Contrary to the popular image of Rizal as a child of destiny, as he whose life was "Preordained," there were many such turning points in his life: when difficult decisions had to be made, when he accepted a course of action because of circumstance, and when he eventually found a way to do what he thought he ought to do. Reading the many letters and diaries and other notes he left behind, I get the impression, not of a dutiful acquiescence to fate, but of an enormous will at work.

It is my contention that, in truth, there was nothing inevitable about Rizal.

II

A hundred and fifty years after his birth, the truth about Rizal is, more or less, plain to see. Through the first-hand experiences he smuggled into his political fiction, through his topical essays and occasion-specific poetry, above all through his letters and diaries, we can make the case that he was his own best biographer. But a reader who wants to know more about Rizal quickly learns that the view is obscured by a thicket of errors.

This should not come as a surprise. The teeming fecundity of Rizal studies all but guarantees this undergrowth. Even the greatest scholars have done their share of fertilizing. Thus, for example, Anderson. Horacio de la Costa SJ, a true eminence in Philippine history and literature (in my view he was the best, the most gifted Filipino writer in English), confused the brothers Taviel de Andrade (De la Costa 1996: 113). Jose was Rizal's bodyguard and friend; Luis his lawyer for the defence. The leading Malayist scholar in the Philippines, Zeus Salazar, thought Rizal decided to annotate Morga's history only in January 1889 or "shortly thereafter" (Salazar 1998: 117). In fact, Rizal was done copying and annotating most of the Morga by December 1888. And so on, and on.

A reader of Rizal's can get discouraged. That was where I found myself, a few years ago. It took some time for me to make the liberating discovery that, though the field of study may be error-ridden, these very mistakes can often lead to the truth. Error has its many uses.

We can construct a typology of the most common errors. The *instructive error* may involve either factual mistakes, or mistakes in interpretation, or both; it is an error, as we may see from the Anderson example above or the examples from Apolinario Mabini and Jean Jaures, Asuncion Lopez Bantug and David P. Barrows below, that can throw unexpected light on a detail or an event or a puzzle in Rizal's life. The *unfortunate error* concerns merely factual imprecision: the wrong date or the wrong place, the wrong age or the wrong name, the result possibly of momentary inattention. Thus, de la Costa and Salazar above; Teodoro Agoncillo below. (I hope those I will make, inevitably, fall ever so gently under this category.) Last, there is the *pernicious error*, a gross misinterpretation driven (not necessarily consciously) by ideology, resulting in a serious misunderstanding. I do not have the space to discuss the errors of this kind perpetrated by the biographers Wenceslao Retana and Austin Craig; I have limited myself only to the Spanish philosopher Miguel de Unamuno.

None of this is to say that to understand Rizal we must only use the most complete editions, the most faithful renderings, of his life and work. Readers of Rizal can make an even more empowering discovery: He has in fact been well-served by *flawed but fateful* versions of his writings. Indeed, some of these versions have had the most influence outside the Philippines, including *An Eagle Flight* (a 1900 version of the *Noli*, by an unknown translator) and "*Selamat tinggal, Tanah koepoedja*" (a truncated 1944 translation of Rizal's famous eve-of-death poem, by the Indonesian journalist Rosihan Anwar, and the subject of Chapter 6 and part of Chapter 7).

Classifying the most common errors helps us clear a path through the thicket; I trust it will help us see Rizal in clearer light.

III

Apolinario Mabini, by popular consensus the Filipino nationalist intellectual second only to Rizal, wrote an account of the Philippine revolution during his Guam exile that privileged the role and especially the novels of Rizal; to the two books he devoted an entire chapter. He wrote *La Revolucion Filipina* in Spanish, and then translated it himself into English, some six years after Rizal's execution. Much more polished translations have since been completed, but in my view Mabini's own version, in his self-taught English, best reflects the cut and thrust of his Spanish-inflected argument.

In it, he wrote, quite unaccountably:

> It was evident that the articles published in a fortnightly review [he means *La Solidaridad*] was not efficient enough to call the attention of the Spanish government. Seeing that Marcelo del Pilar was conducting the publication with rare skill, aided by competent staff, Rizal ceased to be contributor in order to give his works a more convenient and effective form. It was necessary for the Philippine miseries to have a more pathetic expression, that the abuses and the pains they caused might appear to the public eye with the liveliest colours of reality. Novel alone could offer these advantages, and Rizal set on writing novels. (Mabini 1998: 224–25)

Mabini was involved in organizing support, primarily financial, for the Propaganda in Spain from at least 1892, when he joined the Masonic lodge *Balagtas*. He was hard at work reviving Rizal's *La Liga Filipina*, a patriotic association that fell dormant after Rizal was deported to Dapitan, since at least 1893. He was in constant correspondence with del Pilar in Madrid, at least between 1893 and 1895. Not least, several months after the *Noli* first reached Manila in 1887 Mabini was back in the capital as a law student (considerably older than his classmates, because of the interruptions in his schooling); surely he must have been aware of the great controversy that followed in its wake?

"It would have been quite difficult to keep any serious university student unaware of such events," Mabini's distinguished biographer wrote (Majul 1998:16). "And no Filipino sensitive to social discrimination and the nature of the unequal society existing at that time could have disregarded Rizal's message."

Perhaps Mabini may have conflated the work of *La Solidaridad* with another, reform-oriented newspaper published in Spain before the *Noli* became famous, and to which Rizal contributed the occasional article. *España en Filipinas* was a monitory example for the *Soli* — riven by racial antagonism, consumed by financial worry, fatally weakened by political fecklessness ("It is all puerility," Graciano Lopez Jaena wrote Rizal). Though there were many attempts to revive it afterwards, the weekly newspaper lasted only four months, from March to July 1887. To be sure, Rizal finished writing the *Noli* just a few weeks before the newspaper was launched. But as John Schumacher SJ, the definitive chronicler of the Propaganda, notes: "Though its publication early in 1887 slightly preceded the appearance of *España en Filipinas*, [the novel] only began to circulate widely some months later" (Schumacher 1997: 82). It is just possible, then, that Mabini, then teaching at the vibrant provincial centre of Lipa, in Batangas, mistook one newspaper for the other.

Possible, but not likely. In *La Revolucion Filipina*, the chapter on Rizal's novels is preceded by a chapter on *La Solidaridad* and succeeded by a chapter dealing, in part, with the *Liga* — three reform milestones ineradicably linked to Rizal's name. (Indeed, Mabini's insider narrative, like the articles in the only published issue of *Kalayaan*, the newspaper of the Katipunan revolutionary organization, made the connection between reform and revolution explicit.) He prefaces his account of Rizal's novel-writing with a word about del Pilar's "rare skill" in editing the newspaper (well-deserved praise, in the wake of the abbreviated term of Lopez Jaena, the mercurial, discipline-averse first editor). He speaks highly of the *Soli*'s "competent staff" (one driving advantage *La Solidaridad* enjoyed over *España en Filipinas* was Ponce's central presence in the former and near-complete absence in the latter). And he absolutises Rizal's turn to novels, as though it was the novel-writing that caused Rizal to turn his back on the newspaper: "Rizal ceased to be contributor in order to give his works a more convenient and effective form." (In fact, Rizal was busy contributing articles, among other projects, while annotating the Morga and writing the *Fili*.)

Rizal did, however, stop writing for *La Solidaridad*. He did so about a year and a half before he was shipped off to exile in Dapitan, a rustic town on the northern coast of the great island of Mindanao, in July 1892. He stopped, to use the anodyne language of today's corporate culture, because of personality and policy differences; the difference in strategy, however, was the decisive one. Rizal was a one-front general; he insisted the field of battle was back home. Del Pilar wanted to fight on two fronts, even though the campaign in Spain remained without signal victories and consumed most of the materiel being gathered (by Mabini, among others) back in the Philippines.

Five months after his "field of battle" letter, Rizal wrote to the editors of *La Solidaridad* and the members of the reform-oriented *Asociacion Hispano-Filipina*. By then he had settled down in Hong Kong, and had managed to surround himself with many members of his family, his aged parents included. The practice of the "Spanish doctor" in the Crown Colony was doing well, but his mind remained fixed on the battleground. In his letter (Rizal 1933: 298–300), he thanked del Pilar and the editorial staff for *"la campaña que habeis seguido con motivo de los sucesos de Kalamba* — the campaign you have waged on account of the events in Calamba." He was referring to the virtual sacking of his hometown beginning in late 1890; hundreds had been dispossessed, forty heads of family deported, his own relatives scattered. Full of gratitude, the letter was nevertheless written by someone who clearly considered himself a former, not a present, colleague: "*como por algun tiempo he trabajado en sus columnas y con vosotros* — as for some time I worked in its columns and with you."

In it he offered a simple explanation for his decision to stop writing for *La Solidaridad*. "Here I have also written in English for some newspapers, but it is rather for record purposes and for information and nothing more. Without desiring to counsel either newspaper or the *Asociacion*, I believe that at present little can be expected from public opinion in Spain; there the water is up to the neck and it cannot pay much attention to the Philippines" (Rizal 1963b: 661, but with slight revisions).

The explanation is a little disingenuous; as we can judge from the occasional publication of indignant letters from Manila, written in reply to his pieces, his Hong Kong stories had political objectives too. (Or at least they had political consequences. They eventually formed part of the evidence against him in his trial for rebellion and illegal association.) But Hong Kong was only four days' journey from the battlefield. Proximity raised both the sense of possibility and the hope of expectation.

Mabini does not say anything about this conflict in strategy. It is possible he did not know about the initial exchange between Rizal and del Pilar, couched in Rizal's terms of "*paglitaw ng mga bago*" — the rise of the new, hitherto hidden talents among Filipinos (Rizal 1933: 38). Or of the brisk exchange of letters in Tagalog in June and July 1890, discussing Rizal's plan to stop writing temporarily for the *Soli*. Or of the heated letters in mid-1892 to del Pilar, after Eduardo de Lete had written a satirical piece mocking Rizal right in *La Solidaridad*. But it does not seem likely that Mabini was unaware of the fatal differences in matters of leadership and direction between Rizal and del Pilar, in the form these had reached the various councils and circles in Manila in 1891. The controversy had thrown the patriotic elements in Manila in turmoil; partisans had chosen sides between Rizal and del Pilar; ultimately, the Comite de Propaganda had reorganized itself in an attempt (vain, as it turned out) to satisfy Rizal. By then Mabini was an associate, and later an apprentice, of the lawyer Numeriano Adriano, who supported the Propaganda campaign and was executed for it (Majul 1998: 14–16). It beggars belief that Mabini did not know anything about the conflict between the famous doctor and del Pilar, whose brother-in-law Deodato Arellano he was a colleague of. In some of his letters to del Pilar, he had even exchanged news and dispelled rumours about Rizal, who was by then in exile in Dapitan.

At any rate, by the time Mabini wrote La Revolucion Filipina, he certainly had command of more facts. I cannot help but think, then, that his account of Rizal's parting of ways with La Solidaridad, which he attributes anachronously to Rizal's discovery of the expressive advantages of "novel alone," seems to be a deliberate muting, for patriotic reasons, of the "lively colours of reality." In his view, the conflict between Rizal and del Pilar needn't be part of the narrative of the revolution.

About a year before Mabini was banished to Guam by American forces occupying the Philippines, the spellbinding Jean Jaures — "the grandest orator in French history," in the words of Indonesia's founding president Sukarno, himself no slouch in the charismatic oratory department — had occasion to write about Rizal. In a preface to Henri Turot's life of the Philippine revolutionary leader Emilio Aguinaldo, published in 1900, the French legislator recalled Rizal's life and death as "one of the most touching episodes in human history" (the limpid translation of Mitchell Abidor can be found in <http://www.marxist.org>). He praised Turot for including Rizal in his narrative (the account taking up about 30 pages in all).

> *Turot a eu raison de nous donner le detail de ce drame: la vie et la mort de Rizal laissent dans les ames une sorte de frisson sacre, et il parait impossible que le peuple qui a suscite de tels devouements, ne soit pas enfin libre.* [Turot 1900: ix]
>
> Turot was right to give us the details of this drama: the life and death of Rizal sends a sacred shiver into our souls, and it is impossible that the people who aroused such devotion will not finally be free. [Abidor]

Turot depended on Henri Lucas, one of the translators of the first French version of the *Noli*, for many of the details, some rather imprecise, of Rizal's life (Turot 1900: 62). But in offering a summary of Rizal's work based on Turot's second-hand account, Jaures makes the larger, instructive mistake, and falls into the inevitability trap. He writes:

> In Europe [Rizal] fills himself with all of modern science; he returns to the Philippines not to raise it in revolt, but to attempt by a supreme effort to open their master's spirit to the new necessities. But he is seized, judged, and executed ... [Abidor]

Granted, Jaures was writing a preface, and he was under no obligation to sketch "the details of this drama" with a finer pen. But I do not think it would be unjust to characterize his understanding of Rizal's return to the Philippines as the discrete second act of a three-part narrative, instead of the series of false starts and half-measures and eventually resolute decisions that it really was.

Jaures' terms may help make sense of the first homecoming in 1887, but the second return in 1892, prepared in part by several months of patient practice in Hong Kong and anticipated by Rizal's extraordinary attempt to found a Filipino colony — "the new Kalamba" — in Sandakan, in North Borneo, no longer fits his classification scheme. Rizal returned a second time not to "open their master's spirit" (he was done placing his hopes in the reforming capacity of the Spanish), but to open the spirit of his countrymen.

In the "field of battle" letter, Rizal addressed the fundamental condition of the Propaganda: the futility of waging an expensive campaign in Spain without adequate funds. "*Kung walang salapi ay wala tayong malaking magagawa* — If there is no money we cannot do much." The alternative was clear: "*Ang ating maitutulung sa kanila, ay ang* ating buhay sa ating bayan — We can help them [the people back home] with *our life in the country*" (emphasis in the original).

But in the same way that the country should not place its hopes of reform, of freedom and a better life, on the Spanish government, neither should it place its hopes on the Filipino colony in Europe.

> *Ang karamihan ñg mga kababayan sa Europa, ay takot, layo sa sunog, at matapang lamang habang layo sa panganib at nasa payapang bayan! Huag umasa ang Filipinas; umasa sa sariling lakas.* [Rizal 1933: 250–51]
>
> Most of [our] countrymen in Europe are afraid, avoiding the fire, and brave only when far from danger and in a peaceful country. The Philippines should not hope [in them]; [it should] hope in its own strength.

Rizal's second homecoming was against the advice of many, including that of the friend he esteemed the most, Blumentritt. Partly to assuage their fears, he had decided on Hong Kong as a halfway measure. He had even tried to start all over again in North Borneo; the attempt was characteristic of Rizal, a man of projects, and it pleased the most radicalized of his friends, such as Antonio Luna. But throughout it all, his country's shores beckoned. It was only a matter of time before the prospect of living a life that was more useful than writing the *Noli*, or the *Fili*, would steel his will, and draw him back to them.

IV

When was the *Noli* written? In *Lolo Jose*, an affectionate, candid portrait of Rizal steeped in the colours of family lore, Rizal's grandniece, Asuncion Lopez Bantug, categorically states that the

Noli was completed in the last week of June, 1886, in the village of Wilhemsfeld, in the house of the vicar, Pastor Karl Ullmer.

> ... How strange that it was in this atmosphere of happiness and contentment that he completed his sad novel. In the vicarage gardens, under the trees and among the German flowers he loved so much ... he sat, read and wrote. There and up in his room where he kept a map of the Philippines tacked to the wall, he finished the final chapters of *Noli Me Tangere*, working from the last week of April to the last week of June 1886.
>
> He had just turned twenty-five. [Bantug 2008: 77]

And yet documentary proof exists that the last pages of the novel were completed on 21 February 1887. In the original manuscript, after one last line about *"la infeliz Maria Clara* — the unhappy Maria Clara," Rizal writes *"Fin de la narracion"* with a flourish, underscores it, and then notes the place, date, and time: *"Berlin 21 de Febrero 1887 11 ½ Noche Lunes"* (Rizal 1961: unnumbered).

It is possible that he was merely writing a clean copy for the printers; but it seems unlikely that those last pages were based on rough drafts completed from eight months ago. We have Rizal's own testimony, in an 11 November 1892 letter to a former teacher, the Jesuit Pablo Pastells, that he did a lot of editing in Germany. "I admit that I corrected my work in Germany, making many revisions and shortening it considerably; but likewise I had occasion to temper my outbursts, tone down my language and reduce many passages as distance provided me a wider perspective and my imagination cooled off in the atmosphere of calm peculiar to that country" (Bonoan 1994: 139). Much of that editing took place in the Wilhelmsfeld vicarage; it was there where he was most able to bask in that calming atmosphere.

The extant correspondence after Rizal left the Ullmers in late June 1886 shows him asking around for printer's cost estimates, and fielding hints from his friends about the book. "I know already that you have finished the little work," Evaristo Aguirre writes from Madrid on 15 September. Eleven days later he writes again, "I take into consideration the essence and object of your novel and I cherish the hope that it will answer some of our numerous needs ... That the personages are all taken from life and the happenings are true are circumstances that increase the merit of the work ..." Almost a month later, on 21 October, the medical student Maximo Viola, Rizal's faithful travelling companion, reported from Barcelona: "Day before yesterday I was at the house of Daniel Cortezo and there I was told that it was not possible to finish the printing of your work in one year. I was at the Ramirez Printing Press this morning and there they asked me for the printing of your work ..." On 24 October, Aguirre writes again from Madrid, "I am really sorry that, on account of the excessive cost of printing your novel there, we are deprived of its immediate publication that we so much desire" (Rizal 1963b: 56; 59–60; 64; 66).

I take all this to mean that Rizal had finished a complete draft of his first novel by at least the third quarter of the year, or enough of a draft for him to write letters to friends loaded with printing specifications (Rizal 1963b: 64). But even Aguirre's letters suggest that Rizal was not quite done. On 26 September 1886, immediately after talking about his hopes for Rizal's novel, Aguirre writes, "I am sorry I don't know of any military prison as I should like to comply with what you ask me ... I believe that in Manila there is no other military prison except Fort Santiago where there are dungeons under the wall towards the river, where it is completely dark and humid because of its proximity to the Pasig that laps its walls ... In one of them the shipping merchant Mr Mourente caught rheumatism which he remembers perfectly even now that he is established in Hong Kong." Later in the letter, he adds: "Enclosed I send you some scrawled plans of the military prisons of Fort Santiago and of the Bilibid jail. I wish that through them you may form an idea of what those places are" (Rizal 1963b: 60; 62).

And why was that? Perhaps Rizal was at that point in the writing (the last five chapters) where he needed to know where to place members of Manila's moneyed class after the novel's climactic uprising. Or perhaps he had already written the following lines and wanted to expand on them.

> ... The Authorities could not allow that certain persons of position and property sleep in such poorly guarded and badly ventilated houses: in the Fort of Santiago and in other Government buildings, sleep would be much calmer and more refreshing. Among these favored persons was included the unfortunate Capitan Tinong. [Ventura Castro 1989: 354]

That last paragraph of Chapter 59 segues effortlessly into the first paragraph of the next.

> Capitan Tiago is very happy. In all this terrible storm, nobody has thought of him: he was not arrested, not subjected to solitary confinement, interrogations, electric machines, continuous foot baths in underground cells and other more [sic] pleasantries that are well-known to certain persons who call themselves civilized. His friends, that is, those that were (for the man has already repudiated his Filipino friends the moment they were suspected by the Government) had come back to their houses after a few days' vacation in the buildings of the State...
>
> Capitan Tinong went back to his house sick, pale, swollen — the excursion did not do him good — and so changed that he said no word ... [Ventura Castro 1989: 355]

Shades of the rheumatic shipping merchant Mr Mourente!

What does all this tell us about the Bantug account — written in 1936, thoroughly rewritten and first published in 1988, updated in 2008? (The second edition is superb, carefully designed and handsomely produced, and complete with infrequently seen photographs and a compact disk containing copies, among others, of Rizal's correspondence and three major biographies.)

Bantug had been instrumental in the making of other studies of Rizal; the 1968 biography by Austin Coates was especially indebted to her. Through *Lolo Jose*, her lifelong interest in documenting Rizal family lore was itself documented; a good thing, because the value of her research cannot be overestimated. But it may be that, in her recounting of the Rizal narrative, she privileges the memory of the Ullmers, whose descendants she had come to know, at the expense of the documentary evidence. It is pleasing to imagine that the writing of the *Noli* was completed in that two-month idyll in the vicarage, but the conditions under which Rizal wrote, his correspondence with his friends, and not least that notation on the final page of the original manuscript all say otherwise.

The book's cover offers additional confirmation. In an almost microscopic reading of the original manuscript cover of the *Noli*, designed by Rizal himself, Coates intuits "the secret, inner dedication by Rizal to his parents." The dedication is right there on the cover, hidden in plain sight. It includes the date the dedication was written. Coates guesses the month and day: 21 February. But the year is something anyone can see (at least now that our attention has been called to it): 1887.

Another thing. Bantug dates Rizal's request for help from his beloved older brother Paciano in publishing the *Noli* to October — specifically, to one of the most historically important letters[3] in the Rizal canon, that of 12 October 1886 (Bantug 2008: 79). Perhaps this reflects the family tradition that Rizal held off asking for more money from his increasingly hard-pressed family as long as he could. But in fact the first request, or hint, must have been made soon after Rizal left Wilhelmsfeld for Leipzig. A letter from Paciano dated 27 August 1886 reads, in part: "I wish to know how much is the cost of printing a work there in Leipzig or anywhere else, so that I can have ready the amount or borrow it, because the situation of our brothers-in-law does not permit them to help you" (Rizal 1963a: 238). The mail between Germany and the Philippines took from one to two months;

Rizal must have finally told his brother about the novel he had been working on since 1884 in a letter (unfortunately no longer extant) written either in June or early July.

But again, this kind of error is instructive; it teaches us to estimate the weight scholars and critics have assigned to certain pieces of biographical evidence, and at the same time to sift through the evidence ourselves. They are lessons in appreciation.

V

An unfortunate error by the influential David P. Barrows recalls those of both Anderson and Mabini.

A political scientist who later served as president of the University of California, Barrows spent a decade in the Philippines; for most of it he was, effectively, the education minister of the new American colony. From 1901 to 1903, on top of his regular duties, he wrote a history of the newly annexed territory that extended over an area only about a third smaller than California itself. Published in 1905, *A History of the Philippines* quickly became a standard reference. A book review in the March 1906 issue of *The Filipino* magazine (25) may have been one of the first to recommend it, primarily on the strength of Barrows' reputation. "Dr Barrows has studied the Filipino people and their past, and he has written a history which, though condensed, is sound, forceful, readable."

Barrows did not make the mistake of collapsing Rizal's European sojourns into one. He speaks, rightly, of a "second return" in 1892 (Barrows 1905: 282). But in his treatment of Rizal and his work, he commits the error Mabini shared with Anderson: Through a momentary lapse, his chronology places the *Noli* after the *Soli*.

> It was in this latter country [Germany] that he produced his first novel, *Noli Me Tangere*. He had been a contributor to the Filipino paper published in Spain, "La Solidaridad," and, to further bring the conditions and needs of his country to more public notice, he wrote this novel dealing with Tagalog life as represented at his old

home on Laguna de Bay and in the city of Manila. Later he published a sequel, *El Filibusterismo* ... [Barrows 1905: 281–82]

This error in his Rizal chronology (a mental lapse, as far as I can tell) Barrows corrected immediately in subsequent editions; through deft copyediting, he made the correction without changing the shape of the offending paragraph. The first sentences now read: "It was in this latter country that he produced his first novel, *Noli Me Tangere*. He was also a contributor to the Filipino paper published in Spain, 'La Solidaridad'" (Barrows 1914: 281).

In 1924, the book was heavily revised, with entire chapters dropped and new chapters included. "This essentially new book brings the story of the Islands down to date," a publisher's note declared on the copyright page. But the book's time was past; by 1926, Conrado Benitez of the University of the Philippines had written the new standard for public-school use, also titled *History of the Philippines* (Ileto 1997: 65). A news item in the July 1925 issue of *The Philippine Republic*, the Washington, D.C.-based "national organ of the Filipinos in the United States," helps explain the difference in fate between Barrows' revised edition and the original. Datelined Manila, the story on Page 2 announced that "The Government text board has dropped the David Barrows history, a textbook formerly used in the Philippine schools. It was alleged to be anti-Filipino." (An ethnological expert, Barrows had done extensive work with the so-called non-Christian tribes; he had a reputation for being Filipino-friendly.[4] I surmise it was Barrows' vigorous presentation of the argument for continued political union, in the new chapter "Toward Independence, 1914–24," that may have led to the text board's decision.)

Between adoption of the textbook and its abandonment, however, were two decades of instruction and influence. (A pervasive, most insidious influence, according to the eminent Reynaldo Ileto.[5])

Other factual errors are truly unfortunate. In Anderson's 1997 recounting of the writing of the *Noli*, he placed Rizal's age at 26. In fact, Rizal was 25 when he completed his first novel. In *Under Three*

Flags (2005: 163), he placed Rizal's age at his death at 36, instead of 35. But Anderson is in good company; the foremost Filipino historian of the nationalist school and arguably still the most influential today, Teodoro Agoncillo, was even more inaccurate. In *The Revolt of the Masses* (2002: 29), he described the *Noli* as "written at the age of twenty-six." As we have seen, the book was written, on and off, over a period of at least two and a half years, and finally completed on 21 February 1887, when Rizal was four months short of 26.

VI

The pernicious error is an exercise in rank speculation. I do not mean a failed attempt at divining a puzzle in the life of Rizal, or a mere error in interpretation — these honest mistakes are only to be expected in any field of study. By base speculative error I mean interpretations not based on facts but on an assumed but often unarticulated ideology. Some of these errors have been hidden in plain view of scholar and reader alike, the eminence of their interpreters serving as cover. Retana's view that Rizal was the ideal Spaniard, for instance, or Craig's thesis that Rizal was the proto-American.

Of these eminent errors, perhaps none is more erroneous, and no one more eminent, than Miguel de Unamuno and his poetic interpretation of Rizal. I do not mean to suggest that there was no real poetry in Rizal; in fact, and as his own writings would show, Rizal was a true poet in both sensibility and achievement. (Though he came late to poetry, Unamuno was a poet of genuine inspiration too.) I only mean that Unamuno's tragic sense of the poetic — as relentlessly romantic, unsoiled by contact with reality — fails signally to do justice to Rizal.

That Unamuno wrote the eight-part epilogue for Retana's landmark *Vida y Escritos* (in two days, according to the epilogue itself) must be considered a coup for the biographer; Unamuno was the dynamic rector of the University of Salamanca, a leading light of the Generation of '98, and the owner of a growing reputation for literary mastery in all genres. In 1907, the same year Retana's biography came out, he had published his first book of poems. When he wrote the epilogue, his proto-existentialist masterpiece *Del Sentimiento Tragico de la Vida en los Hombres y en los Pueblos* (better known by its influential English version, *The Tragic Sense of Life*) was still six years in the future. But the religious crisis that had changed his outlook, and deepened his despairing view of the eternal conflict between thought and action, had already taken place.[6]

The *Diario intimo* he kept during and immediately after the crisis gives witness to his obsession with mortality (many entries begin with the word "Death," punctuated with a period) and to the great tension that existed between his faith and his reason, a conflict he resolved through an act of will — understood, however, in the specifically Christian sense, as a surrender to God's own will. His last notebook begins and ends with a meditation on Christ's basic prayer: "Thy will be done. This cry encompasses all prayer. God is asked for what must be in any case: that His will be done" (Unamuno 1984: 80–81).

Two years before writing the epilogue on Rizal, Unamuno had published *La Vida de Don Quijote y Sancho,* the first of his books to be translated into another language (Unamuno 1984: 221) as well as an examination of the meaning of Don Quixote's pursuit of spiritual values in the desert of Spain's arid materialism. It was precisely on this point, Rizal as a kind of Quixote, that Unamuno's epilogue begins to engage Retana's biography.

> "*Quijote oriental*" *le llama una vez Retana, y esta asi bien llamado. Pero fue un Quijote doblado de un Hamlet; fue un Quijote del pensamiento, a quien le repugnaban las impurezas de la realidad.* [Retana 1907: 476]
>
> Retana also called him an Oriental Don Quixote, and indeed this title describes him aptly; but he was Don Quixote with the substance of Hamlet, a Don Quixote only in thought, who had the greatest repugnance for reality with its impurities. [Unamuno 1968: 5]

This is meant to be praise, but in fact it is a gross misreading of the character of Rizal. Trinidad Pardo de Tavera, the "quintessential ilustrado" (Mojares 2006: 121) whose scholarly work Rizal admired and who knew Rizal on familiar terms, had no patience for this or any other display of "ignorance." In a lengthy analysis of "The Character of Rizal" in that early high-water mark of Philippine historiography, the bilingual *Philippine Review/Revista Filipina*, Pardo chose to respond to Retana's "carefully written work" because of a fundamental discovery: "*I have failed to find in it a study of the character of the martyr.*" (Pardo 1917: 41, his italics. Pardo's Spanish original appeared in the May 1917 issue; the fine English translation, presumably by the review's redoubtable editor Gregorio Nieva, that unsung hero of Philippine historical research who bridged the Spanish and the American eras, came out the following month. All the quotations I borrow, with their emphases, are from the English version.)

> I shall not undertake to attack his detractors who, to be sure, were not all actuated by political or religious hatred or resentments of a political nature. It is clearly to be seen that many of these attacks were the result of IGNORANCE, that IGNORANCE which succeeded in getting him deported, imprisoned and murdered; that IGNORANCE which he fought, which we go on fighting, and which the generations after us will still have to fight. [Pardo 1917: 42]

While making allowances for Unamuno's good faith (and Retana's too), Pardo proceeds to wage war on their well-intentioned ignorance. "I can not and must not pass over in silence that which is not only contrary to the real facts brought to the public knowledge by that same book [that is, Retana's biography], but which attributes to Rizal defects of importance that were never his."

To Unamuno's easy view that "Throughout his entire life he was nothing but *an impenitent dreamer, a poet*," Pardo replies: This "is a figure of speech not based on anything real, a statement unsupported by any act or any moment of the life of Rizal. He desired the advancement and welfare of the Filipino people. Did he desire anything unrealizable? His dream was to conquer, by reason, an era of liberty and rights for his people. How far is this dream of his unrealizable?"

To Unamuno's blithe view that "Rizal was a poet, a hero of thought and not of action ... Rizal, the valiant dreamer, appeared to me a weak and irresolute man for action and life," Pardo replies: "He preached *tolerance* and was *tolerant*; he advocated *study* and *studied*; *sincerity*, and was *loyal*; *valour*, and *died without flinching*; *work*, and *worked* as an author, physician, sculptor, mason, printer, and farmer."

And to Unamuno's dreamy view that "He was a Quijote of thought, who *looked with repugnance upon the impurities of reality*," Pardo replies: "What reality repelled him? ... neither Rizal nor [I] myself understand what the 'impurities of reality' are so long as they are not *realities* become *impure after they had ideal life*. Unamuno's opinions are a complete misrepresentation of the tendencies and character of Rizal and are unsupported by any known fact" (Pardo 1917: 42–43; all emphases are in the Spanish original too).

There is another thing: Unamuno helped Retana decipher the coded language Rizal sometimes used in his diaries, something the university rector took not a little satisfaction in (Retana 1907: 74; 90). It seems astonishing to me that his close study of the Madrid journal — which shows Rizal making a life even under straitened circumstances, doing without food for stretches at a time, scheduling self-improvement sessions by watching Shakespeare's plays and the like, excelling in his studies and extra-curricular projects despite what was effectively genteel poverty — makes Unamuno conclude that Rizal was not only impractical but irresolute!

Unamuno's opinions, however, have had a remarkably long shelf life. One of the most intellectually vigorous attempts to investigate the meaning of Rizal, the 1968 anthology *Rizal: Contrary Essays*, edited by Petronilo Bn. Daroy and Dolores Feria, gave pride of place to what it called "Unamuno's seminal study of Rizal," six decades after it first saw print. (The English translation by Antolina Antonio, however, presents only the first three parts of Unamuno's lengthy essay.) Studies on Rizal today continue to reference Unamuno's essay (although I cannot help but think that those who cite it as "Rizal: The Tagalog Hamlet" labour under the misimpression that the Antonio version is complete. The epilogue itself is titled simply "Rizal.")

What explains the continuing influence of Unamuno's erroneous views? Some of it must be due to the Spanish philosopher's great fame, especially in the first half of the twentieth century; his novels and plays had turned out to be a foreshadowing of the modernist advance in literature, his study of Kierkegaard and his exploration of the tragic sense of life a prefiguring of existentialist themes. The citations describing "the famous Unamuno" or some such variation are thus a subtle appeal to celebrity-as-authority. (Even Retana, writing at the turn of the twentieth century, could not stop himself; he refers to *"el ilustre* Unamuno," *"el gran* Unamuno," and so on, in his own text.) But some of it must be due to the ascendancy of the extreme nationalist orientation in Philippine historical studies, which popularized the great divide between true revolutionaries and mere reformers — with Rizal on the wrong side of the divide. Hence, Rizal as the irresolute dreamer, the Tagalog Hamlet.

The vexing biography of Trinidad Pardo de Tavera must have been a factor too. In a hundred years of Rizal studies, his was the most penetrating criticism of Unamuno's perspective — and yet that critique, until today, remains decidedly on the periphery. I fear Pardo's decade of service in the American colonial government, culminating in his years as the senior Filipino member of the Philippine Commission, marked him for life and may have resulted in a drastic discounting of his views.

Mojares, in his magisterial group study of the lives of Pardo, Pedro Paterno, and Isabelo de los Reyes, summed up the matter succinctly: "The pious nationalism of twentieth century Philippine historiography cast him as one of the procrastinators and collaborators in the 'struggle for independence' .... In the late 1940s and 1950s, in the context of the Huk rebellion and the influence of Marxism on Filipino intellectuals, class-based interpretations of the national history made Pardo even more unpopular. He was a convenient sign (together with men like Paterno and even Rizal) for a vacillating, opportunistic middle class[7] ..." (Mojares 2006: 228).

To be sure, Pardo did not think Rizal was ever a revolutionary.

> It is true he always feared revolution, and, what is more, he rejected it, as we all know, and it is thoroughly fantastic to say that *in his innermost soul he desired it*. These are gratuitous, unfounded, unlooked for opinions and come as a surprise from him who uttered them. [Pardo 1917: 43]

The words in italics are from Unamuno, but the sentiment is characteristically Pardo's. I will discuss the issue of Rizal as a revolutionary in later pages; may it suffice to say for now that this particular sentiment is more a reflection of Pardo than it is of Rizal, and that nevertheless Pardo was yet right: a man who was fatally aware of the deathly consequences of revolution could not have secretly desired it in his innermost soul. That would be merely poetic.

Pardo criticized both Unamuno and Retana (who was a friend of his and a regular correspondent) not only for their sweeping, rhetorical interpretation of Rizal but also for their selection of detail — the kind that lent itself, precisely, to sweeping, rhetorical interpretations.

> The fact that these [virtues] are positively known to have been his qualities of character makes me reject as false two statements attributed by certain persons to Rizal and alleged to have been made by him before his death. One is to the effect that shortly before being executed, he said to his confessor: "My presumption has ruined me." [Pardo 1917: 52]

To this alleged fact (Retana 1907: 431), Unamuno responds in character, by improvising a rhetorical rhapsody. He begins with a denial: "What is that about presumption? A person admitting that he is presumptuous has never had that fault." He becomes indignant: "The presumptuous ones were the others; the presumptuous ones were the barbarians who, over his body, uttered, as an insult to God, that sacrilegious "Viva España." He waxes expansive, and Biblical: "Yes, his presumption *caused his downfall in order that his race might rise*, because every one who wishes to save his soul will lose it and he who lets it be lost will save it." He ends by redefining presumption, thus turning the tables on Rizal's critics: "yes, his only presumption, the consciousness that in him there lived an intelligent, noble race, a race of dreamers..."

It sounds stirring, even ennobling; the momentum of the language carries us away. But to Pardo, the Spanish philosopher was talking through his hat. "Unamuno, inspired by a noble sentiment, errs in pronouncing these words, with regard to which I will say, *basing my affirmation on real facts*, that [Rizal's] dignity was not presumption, his firmness of character was not presumption, his self-denial was not presumption." Unamuno's neat reversal of terms works only if the issue were in black and white. But: "A person can not be PRESUMPTUOUS who acknowledges the shortcomings of his race and proclaims as a remedy for their redemption study, work, and the practice of the civic virtues" (Pardo 1917: 52).

Here we have a clue to the secret of Unamuno's rhetoric; his antitheses rely on balance, not merely between the sonorous periods but between ideas. But what, in truth, is the opposite of Rizal's own balanced views: his recognition of "the shortcomings of his race," his emphasis on the redeeming value of labour and suffering, his belief in the good example?

This first false statement (an absurdity, Pardo calls it) is kin to the second. (Indeed, they share the same source: Pastells' *La Masonizacion de Filipinas — Rizal y su obra*.)

> Nor can we accept as true the other statement attributed to him at that moment: "It is in Spain and in foreign countries where I was ruined." [Pardo 1917: 52]

Pardo recoils from the implications, not only because Rizal "knew fully well that he had never been ruined," but also and mainly because the two statements, together, represent Rizal as "a *presumptuous mesticillo*, according to the traditional formula, utterly ruined by the atmosphere of Spain and the foreign countries, because his narrow brain was not made for any climate or civilization outside of those of the Philippines." The two statements, together, make Rizal "confess in an indirect way *that his execution was just*, because he himself acknowledged that *he had been ruined*" (Pardo 1917: 52–53).

Here, then, are the wages of impenitent lyricism — but Unamuno's, not Rizal's.[8]

The philosopher's own personal courage cannot be gainsaid. When Primo de Rivera (the son and namesake, as it happens, of the man who was twice governor-general of the Philippines) mounted a coup in Madrid in 1923 and declared a dictatorship, Unamuno served as a symbol of resistance. At the height of the Spanish Civil War, he stood up, literally, to the bullying of a Loyalist general.[9] (The general responded to Unamuno's courageous admonition by shouting "Death to intelligence! Long live death!")

But Unamuno's poetic view of Rizal, like Retana's, is not only speculative; it is ultimately metropolitan. That is to say, it may have boldly criticized Spanish colonialism, but in fact it shared the assumptions of the former metropole. In that sense, it strips Rizal's courageous sacrifice, on behalf of a colony, of its full meaning.

VII

In my own view, Unamuno's worst excess was not his idea that Rizal was repelled by *las impurezas de la realidad* (this is, on reflection, a mere mirroring of the philosopher's concern about the divide between thought and action); it is his notion (reflecting his own tragic sense of life) that Rizal was a passive participant in his life's drama.

> *Rizal previo su fin, su fin glorioso y tragico; pero lo previo pasivamente, como el protagonista de una tragedia griega. No fue a el, sino que se*

> *sintio a el arrastrado. Y pudo decir: Hagase, Señor, tu voluntad y no la mia!* [Retana 1907: 477]
>
> Rizal foresaw his end, his tragic and glorious end, but like the principal character in a Greek tragedy, he foresaw it passively. It was not he who was the actor; rather it was as if some undertow had swept him into the role, and he could say, "Lord, Thy will be done, not mine!" [Unamuno 1968: 6]

Rizal's diaries make clear that he used similar religious phraseology too. But "Thy will be done" — the meaning Unamuno gives to it is nothing more than projection. He is reading his own "inner biography" (a concept he discussed in Unamuno 1921: 38) into Rizal's tragic life.

It is very likely that Rizal did foresee his end. The order of his arrest, when he was again on his way to Spain to board the ship that would take him to Cuba, came as a real shock; perhaps his four years in exile had dulled his sense of risk. But the day he spent in notorious Montjuich prison in Barcelona, the month it took to return to Manila, the two months he was kept in detention, the fortnight it took for the legal process to find its preordained way to a death sentence, the twenty-four hours he had between proclamation of the sentence and execution — he had plenty of time not only to contemplate his death but also to die on his own terms.

Rizal, however, was no passive spectator. (The Asians who held his "great struggle" up for emulation, such as Sukarno, or Shaharuddin bin Maaruf in *Concept of a Hero in Malay Society*, certainly did not see him that way.) He was a kinetic actor in his own drama, actively working not to avoid the fire, or flee from danger, or seek the solace of life in a peaceful country — to use the terms of his own counsel in his letter about the field of battle. As a consequence, he was perpetually wrestling with his will. To Unamuno, struck by the seeming inevitability of Rizal's death and conditioned by his own preoccupation with mortality, he was the passive hero in a Greek tragedy. In reality, Rizal's wilful embrace of an entirely avoidable death was positively, eminently, Shakespearean.

Notes

1. Teodoro Sandiko, the young Latin teacher who taught Spanish on the sly to the now-famous "women of Malolos," in Bulacan province. In 1888, the women petitioned the governor-general of the Philippine colony for the privilege of learning Spanish; their request sharpened the conflict between the town and its truculent parish priest. In February 1889, Marcelo del Pilar asked Rizal to write the women a message of encouragement; he complied immediately. The result was, after his translation of *Wilhelm Tell*, Rizal's longest work in Tagalog.
2. A feature in the *Philippines Free Press* of 25 December 1948 tells the story of how Rizal recruited Perfecto Rufino Riego, a cabin boy on a ship that plied the Manila-Hong Kong run, to help smuggle in *buri* sacks full of copies of the *Noli*. Augusto de Viana's *The I-Stories*, a helpful compendium of "alternative" eyewitness accounts of the Revolution and the Philippine-American war, recounts the interesting details (De Viana 2006: 7–13). There are some inconsistencies in Riego's account (by the time the story came out he was already in his eighties), but the basic facts seem authentic.
3. In this letter, Rizal searches for the Tagalog for *Freiheit* or liberty; he has just translated Schiller's *Wilhelm Tell* and confesses to his inadequacy: "I lacked many words." He mentions del Pilar's use, in the translation of Rizal's first essay written in Spain, "*El Amor Patrio*," of the words *malaya* and *kalayahan* — an indication that the word Filipinos use today to refer to freedom, *kalayaan*, may have been forged in the smithy of the Propaganda. Also in this letter he speaks frankly of his ambition: "It is very painful for me to give up publishing this work on which I have worked day and night for a period of many months and on which I have pinned great hopes. With this I wish to make myself known…" (Rizal 1963a: 243–45).
4. A passage from "A Friendly Estimate of the Filipinos," an essay Barrows wrote for *Asia Magazine* in November 1921, quoted in Serafin E. Macaraig's *Social Problems* (1929: 106), is worth reproducing; it turns the whole issue of alleged Filipino indolence upside down. "… Filipinos are willing workers. They are early risers, so that by ten o'clock in the morning they have accomplished the better part of the day's work; and if, at this period, belated and late-rising foreigners desire to requisition their services, their indifference will give rise to reproaches of indolence."
5. "Barrows' *History of the Philippines* exhibits the first textbook plotting of Philippine history along the medieval-to-modern axis. It is, in effect, a narrative of transition that makes the reader see failure, or at least lack and inadequacy, in the thoughts and actions of Filipinos, until their race

has become fully hitched to the bandwagon of European history" (Ileto 1997: 65).
6. Allen Lacy's introduction to *The Private World: Selections from the Diario Intimo and Selected Letters 1890–1936* (1984) is most enlightening on Unamuno's religious crisis of 1897. Unamuno's biography is outlined in that same book, as well as in Salvador de Madariaga's interesting if somewhat breezy introduction to the 1921 edition of *Tragic Sense of Life*; his philosophy is discussed in great depth in Julian Marias' *Miguel de Unamuno*, translated by Frances Lopez-Morillas (1966); see, for instance, "Unamuno's Theme" (11–30). I have also profited from online profiles of Unamuno, especially the one written by Petri Liukkonen available at <http://www.kirjasto.sci.fi/unamuno.htm> and the entry in Britannica Online available at <http://www.britannica.com/EBchecked/topic/613982/Miguel-de-Unamuno>.
7. But even the arch-nationalist Agoncillo quoted him when his well-phrased views proved convenient. For instance, in *The Revolt of the Masses* (2002), he quotes Pardo at length, first on the impact the *Noli*'s expose of conditions in the colony had on the "prestige [of] Spanish civilization in the Islands" (29–30) and then in a candid but sympathetic portrait of Aguinaldo (180). But aside from Mojares' superb *Brains of the Nation*, I cannot find a citation for Pardo's deconstruction of Unamuno in the major texts.
8. An alternative reading of Unamuno's antitheses is suggested in a letter he addressed to Jose Ortega y Gasset a year before he wrote the epilogue: "Every day, friend Ortega, I feel more and more impelled to make gratuitous assertions, more given to arbitrary statements, to the passionate stance, and every day I am more rooted in my own form of anarchism, which is the true form .... If you only knew, my dear Ortega, the travail I undergo to give birth to what they call paradoxes!" (Unamuno 1984: 180). In his Author's Preface to J. E. Crawford Flitch's translation of *The Tragic Sense of Life*, Unamuno also said: "The truth is that, being an incorrigible Spaniard, I am naturally given to a kind of extemporization ..." (Unamuno 1921: 34).
9. A moving account of the encounter in the packed Ceremonial Hall of the University of Salamanca between university rector Unamuno and General Jose Millan Astray can be found in *The Private World* (Unamuno 1984: 263–71). The author, Luis Portillo, described the philosopher's eloquent defiance as "Unamuno's Last Lecture." Unamuno died two months later, on 31 December 1936.

A RIZAL CHRONOLOGY

1861

19 June   Rizal is born in the town of Calamba, in the province of Laguna, on the island of Luzon, to Francisco Rizal Mercado and Teodora Alonso. He is the couple's seventh child; his only brother Paciano turns 10 years old the same year.

22 June   Rizal is baptized as Jose Rizal Mercado, bearing his father's full surname. Rizal was added to the Mercado family name after the Claveria decree of 1849.

1868   Multatuli's *Max Havelaar* (first published in 1860) is translated into English by Baron Alphonse Nahuijs. Twenty years later, Rizal reads Multatuli in London, most probably in the English version. This sweeping indictment of Dutch misrule in Java helps lead Rizal to found a secret society with a pan-Malayan orientation.

1869

17 November   The Suez Canal is opened. The new passage reduces travel time between Spain and its Philippine colony from half a year to just about a month, sparking a boom in travel from the Spanish peninsula to the islands and vice versa. In time, families of means begin sending their sons to study at the universities in Europe. Rizal crosses the Canal five times: in 1882, in 1887, in 1891, and twice in 1896.

1872

17 February   The Filipino priests Mariano Gomez, Jose Burgos, and Jacinto Zamora (known to later generations as the martyrs Gom-Bur-Za) are executed, for alleged

	involvement in the Cavite Mutiny the month before. The student Paciano Rizal, a *protégé* of Burgos', returns to the province to escape government attention.
26 June	Rizal is enrolled at the Ateneo Municipal, the Jesuit school established only two years before he was born. To limit any fallout from Paciano's association with Burgos, he is enrolled as Jose Rizal, without the second family name. He graduates with the highest honours in 1877.
1878	Rizal enrols at the venerable Dominican University of Santo Tomas, the only school of higher learning in the Philippine colony. It was founded in 1611.
1879	
22 November	Rizal writes "A la Juventud Filipina" as an entry for a literary competition; the poem, which speaks of the Filipino youth as *"bella esperanza de patria mia —* the fair hope of my country," is used as evidence of Rizal's separatism in December 1896, when he is tried for rebellion and illegal association.
1882	
3 May	Rizal sails for Spain, with neither his parents' knowledge nor permission. He is to continue his studies in medicine, and to meet a higher purpose. In a letter to his parents, he wrote: "I too have a mission to fill, as for example: alleviating the sufferings of my fellow-men."
9 May	He arrives in Singapore; it is, as he dutifully notes in his diary, his first "foreign country."
20 August	His first published piece — "*El Amor Patrio*," written soon after he arrived in Spain — appears in the new

bilingual newspaper in Manila, *Diariong Tagalog*. A Tagalog translation is prepared by Marcelo del Pilar.

1884

21 June   Rizal receives his licentiate in medicine from the Universidad Central de Madrid. His licentiate in philosophy and letters is awarded the following year.

25 June   At a special banquet in honour of the prize winning Filipino painters Juan Luna and Felix Resurreccion Hidalgo, Rizal offers a *brindis* or toast that Madrid newspapers describe as thoughtful and residents in the Philippines see, inevitably, as subversive. Rizal's assumption of the leadership of the Filipino colony in Spain may be said to begin on this day.

1886

31 July   He begins a decade-long correspondence and a lasting friendship with the Austrian scholar Ferdinand Blumentritt. In an early letter, Blumentritt informs Rizal about the existence of a rare copy of Antonio Morga's early seventeenth century history of the Philippines.

1887

21 February   Rizal completes the final draft of *Noli Me Tangere*, his first novel. It would make him the most famous man — and to Spaniards the most dangerous — in the Philippines.

13 May   Rizal, accompanied by his "*landsmann*" Maximo Viola, visits Blumentritt for the first and only time in Leitmeritz (present-day Litomerice). They stay for four days.

26 July On the voyage back to the Philippines, Rizal makes a stopover in Singapore and then, on 30 July, in Saigon (present-day Ho Chi Minh City).

5 August Rizal arrives in Manila; he had spent five years and a month in various parts of Europe. He soon begins a lively medical practice, acquiring a reputation as "the German doctor."

1888

3 February Under pressure from the colonial government and the religious orders, Rizal leaves for Hong Kong. He writes Blumentritt: "They forced me to leave my country."

28 February Rizal arrives in Japan. It is a happy interlude. On 13 April he leaves Yokohama on board the *Belgic*, bound for the United States. On the ship, he makes the acquaintance of Suehiro Tetcho, who would later write a Japanese novel set in the Philippines that was influenced by both the *Noli* and Rizal's own biography.

1 March Local officials in the Manila province issue the Manifestation of 1888, an unprecedented petition seeking the expulsion of the friars from the Philippines. A biographer notes: "It was the first public outcome of the influence of *Noli Me Tangere*."

28 April Rizal arrives in San Francisco, where he together with other Asians are placed under quarantine. In May he crosses the continental United States via rail. The emerging power leaves him unimpressed. He leaves New York for Liverpool on 16 May.

2 June Rizal arrives in London. He would spend the next several months doing research at the British Museum, and copying the Morga by hand.

6 December An unusually excited Rizal writes Blumentritt to tell him of a wonderful discovery: He has just read Multatuli's "extraordinarily interesting" novel about Dutch misrule in Java, *Max Havelaar*.

1889

15 February The first issue of *La Solidaridad*, the Filipino newspaper founded to advance the Propaganda in Spain, is published in Barcelona. Graciano Lopez Jaena serves briefly as chief editor.

March–May In quick succession, Rizal organizes the Kidlat Club, the Indios Bravos, and the secret society "Rd. L. M." He and other Filipino expatriates attend the Paris Exposition.

October (?) Rizal's annotated Morga, which bears a publication date of 1890, comes off the press. Blumentritt writes: "This edition with your erudite notes will glorify your name."

15 November The first issue of *La Solidaridad* is printed in Madrid, the newspaper's new base. Marcelo del Pilar, the new chief editor, serves in this post until the newspaper's very last issue, in 1895.

1891

September *El Filibusterismo*, his second and "darker" novel, is published in Ghent, Belgium.

October (?) Rizal writes his "field of battle" letter, explaining his decision to return to the country, for good. "The field of battle is the Philippines: that's where we should meet."

18 October Rizal leaves for Hong Kong, where he arrives on 20 November; his second European sojourn had lasted three years and four months.

10 November	Rizal arrives in Singapore for the third time. "I found Singapore much altered with many jinrikshaws and with a steam streetcar."
14 November	Back in Saigon, the assiduous correspondent notes: "At 12 o'clock we went ashore and proceeded to the telegraph station to send a telegram to Hong Kong. Four words (2 dollars and 14 cents). Post cards at 2 cents."
6 December	Most of Rizal's family, including his father and Paciano, reunite in Hong Kong. His mother will follow in several days. He later writes Blumentritt: "Here we are all living together, my parents, sisters, and brother, in peace and far from the persecutions they suffered in the Philippines."

1892

7 March	Rizal visits Sandakan, in northern Borneo. He makes plans to found a Filipino settlement.
26 June	Rizal returns to the Philippines a second time. He meets the governor-general that same night, and wins pardon for his father.
3 July	The organizational meeting of the Liga Filipina, a patriotic association, is held in the residence of Doroteo Ongjunco. The event would later be used in Rizal's trial, as a crucial link in the prosecution's case.
6 July	Rizal is arrested in the governor-general's palace, and then detained at Fort Santiago for a week; on 15 July, he is deported to Dapitan, in the northern part of the island of Mindanao.
7 July	News of Rizal's arrest is published in the *Gaceta de Manila*. On the same day, Andres Bonifacio et al found the revolutionary organization Katipunan.

1894

February — Governor-General Ramon Blanco meets Rizal in the cruiser *Castilla*, off the waters of Dapitan. He offers the exile the chance to relocate to Luzon.

1895

Rizal meets Josephine Bracken, who would eventually live with him in Dapitan.

1896

3–4 May — A grand assembly of the Katipunan, which is under threat of discovery, resolves to consult Rizal about the planned uprising.

1 July — Pio Valenzuela, the Katipunan's emissary, confers with Rizal in Dapitan.

6 August — Rizal arrives in Manila, from Dapitan. On the same day, the Katipunan attempts to rescue him, but he declines the opportunity.

29 August — At nine in the evening, the Katipuneros rise up in arms; it is the beginning of the Philippine revolution.

3 September — Rizal leaves for Spain, hoping to serve as a military doctor in Cuba.

8 September — Another Singapore stopover. "In the morning we slowly entered Singapore and we docked beside the wooden pier. The peddlers do not go on board but display their goods on the pier. I have observed some changes. There are more Chinese merchants and fewer Indian."

30 September — Wenceslao Retana's "Un Separatista Filipino — Jose Rizal" is published in *La Politica de España en Filipinas*, in Madrid. The vitriolic article helps influence the prosecution's case against Rizal, when he is charged in December before a Spanish court-martial.

3 October	Rizal arrives in Barcelona, but is allowed to disembark only on 6 October; after a few hours in notorious Montjuich prison, he is ordered to sail back to the Philippines on the same day, this time as a prisoner.
3 November	Rizal arrives in Manila, and is immediately imprisoned in Fort Santiago.
15 December	Rizal writes his controversial manifesto addressed to "certain Filipinos," appealing to them to stop the insurrection. The judge advocate-general, however, refuses to allow publication because "far from promoting peace, [it] is likely to stimulate for the future the spirit of rebellion."
19 December	An article predicting that if the rebellion in the Philippines were to succeed, the islands would be at risk of Japanese expansionist ambitions is printed in *Java Bode*, in Batavia (present-day Jakarta).
26 December	The Spanish court-martial finds Rizal guilty of the crimes "of founding illegal associations and of promoting and inciting to the crime of rebellion."
29 December	Rizal is informed that he has been sentenced to die the following morning, by musketry. At night, Rizal's most famous poem, "Mi Ultimo Adios," is completed.
30 December	Rizal is executed. The time of death: 7 o'clock in the morning.

1897

16 January	News of Rizal's execution reaches Batavia, present-day Jakarta.

1898

12 June	Emilio Aguinaldo proclaims Philippine independence. On the same day, Apolinario Mabini joins Aguinaldo's as his chief adviser.

30 December The first official "Rizal Day" is commemorated, following a decree issued by Emilio Aguinaldo, president of the revolutionary government. The year before, Aguinaldo and other revolutionary leaders exiled to Hong Kong marked Rizal's first death anniversary with simple rites.

1899

3 April Antonino Guevara y Mendoza, the revolutionary known as Matatag (Firm), completes his *History of One of the Initiators of the Filipino Revolution*. In this slim volume dedicated to Emilio Aguinaldo, Matatag pays special tribute to "*el inolvidable Dr Rizal* — the unforgettable Dr Rizal."

1900 Mariano Ponce writes *History of the War for Philippine Independence*; it is subsequently translated into Japanese in 1901 and Chinese in 1902. The latter version becomes "perhaps the single most influential text" on Chinese interpretations of the Philippine revolution.

1901

23 March After a year and a half on the run, Emilio Aguinaldo is captured by American occupation forces in Palanan, Isabela, in northern Luzon.
The Indische Bond, a mutual aid association said to be inspired by the Philippine revolution, is formed in the Dutch East Indies.

1905

May The Russo-Japanese War ends in Russian humiliation. The victory of the Japanese emboldens Asia's emerging nationalists.

1912

30 December   The now-iconic Rizal Monument in Manila, built at the site of his execution through a public subscription, is inaugurated.

1913

31 March   Artemio Ricarte, Filipino revolutionary general and staunch anti-American, completes a proposed Constitution for what he calls the "Rizaline Republic."

15 May   E. F. E. Douwes Dekker's essay entitled "Rizal" is published in *Het Tijdschrift*. It is the first in-depth look at the Filipino hero in the Dutch East Indies; it also reflects the "Indo" pioneer nationalist's view at the time, of a nationalist movement under mestizo leadership.

June–July   Douwes Dekker's articles on the Philippine Revolution appear in *De Expres*, in the Netherlands Indies.

1921

30 November   The first official holiday to mark Andres Bonifacio's birthday, mandated by a law sponsored by Senator Lope K. Santos, is celebrated.

1922

Labour leader Hermenegildo Cruz publishes *Kartilyang Makabayan*, a primer on Bonifacio and the Katipunan. The effort to distance the founder and his revolution from Rizal's legacy is now apparent.

1925

July   The Indonesian nationalist Tan Malaka, representative for Southeast Asia of the Communist International, arrives in Manila. He will be based in the Philippine capital, on and off, for the next two years.

1926
November The communist uprising in West Java fails.

1927
January The communist uprising in West Sumatra fails. Tan Malaka had warned his colleagues that an uprising at this time was premature.
Artemio Ricarte, a general in the Philippine revolutionary army, publishes his memoirs in Yokohama. In it, he acknowledges the revolution's debt to Rizal.
Santiago Alvarez, another ranking revolutionary general, begins writing his memoirs.

1938 In what is possibly the first mention of Rizal in a Malay-language publication, nationalist Ibrahim Haji Yaacob references Rizal in *Majlis* (The Council), the newspaper he edits. "He was the father of the Filipino's struggle against western colonialism."

1942
10 October Sukarno, the Indonesian nationalist leader, speaks of "Jose Rizal y Mercado" for the first time. (At least it is the earliest reference on record.) He would reference Rizal numerous times, especially during his term as Indonesia's first president.

1943
30 December *Asia Raya* publishes a front-page profile of "Jose Rizal y Mercado."

1944

7 September — The so-called Koiso Declaration: Prime Minister Koiso of Japan "announces the future independence of all Indonesian peoples." It galvanises Indonesian nationalists.

30 December — An Indonesian translation of "Mi Ultimo Adios," by the young journalist Rosihan Anwar, is published in the Jakarta newspaper *Asia Raya*. At night, Rosihan reads the translation on Jakarta radio.

1945

17 August — Sukarno proclaims Indonesian independence. On the same day, Jose Laurel issues an order officially declaring an end to the second (Japanese-sponsored) Philippine republic.

10 November — The iconic Battle of Surabaya, between Indonesian rebel youth and British forces protecting Dutch interests, begins. Sent by Sukarno et al to monitor the situation, Rosihan Anwar spends the next three days in the city, at the time of the fiercest fighting. On his way out, he is shown a pemuda magazine printed on "bad paper." Inside he finds his translation of Rizal's farewell poem.

1946

July — Rosihan Anwar's translation of "Mi Ultimo Adios" is reprinted as part of a special issue on Philippine independence in *Bakti*, a revolutionary magazine published in Mojokerto, in East Java.

1948

Tan Malaka publishes his memoirs; the English translation by Helen Jarvis won't appear until 1991.

1950   *Jose Protasio Rizal: Pelopor Kemerdekaan Bangsa Pilipina* (Pioneer of Philippine Independence) is published in Jakarta as part of a series on heroes (the list includes Kartini, Gandhi, Sun Yat-sen). The Indonesian translation of F. W. Michels' Dutch original is by the poet Amal Hamzah. "Selamat Tinggal," a new, more complete translation of "Mi Ultimo Adios," presumably by Hamzah himself, is included.

1956
May   Teodoro Agoncillo's *The Revolt of the Masses* is published; it quickly becomes the standard account of Bonifacio and the Katipunan, and while acknowledging a deep debt to Rizal's role effectively damns him as a mere reformer.

12 June After prolonged and acrimonious debate, the Philippine legislature passes a law (Republic Act 1425) requiring the study of Rizal. "Courses on the life, works and writings of Jose Rizal, particularly his novel *Noli Me Tangere* and *El Filibusterismo*, shall be included in the curricula of all schools, colleges and universities, public or private ..."

1961
4 December The five-day International Congress on Rizal convenes in Manila, to mark Rizal's centenary. On 7 December, Indonesian journalist Rosihan Anwar presents a paper on "Rizal's Name in Indonesia" and reads his 1944 translation of Rizal's "Ultimo Adios."

1969

30 December — Renato Constantino reads "Veneration without Understanding" as the year's Rizal Day Lecture. It has since become the standard critique of Rizal's place in the Philippine pantheon of heroes.

1975

Tjetje Jusuf's translation of *Noli Me Tangere (Jangan Sentuh Aku)* is published in Jakarta.

1977

19 January — *The Myth of the Lazy Native*, by Syed Hussein Alatas, is published together with *Intellectuals in Developing Societies*. Both books discuss Rizal's work as public intellectual and incipient sociologist.

30 December — Chandra Muzaffar, who studied Rizal under Syed Hussein Alatas, founds ALIRAN (the Nationalist Consciousness Movement) on Rizal's death anniversary. "I chose 30 December, the day of his martyrdom."

1983

The first edition of Benedict Anderson's influential *Imagined Communities* is published. It reintroduces Rizal, and especially the *Noli*, to a worldwide audience.

1984

Shaharuddin bin Maaruf publishes *Concept of a Hero in Malay Society*, a courageous survey of pernicious influences on the Malaysian idea of heroism. The book recommends Rizal as one of three ideal heroes to emulate. In 1994, the Malay translation receives a Commendation from the National Book Development Council of Singapore.

1994

Tjetje Jusuf's translation of *El Filibusterismo (Merajalelanya Keserakahan)*, based on Charles

Derbyshire's English translation (*The Reign of Greed*), is published in Jakarta.

1995

2–3 October   Malaysia hosts the International Conference on Jose Rizal and the Asian Renaissance, with Deputy Prime Minister Anwar Ibrahim as convenor and a keynote speaker. "We associate Rizal and his like, such as Muhammad Iqbal and Rabindranath Tagore, with the Asian Renaissance because they are transmitters *par excellence* of the humanistic tradition."

1997

28–30 August   Jakarta hosts the International Conference on the Philippine Revolution and the First Asian Republic. Rosihan Anwar's translation of "Mi Ultimo Adios" is included in the record of the proceedings.

1999

May   Pramoedya Ananta Toer, Indonesia's greatest novelist, accepts an honorary doctorate from the University of Michigan. In a post-event interview, he acknowledges the writers who have inspired his work: John Steinbeck, William Saroyan, Emile Zola, Maxim Gorky, and Jose Rizal.

1

Turning Points

He was, self-evidently, a man of projects. From his letters and diaries, and from the accounts of those who knew him best, we get the impression that Rizal was incapable of standing still, of doing nothing. He always had something *going on*.

His closest friends, like the tireless letter-writer Evaristo Aguirre, understood. "Do not be surprised that I have delayed answering your esteemed letter of 10 November," Aguirre writes at the end of January, in 1887, by way of excusing his "prolonged silence" in corresponding with Rizal. "It was because, not long after having received it, I was told that you had gone to Italy, through a notice from Ceferino de Leon, on account of your chest ailment; it was only on the night of 31 December, when we gathered, that I found out that your trip was not certain, but simply an idea or a project [*un proyecto*] of yours, as yet undecided."[1]

A Spaniard born in Kawit (Cauit), Cavite, just south of Manila, and in the 1880s a student in Madrid, Aguirre considered himself a pure Filipino and shared Rizal's sense of patriotic obligation; if anything, his nationalism was a step ahead of Rizal's, and by the time *La Solidaridad* was launched in 1889 as the flagship of the Propaganda campaign to publicise the evils of Spanish colonial rule in the Philippines, he already recognized the futility of political agitation in Spain. Like Julio Llorente, another friend of Rizal's, he had been disillusioned by the intrigues and the insipidity of the short-lived

España en Filipinas, the *Soli*'s forerunner. The biographer Leon Ma. Guerrero professed some impatience with Aguirre's kilometric letters, but as John Schumacher SJ, the definitive chronicler of the Propaganda, noted less than a decade after *The First Filipino* appeared in print, Aguirre's letters were "a principal source for the events of this period" (Schumacher 1997: 59; the first edition of Schumacher's *The Propaganda Movement* came out in 1973).

Aguirre's letters help paint a portrait of Rizal as perpetually engaged in one undertaking after another. We can follow the progress of some of the projects that reached completion: Rizal's "grand tour" of Europe before returning home, the translation of Schiller's *Wilhelm Tell* and of some tales of Hans Christian Andersen, above all the making of the novel that would seal both Rizal's fame and fate, the *Noli Me Tangere* (Rizal 1963b: 59–60; 66; 70; 87–88). But we can also trace those projects that were for various reasons never finished, what we can call Rizal's false starts: for instance, a translation of Goethe's *Faust*, the studies of Sanskrit, or "that other novel with a historical background that you have in mind" (Rizal 1963b: 75; also 70).

Other letters in the ample Rizal correspondence add colour to the portrait. One from Rizal in Berlin to his great friend Ferdinand Blumentritt in Leitmeritz (present-day Litomerice, in the Czech Republic) speaks of two major projects: "I am planning to translate into Tagalog the travels of Jagor as soon as I finish the translation of Waitz ... I hope to be able to finish this work in spring" (Rizal 1963c: 44). In fact, the translation (into Spanish) of the fifth volume of Theodor Waitz's *Anthropology of Primitive Peoples*, an undertaking for which Rizal had initially allotted three weeks (Rizal 1963c: 27), was never completed; the translation of Feodor Jagor's account of his travels to the Philippines never begun.

Another letter, sent by Rizal from his Dapitan exile to his brother-in-law Manuel Hidalgo, talks of a business venture. "Here I have formed a partnership with a Spaniard to supply the town with fish of which it lacks .... If you wish to sell me your *pukutan* [a dragnet for deep-sea fishing] at an agreed price, and if it is still in good condition, I would buy it" (Rizal 1963a: 354). But nothing came of this plan, or the partnership.

A bare list of plans mulled or projects uncompleted can fill up several pages. They include the proposal to publish an anthology of writings by Filipinos in Spain; the attempt to read Dutch scholarship on the Philippines; the plan to read up on colonization ("I am studying all the books about colonies that have been published" — Rizal 1963e: 124); the campaign to persuade Blumentritt to write a history of the Philippines; his enrolment in additional French classes to master the language, in order to write a novel in French; the project to found a Filipino colony in Sandakan, in North Borneo; even the founding of La Liga Filipina in 1892 — these and many others in various stages of initiation throw a different kind of light on Rizal's character. The completed work on the *Noli*, the annotated edition of Morga's *Sucesos de las Islas Filipinas*, and the even more subversive second novel, *El Filibusterismo*, demonstrate Rizal's extraordinary willpower. They were written and published under severely trying circumstances. (The waterworks system he constructed in Dapitan is proof of the same kind: it was completed with meagre resources, without explosives, using material that was ready to hand.) But the many unfinished projects — these tell us something fundamental about Rizal's character too. He was eminently practical; that is to say, he had a bias for activity.

(He dispensed equally practical advice: read the complete works of Voltaire, he wrote Marcelo del Pilar; study Italian to read Antonio Pigafetta's account of Magellan's voyage to the Philippines, he implored the Filipino community in Spain; bring a printing press to the Philippines, he urged Mariano Ponce.)

What seems striking about all these projects, those that came to pass and those that didn't, those that were exercises in self-improvement and those that were initiatives in nation-forming, is that they were all animated by a sense of the possible.

Can the same be said of his plan to serve as a military doctor in Cuba? The idea, first suggested by Blumentritt and enthusiastically seconded by Antonio Ma. Regidor, was cobbled together out of an exile's desperation; the reprieve from his Mindanao exile that he had been led to expect (perhaps a transfer to Luzon or, if that proved politically untenable, "my passport to the Peninsula to restore my broken health") never materialized.

Governor-General Ramon Blanco had met Rizal off the coast of Dapitan in late 1894, and offered to relocate the exile to Luzon. Nothing came of it, however. "Since Your Excellency had the kindness to promise me my transfer to Ilocos or La Union, many months have passed," Rizal wrote Blanco on 8 May 1895. "I see that no alternative remains to me but to accept what Your Excellency had deigned to propose to me when you were here on board the Castilla, which is my passport to the Peninsula to restore my broken health" (Rizal 1963e: 324).

When he finally asked permission to serve in Cuba late in 1895, a year had passed since the promise of a transfer to Luzon was made; by the time he received the governor-general's authorization, in a letter dated 1 July 1896 but received 30 July, he had already marked his fourth anniversary as an exile.

"This letter upset my plans," he wrote Blumentritt while en route to Spain for the third and last time, in a letter pivotal to any understanding of Rizal's conduct in his last few months, "for I was not thinking of going anymore to Cuba in view of the fact that more than six months had already elapsed since I filed my application; but fearing that they might attribute [my decision] to something else if I should now refuse to go, I decided to abandon everything and depart immediately" (Rizal 1963d: 536).

But Cuba wouldn't have been an option (the last in a short and desperate list) if Rizal had not been in Dapitan in the first place, and he wouldn't have been deported to Dapitan if he hadn't risked returning to the Philippines a second time. Coming home in 1892 was not only against the advice of friends like Blumentritt and Regidor — "I only regret that on account of his youthful inexperience he had ignored my counsel when he put his head in the mouth of the wolf, giving credit to the empty talk and supposed integrity of the wicked [Governor-General Eulogio] Despujol," Regidor wrote Jose Ma. Basa in 1895, more than three years after Rizal walked into the wolf's lair (Rizal 1963e: 336). It was also "harshly" criticized by others who, in Apolinario Mabini's choice summary, thought it was "a useless and a childish display of rash valour" (Mabini undated: 183).

Rizal could have stayed in Hong Kong where he had a successful medical practice, or gone back to Europe where he was a member of several scientific associations, or taken up the proposal of the new Comite de Propaganda to serve as the campaign's diplomatic representative to other countries (Schumacher 1997: 270–71). These were all honourable alternatives, and he knew and admired compatriots who had chosen or been forced by circumstance to accept alternate destinies.

Trinidad Pardo de Tavera, scholar-turned-politician,[2] for instance. Jose Alejandrino, a general in the revolution who had assisted in the printing of the *Fili* in Ghent, Belgium, recorded Rizal's high opinion of the doctor and linguist. "Rizal, with his habitual high sense of proportion and justice, told me without any false modesty that Dr T. H. Pardo de Tavera deserved to appear ahead of him in the encyclopedias for his linguistic works, especially for his reform of our alphabet with the resulting improvement in our spelling" (Alejandrino 1949: 6). Indeed, in Rizal's proposed reform of Tagalog orthography (a project successfully completed), he references Pardo at least seven times (Rizal 1933: 10–21).

The anti-friar Jose Ma. Basa was another example. Exiled from the Philippines for alleged complicity in the Cavite Mutiny of 1872, Basa ended up a successful businessman in Hong Kong. From its busy harbour, he served, essentially, as the Propaganda's transhipment hub. The Propagandists in Europe sent him Rizal's books, del Pilar's pamphlets, and other subversive material, and he found ways to smuggle them into the Philippines. Rizal paid him great respect, sharing confidences and even recruiting the much older man into his secret society, the "Rd. L. M." When a reversal of fortune overtook him, Rizal wrote to his mother, then still in Hong Kong, on 19 October 1892: "I am sending Don Jose Basa 200 pesos on the pretext that they are to cover household expenses. On no account must you take any money from him, for I owe this gentleman a number of small amounts when he was rich and I was a student, and now that he has come down in the world I want to repay him the small expenses I occasioned him in the past" (Guerrero 2007: 361).

Then there was the example of the advocate Regidor, a political refugee who, despite a humiliating exile as a Spanish-trained lawyer in Victorian London, managed to keep himself heavily involved in Philippine affairs. Banished to the Marianas like Basa and Pardo's beloved uncle Joaquin Pardo de Tavera after the 1872 mutiny, he was one of the first and most enthusiastic readers of the *Noli*; his lengthy letter of 3 May 1887 offers the second most detailed critique available of the novel's first printing (after Blumentritt's extended review).

> Today I have finished reading your most interesting book, and I must tell you candidly that I have not read a more truthful or more graphic description of our much slandered and chastised society. Who does not know "Fr Damaso"? Ah, I have met him; and though in your brilliant characterization in your novel he wears the habit of the dirty Franciscan, always rude, always tyrannical, and invariably corrupt, I have met him and studied him in real life in the Philippines. [Rizal 1963b: 110]

The paragraph continues for several more lines, comparing other Damasos in Augustinian habit or Recollect tunic; it is followed by nine more paragraphs dealing with specific characters in the *Noli*. To readers who all too readily assume that Crisostomo Ibarra is only Rizal in disguise (an error committed not only by modern-day Filipinos who cannot read Spanish but also by turn-of-the-century

Spaniards, such as Rizal's first biographer Wenceslao Retana), Regidor's discussion of the novel's lead character should give pause:

> If all these characters portray perfectly social life in the Archipelago, what can I say about "Ibarra" whose life and misfortunes are similar to mine and my humble history. I don't know if some one will dare question the absolute reality of this victim of despotism and colonial corruption; but if such a thing should happen, I can point out to him historical facts ... If he [that is, Ibarra] is pure idealization, the greater is the merit of the author; for he must be a great artist indeed who can reproduce on one canvas the typical and salient lines of three or four different faces and succeeds to make the beholder recognize with every change of light the exact likeness of a dear friend who died on the scaffold, in prison, in exile, or in disgrace... [Rizal 1963b: 111–12]

This introspective note seems out of character in the extant letters of Regidor or the anecdotes about him found in the correspondence of both Rizal and del Pilar. The other letters portray him as a man with a pragmatic streak, and it was this pragmatism that must have emboldened some friars to reach out to Rizal and del Pilar through him (see Rizal 1931: 290–92). Perhaps it was this same quality that made him hesitate from honouring his offer to underwrite the cost of Rizal's second book, the annotated history by Morga — there was no market for it. "It was not a very successful venture in any sense," notes Guerrero (2007: 221). Coates has an account more sympathetic to Regidor, but in my view he misreads part of the evidence.[3]

But Regidor continued to make himself useful, to Rizal and to the widely scattered expatriates. He contributed to the Spanish press (Schumacher 1997: 190), negotiated for Rizal's release from exile (Rizal 1963e: 335), wrote a faulty but not altogether unreliable account of the events of 1872 (Schumacher 1991: 91–90). In later years, he served as willing source for historians and researchers.

He was one of six individuals (Saturnina Rizal and Mariano Ponce were among the others) that the American biographer Austin Craig depended on to write his *Life, Lineage and Labours of Jose Rizal*, a debt he acknowledged 15 years after the fact, in the foreword to his *Rizal's Life and Minor Writings*. Craig's belated portrait of Regidor is not without its pathos.

> "Dr Antonio Regidor y Jurado, the real leader of the civil agitation in the Philippines under the liberal regime of 1868, returned to Manila after over a third-of-a-century's absence to find himself almost forgotten and the affairs in which he had played so important a part practically unknown. His long residence in London made him Anglo-Saxon in his outlook and he could anticipate my difficulties in understanding the complex situation that led up to his exile for alleged complicity in the fabulous Cavite conspiracy... In his conversations and explanations he did not use that reserve which have made his writings less esteemed by persons who forget the conditions under which he wrote." [Craig 1927: x]

Perhaps it's best to remember Regidor in his prime. "If you knew how he loves our native land!" Rizal wrote to Blumentritt in 1888, some two months after settling down in London with Regidor's help (Rizal 1963c: 194). "He is the only one who sacrifices everything for her — life, money, and health! I don't know of any other compatriot as enthusiastic as he is."

Pardo, Basa, and Regidor shared a common history: They were all liberal reformists formed by the events of 1872. (The overly cautious Pardo, who came under his uncle Joaquin's guardianship when he was seven years old, once wrote of those events as an "open wound" — Mojares 2006: 123; 125.) This bond touched Rizal to the quick, because he was himself shaped by 1872: the execution of the Filipino priests Mariano Gomez, Jose Burgos, and Jacinto Zamora had arrested his brother Paciano's career, forced Rizal to drop his full family name when he enrolled at the Jesuit school in Manila, and changed his entire outlook. In a word, it politicised him.

"Without 1872," he wrote Ponce on 18 April 1889, "there would not be now either a Plaridel, or Jaena, or Sanciangco, or would there exist brave and generous Filipino colonies in Europe; without 1872 Rizal would be a Jesuit now and instead of writing *Noli Me Tangere*, would have written the opposite. At the sight of those injustices and cruelties, while still a child, my imagination was awakened and I swore to devote myself to avenge one day so many victims, and with this idea in mind I have been studying and this can be read in all my works and writings. God will someday give me an opportunity to carry out my promise" (Rizal 1963b: 321).

The formation of a virtuous people as the perfect revenge: To this idea, the mature Rizal remained constant, as all the personal accounts attest; it was his single most sustained act of will. But the promise, the work of vengeance, could be carried out by various means; hence the many projects, the false starts, the hesitations and sudden resolutions, the twists and turns in a life that has been misrepresented as a single, straight, inevitable line.

Two turning points, in particular, are fundamental to understanding Rizal's legacy in the Southeast Asian imagination.

THE MALAY TURN

In 1889, Rizal ended a long letter to a racist colonial official by counting himself as among "the unfortunate Malays of the Philippines" (Rizal 1963e: 119). That self-identification came at some cost.

Almost from the beginning of the Spanish conquest, the Spaniards already saw the natives of the Philippines as Malay. "The Spanish colonists recognized early that their '*Felipinas*' and its inhabitants belonged to a greater and cultural totality," writes Zeus Salazar, the preeminent scholar on the Filipino's Malay identity (Salazar 1998: 111). "The native '*Indios*' were, in their view, quite clearly related to the '*Malayos*,' particularly those of Malacca and Sumatera."

In fact, proto-Filipinos had become part of the Malay world well before the Spaniards set foot on the Philippines. Salazar surveys the proofs that are now standard: Malay words burrowed deep in Philippine vocabularies; the remains of several *balangays*, the "migrant clan boat" used in Malay-Indonesian trade, excavated in Butuan, in Mindanao; not least, the "Laguna copper-plate inscription" in Kawi script, dated to AD 900 and accepted as the product of a "Malay-speaking nexus of trade and culture contact" (84). He then concludes:

> The coastal trading communities of the Philippines were thus part of an ecumene where Bahasa Melayu was the lingua franca and Malay cultural norms had acquired wide currency. They did not cease to be part of that world when Spain took over the Philippines. [Salazar 1998: 88]

But after Filipino-Spanish forces withdrew permanently from Ternate, in the Moluccas, in 1663, about a hundred years after the Spanish contact, "there was relative eclipse [in Luzon and the Visayas, but not in Mindanao] of both [the use of] the Malay language and the contacts that had spread it" (81–82). When over two centuries later Rizal's generation began to rediscover its Malay roots, Mojares narrates, they "had to rely on European sources in theorizing 'Malayness.' Western-educated, they mined early Spanish chronicles and modern European scholarship in the cultural sciences — reading authors like Wilhelm von Humboldt, Johann Blumenbach, and Alfred Russel Wallace — in constructing the Filipino Malay identity. They discovered Asia by way of Europe" (Mojares 2009: 2).

The prominent Southeast Asianist Anthony Reid places on Blumentritt's shoulders the entire burden of Rizal's Malay turn. "Their principal link to it was the Austrian Ferdinand Blumentritt (1853–1913), who continued the tradition of comparative ethnography by a detailed study of the Philippines," he writes. "Through his extensive correspondence with Blumentritt, Rizal became convinced that his people were 'the six million oppressed Malays', and he himself a 'Tagalog Malay' " (Reid 2010: 98–99).

This seems to me a mistake, at least in nuance. It *was* Blumentritt who got Rizal to first think seriously about his Malay roots. But what he actually did was to introduce Rizal into a thriving milieu filled with the sense of possibility. Salazar traces three sources of the Propagandists' rediscovery of their Malayan identity: first, "conservative elements in Spain as well as European friends of Filipinos themselves ... categorized them as Malays, the Spaniards often with the intent to disparage" (1998: 115); second, the Propagandists enjoyed "intimate contacts with European liberals and scholars with positive views about Malays and Malay civilization" (116); and third, the exciting context heightened "their intense interest in the historical roots of their country, which made them seek and read all available works, whether Spanish or foreign, on the subject" (117).

With Rizal, the intense interest inevitably took the form of a series of projects. The Exposition Universelle de Paris in 1889 (the famous one, for which the Eiffel Tower was built as the entrance arch) prompted an organizing binge. Anticipating the exposition, he had founded an international association of Philippine scholars and planned to convene a congress on Philippine studies (the logistics of securing approvals and clearances, however, defeated him). Immediately after arriving in Paris from London, he had gathered his fellow Filipinos and formed the Kidlat ["Lightning"] Club as a means to view the attractions of the exposition together. Impressed by Buffalo Bill and his show featuring skilled Indian braves, he reorganized his network of compatriots into the Indios Bravos, a society of Filipinos defiantly proud of their "indio" status. And he started the secret society "Rd. L. M."

One of the Indios Bravos, Baldomero Roxas, recalled that "at the time, they were frequently talking of the misfortunes of the Javanese people and that in this connection, Rizal was always referring to the book of Multatuli[4] which dealt on the life of the oppressed Javanese people" (Lopez-Rizal 1960: 69). The discussions led to the founding, with a select few, of the "Rd. L. M."

Only two letters referencing this secret society survive. One is from Rizal in Paris to del Pilar in Madrid, asking for help for a secret brother in need (Rizal 1931: 235). The other is from Rizal in Paris to

Basa in Hong Kong, announcing the formation of *"la Sociedad R.D.L.M."* and instructing Basa on protocols and countersigns (Rizal 1931: 221–23).

On the face of it, the society's mission seemed innocuous:

> Well now, inspired by your zeal and activity, we have decided to establish a society whose only purpose is the diffusion in the Philippines of all useful knowledge, be it scientific, artistic, literary, etc. It imposes no other obligation on the members except to favour one another when it concerns the propagation of a useful knowledge .... We make you our correspondent and you will continue acting as you have done until now, endeavoring to have at your command Chinese, sailors, servants, etc. to further the purposes of our society which are the diffusion of education in our country. Neither religion nor politics has anything to do with it. [Rizal 1963b: 373]

This seems passing strange, especially when the new society required a secret countersign on all its correspondence "for your letter to receive special attention or your order to be carried out," and given that Basa was requested to burn the letter right after reading, without communicating "its contents even to your subordinates" (374). I am particularly intrigued by what Rizal could have meant by "the propagation of a useful knowledge" and "the diffusion of education" that could be accomplished only with the help of Chinese, sailors, and servants.

Leoncio Lopez-Rizal studied the matter closely. He found that a bilingual newspaper published in Lipa, Batangas in 1899, during the Philippine-American War, and carrying the unusual name *Columnas Volantes de la Federacion Malaya*, was edited by Gregorio Aguilera — an original member of Rizal's "Rd. L. M." (Aguilera is among the five members Rizal mentions by name in the letter to Basa.) Indeed, Aguilera's own pseudonym when he wrote for *Columnas Volantes* was "R. del M."

The newspaper's original idea, Lopez-Rizal notes, "was to publish something as an organ of the Filipino people marching ahead and together with the Malayan people as a federation, which obviously was what the Director and founder of the bi-weekly had in mind, an idea that presumably he brought from Europe and was related to the R.D.L.M." (Lopez-Rizal 1960: 70).

Given these tantalizing details, Lopez-Rizal reaches a tentative conclusion:

> May we not believe and presume, therefore, that these "ideas politicas" [of editor Aguilera] were the ideas acquired from his conversations and discussions with Rizal, del Pilar, Ponce, B. Roxas and others when they organized the Society in Paris? May we not also presume that this was the same purpose of the R.D.L.M., which, he, the only one alive to know the secret, was trying to carry out? [71]

Rizal's nephew seems to be on solid ground when he finally arrives at the meaning of "Rd. L. M." — and the possible real motive for Rizal's Borneo project.

> It is my personal belief that Rizal's intention to settle and found a colony of Filipinos in Borneo was not merely to have a place where Filipinos could live and work with more liberty as well as free themselves from the oppressive conditions in the Philippines; not necessarily to become farmers, for the extension of land that he (Rizal) originally secured was not enough for the said purpose but for something else more important, which is to have freedom of action to attain the aims of the R.D.L.M. Society which, to me, means no other than the "Redemption of the Malay Race." [72]

Thus, "Rd. L. M." as *Redencion de los Malayos*.

He is careful to state that his conclusions are "mere conjecture and speculation," but this word of caution has not stopped biographers, historians, and polemicists (even those citing Lopez-Rizal) from giving "*Redencion de los Malayos*" as the definitive meaning of the enigmatic initials.[5]

The "Rd. L. M.," however, was underground work. Above the ground, Rizal was hard at work reimagining the Filipino past, this time as a Malay laying claim to his history. He read all the available chronicles, corresponded with the leading scholars. He wrote furiously, filling the pages of *La Solidaridad* and his annotations to Morga with references to the pre-Spanish Philippines as a Malay polity.

"What will the Philippines be a century hence? Will it continue to be a Spanish colony? If this question had been asked three centuries ago when, at the death of Legazpi, the Malayan Filipinos began little by little to be disillusioned, and finding the yoke burdensome, tried in vain to shake it off, without doubt the answer would have been easy" (Rizal 2007: 133). "The Malayan Filipinos before the coming of the Europeans carried on an active trade, not only among themselves but also with all their neighboring countries" (Rizal 2007: 233). "*Las tradiciones antiguas hacian de Sumatra como el origen de los Indios Filipinos* — Ancient traditions make Sumatra as the origin of the Filipino Indios" (Rizal 1991: 259). This was heady stuff, and Rizal knew it.

The Malay turn had given him an unexpectedly powerful weapon against Spanish and even European presumption: history. Schumacher sums up the shock of rediscovery in magisterial fashion.

> For Rizal history was at the very heart of his nationalism. It served as a weapon to combat the pretensions to beneficence of the colonial power. It provided an explanation of the contemporary situation of the Philippines as well as a picture of the glorious past destroyed by Spanish intrusion. It offered the key to national identity and corresponding orientations for future national development, as well as examples to emulate in the nationalist struggle. Finally, it provided a legitimation of the struggle for freedom and the destruction of colonial rule. Rizal accepted Western historical research with its rigorous methodology, and wished his work to be judged by those standards. But at the same time he wrote as a Filipino and an Asian, and worked intensely to read once more through Asian eyes the accounts that had come from European pens. European methodology could be used to give a Filipino meaning to the history of his people. [Schumacher 1991: 108]

THE TURN TO TAGALOG

Some scholars and historians have remarked on Rizal's turn or return to his native tongue, but mostly in passing. "To emphasize the role of language in this effort at solidarity and unity, he began to write his colleagues in Tagalog," Jovita Ventura Castro wrote in the introduction to *The Revolution* (1992: 11), the most faithful translation of the *Fili* — and then left it at that. The most programmatic of Rizal's biographers, Gregorio Zaide, reserves only four paragraphs to Rizal's Tagalog writing, combining it with his advocacy of a new orthography (2008: 169–70). "In spite of his European education and his knowledge of foreign languages, Rizal loved his own native language," the first paragraph began.

Author and academic Nilo S. Ocampo is one of the very few who have studied Rizal's use of Tagalog in real depth and consuming detail. His *May Gawa na Kaming Natapus Dini: Si Rizal at ang Wikang Tagalog* (2002) is bracing, a necessary corrective to the notion shared widely in the Philippines that Rizal, except for a literal handful of pieces, wrote exclusively in Spanish. The title is borrowed from Rizal's last (extant) letter to Ponce, written in his last month in Hong Kong while preparing to return to the Philippines; cast entirely in Tagalog, the letter expresses Rizal's appreciation for Ponce's loyalty and then, characteristically, proposes a project: for Ponce to return to the Philippines with a printing press. "*May gawa na kaming natapus dini,*" Rizal adds — a resonant line that could be rendered as "We have some completed work here."

In fact, Rizal never stopped writing in Tagalog. It was the language most of his sisters used in their letters, he exchanged scholarly notes on the language with Blumentritt and other specialists, and he was always ready to translate works he thought would be useful back home: Schiller's *Wilhelm Tell*,[6] five of Hans Christian Andersen's stories, even (when he was in Hong Kong) "The Rights of Man" as proclaimed by the French Constitutional

Assembly in 1789. He also attempted several times to begin a third novel, in Tagalog.

All together, Rizal's Tagalog writings constitute a substantial body of work. Ocampo writes: *"sunod sa Espanyol na makabuluhang korpus ang kanyang mga akda sa wikang Tagalog, at litaw sa mga ito ang kanyang angking husay* — Next to Spanish as a significant body of work are his writings in the Tagalog language, and in them his natural skill stands out" (Ocampo 2002: 23).

This fact, at the beginning of the second decade of the twenty-first century, is still not generally known (in the roughly parallel fashion, I suppose, that the Indonesian novelist Pramoedya Ananta Toer's work as a historian remains generally unrecognized). To the uninitiated, Ocampo offers a schematic view of Rizal's work in Tagalog.

> *Mapapangkat sa tatlong bahagi ang kaugnayan niya sa wikang Tagalog: una, sa mga orihinal na sulatin sa Tagalog, karamihan mga sulat sa pamilya at kasama sa propaganda at yaong panimula sa ikatlong nobela; ikalawa, sa mga salin sa Tagalog; at ikatlo, sa akda tungkol sa wika at panitikang Tagalog sa Espanyol, Aleman, at Inggles.*
> [Ocampo 2002: 24]

> His involvement in the Tagalog language can be grouped into three parts: first, the original writings in Tagalog, mostly letters to family and colleagues in the Propaganda and the start of the third novel; second, the translations in Tagalog; and third, the works about Tagalog language and literature in Spanish, German, and English.

But it was in his correspondence with del Pilar and Ponce, the engines of the Propaganda in Spain, that Rizal's turn to Tagalog is most marked — and most useful to the modern reader. Of the surviving letters, there are 45 entirely in Tagalog, plus eight more partially written in the language, exchanged between 21 July 1888 (when Rizal was newly settled in London) and 15 June 1892 (when Rizal was preparing to depart Hong Kong for Manila). The first was a mere postcard from Rizal to Ponce; the last was the letter asking Ponce to consider going into the underground printing business.

Ocampo tallied only 28 letters exchanged by the three Propagandists, including two partially written in Tagalog (2002: 565–68). But in fact a page-by-page review of both the *Epistolario Rizalino* and *Epistolario Pilar* yields a total of 53 — almost twice as many.[7] (The total includes seven exchanged between Ponce and del Pilar).

I expected to trace the start of this turn to mid-February 1889, when del Pilar asked Rizal to write a letter of encouragement in Tagalog to the women of Malolos who had bravely petitioned for the privilege to be taught Spanish. But in fact the Tagalog writing started before that, and then petered out after. It surged again, and then dissipated. And then it gathered up again, only to dissolve once more in the sea of Spanish the propagandists swam in. It came and went in waves.

What prompted the occasional burst of Tagalog writing? The original reason seems to be clear, from the circumstance. In the writing of postcards, Tagalog provided an additional layer of privacy.

Of the 45 letters written fully in Tagalog, at least 12 were postcards. The very first letter in the Tagalog correspondence, from Rizal to Ponce, was a *tarjeta postal* postmarked 21 July 1888 in London. In it, Rizal acknowledged receipt of a copy of *La Publicidad*, the republican newspaper published in Barcelona and generally sympathetic to Filipinos, thanked Ponce for introducing him to the work of Piping Dilat (Wide-Eyed Mute), and finding in that article a reason to hope that "*nagsisitubu na ang mga anak na maalam magmahal sa kanilang ina* — the children are growing who know how to love their mother." He then asked: "*Sino po si 'Plaridel'?* — Who is 'Plaridel'?"

The answer, as it happens, bore dramatic consequences for Rizal and his many projects. Both Plaridel (an anagram) and Piping Dilat were pseudonyms of del Pilar, Rizal's only real equal in political writing and his superior in polemical cunning, and the most important new ally he would find in his second European sojourn. Their alliance did not end well, but even after the recriminations and resentments both Rizal and del Pilar continued to think of each other on friendly terms.

(A letter of Rizal's shows that he was aware of del Pilar's Tagalog translation of "*El Amor Patrio.*" It was the first essay Rizal wrote on foreign soil, in 1882, and the first of his many pieces to be published in a newspaper, in this case the bilingual and short-lived *Diariong Tagalog*. He did not know then that his translator was in fact the same Plaridel.)

Rizal and Ponce, and eventually del Pilar too, when he arrived in Spain, used postcards for their convenience: they were cheaper and faster. Rizal the penny-pincher knew the economics of postage intimately, and it is no surprise to discover that all but two of the 12 postcards in Tagalog were from Rizal to Ponce, who had a gift for the logistics of editing. While even the longer letters contained instructions about submitted articles or queries about editing, or the various details involved in the administration of an international publishing venture, the postcards were pre-eminently occupied with these practical, time-bound matters.

Thus, for example, the postcard of 26 May 1889, sent from Paris:

> *Kaibigan: Kasabay nito ang sagot ko kay Barrantes. Ypalimbag ninyo kung sakali akala ninyong nagmamarapat. Ylagay ninyo ang ngalan ko man o ang Laong Laan. Sabihin mo kay Plaridel at kay Jaena na sila na ang bahalang magputol o magalis ng labis na hindi nila maibigan. Ako ang nasagot ng ano pa man.* [Rizal 1931: 182]

> Friend: With this is my reply to Barrantes. Print it if you think it worthwhile. Put my name or Laong Laan. Tell Plaridel or Jaena to cut or remove any excess they would not like. I will answer for anything.

Or the postcard of 19 July 1889:

> *Abay: Tinangap ko ang Sol:, salamat. Mayroon ditong isang kababayang maganak na nasuscribe sa Sol: mula sa No. 1, ang ngalan ay si Mme. Boustead, 3 Rue des Bassins, Paris. Kaya nga inyo siyang padalhan ng lahat ng numero sampu ng recibo ...* [Rizal 1931: 212]

> Colleague: I received the [latest issue of La] Solidaridad, thanks. There is a family of compatriots here who wish to subscribe to the Sol, starting with issue No. 1, the name is Madame Boustead, 3 Rue des Bassins, Paris. Therefore send her all the issues, together with the receipt ...

(He was to repeat this request at least once, and make other, similar requests; apparently, subscriptions then, as now, seemed to be vulnerable to the vagaries of the post.)

But the three leading Propagandists also learned to use Tagalog to wrap delicate matters in secrecy, or to bind themselves to it. Most of their letters, Rizal's especially, were meant to be read in company, to be passed from hand to hand, to be copied and circulated (indeed, copies of some of Rizal's letters were found by the raiding party that broke into the warehouse where the revolutionary organiser Andres Bonifacio was employed, and used as evidence in his trial for rebellion). A few were meant to be strictly confidential.

Rizal's letter from Paris to del Pilar in Madrid, dated 4 November 1889, provides the perfect example.

> Kaibigang Selo: Ang may taglay nitong sulat ay isang lihim na kapatid natin sa Rd. L. M. no. 2 ang taas. Walang sukat at dapat maka-alam na siya'y kapatid kundi ikaw lamang at ako. [Rizal 1931: 235]

> Friend Selo: The bearer of this letter is a secret brother of ours in Rd. L. M., of the second degree. No one should know he's a brother but you and me."

The secret brother in Freemasonry whom Rizal recommended to del Pilar's offices was a Filipino priest — "most likely Father Jose Chanco," in Schumacher's considered view (1997: 239) — who needed the help of the highly placed Masonic friends of Del Pilar and Julio Llorente. "*Kaya nga,*" Rizal wrote, "*alinsunod sa pangako niya sa akin na tayo'y tutulungan niyang lihim, sa lahat ng makakaya, iniaalay ko naman sa kaniya ang ating tulong—* That is why, following his promise to me that he will help us secretly, to the utmost, I am offering him our help."

Towards its close, the letter sounded a note that would be struck again in the next several weeks. "*Ano ang dahil at di sumusulat sa akin ang mga I.B. ng Rd. L. M.?* — What is the reason and the I. B. [Indios Bravos] of Rd. L. M. don't write to me?"(Rizal 1931b: 236)

On 22 November, he writes del Pilar again about the Indios Bravos: "*Ybati mo ako sa lahat ng I.B. Bautista, Aguilera, iba pa. Ano ang lagay ni Llorente?* — Send my greetings to all the I. B. [Indios Bravos] Bautista, Aguilera, and others. How is Llorente doing?" (Rizal 1931b: 243) And then again on 5 December, in a lengthy letter in Spanish, he suddenly inserts a short paragraph in Tagalog: "*Sinulatan ko na si I.B., nguni at hindi pa ako sinasagot. Kailangan kong matanto kung bakit at ang mga I.B., ay ayaw sumagot sa aking mga sulat* — I already wrote I. B. but he has not answered. I need to know why the I. B. don't want to answer my letters" (Rizal 1931: 257).

The three Propagandists had a third reason for writing in Tagalog: They wanted to make a point. Done half right, the point could be misunderstood as nothing more than language tokenism. Rizal's letter to Ponce and the writers of the *Soli* dated 18 April 1889, for example, began in Tagalog: "*Tinangap ko ngayon ang sulat mo sampu ng Sol:d. Totoong magaling ang numerong ito, at pagaling ng pagaling* — I received today your letter together with the Soli. This issue is really good, and [the paper is] getting better and better" (Rizal 1931: 165). And then this slender paragraph in Tagalog is followed by 11 more in Spanish, most of them robust. (This is the same letter where Rizal spoke of the life-defining events of 1872.)

But after Rizal returned to Europe in 1888, practically chased out of the Philippines because of the *Noli*, he gained a better sense of the Tagalog language's possibilities. To be sure, even before he went home the first time he had already translated the great Schiller into Tagalog. But since his return the thought of writing another novel in French had receded, and he worried about Tagalog translations of his own works.

He wrote a lengthy letter in Tagalog to the women of Malolos — a sociological tract in all but name on the status of women in colonial, theocratic society. He dedicated himself to reforming Tagalog orthography. And he engaged his closest allies del Pilar and Ponce in bouts of Tagalog letter-writing.

For instance, on 28 May 1890, he wrote del Pilar to tell him he was taking a break from writing for the *Soli*. "*Sadya akong hindi nagpadala sa iyo ng articulo sa ating Sol: upang makapahinga ang mga nabasa at makasulat naman ang iba nating mga kababayang dapat makilala ng lahat* — I purposely did not send you an *article* for our Soli, so that our readers can rest and our other countrymen who should be known to all can write" (Rizal 1933: 38).

An anxious del Pilar responded deferentially. "*Sakaling may ipinagkulang ako sa iyo — bagay na malayong kusain ko — ay mangyari sanang ipaunawa mo at nang maalaman ko naman ang sukat kong pag rikahan*" (Rizal 1933: 58). Here del Pilar strikes a disconcerting tone, one that echoes Mabini's own deferential letters to del Pilar. Del Pilar's reply can be translated thus: "If I have failed you — something I do not remotely intend — please let me understand so I would know what to make amends for."

Rizal sought immediately to clear the air. "*Napakalayo naman ang abot ng iyong munakala sa pag-isip mong ako'y hihiwalay sa Sol. dahil sa sama ng loob* — Your speculation is too far off, in thinking that I will separate from Soli because of resentments" (Rizal 1933: 60).

This exchange is important not only because it foreshadows the final break between the two leaders of the Filipino colony in Spain, in 1892; it also shows how both Rizal and del Pilar strove to conduct the beginnings of a long-running argument over questions of audience and Propaganda strategy entirely in Tagalog.

The real significance of the Tagalog correspondence, thus, lies in the Propagandists' quest for authenticity. Ponce and del Pilar responded to Rizal's Tagalog letters with gusto, and it must be said that del Pilar was a much more vivid letter-writer than Rizal — his letters to his wife Chanay, written entirely in Tagalog, are Chekhovian in their humor and humanity — but it was in fact Rizal who began the turn to Tagalog. To forge a unity of purpose, he felt it was, as always, necessary to set an example. And because the question of language was becoming more and more central to their attempt to found a nation, he began writing to his closest allies in Tagalog. One consequence of this turn remains under-appreciated by Filipinos, even today: Some of the most important letters in the Rizal canon were written in their own language.

Notes

1. The translation is by Encarnacion Alzona, the overworked official translator of the Jose Rizal National Centennial Commission of 1961; I have revised her version, to include words in the Spanish original that were inadvertently excluded in the translation, and to restore the original punctuation (see Rizal 1930: 221; Rizal 1963b: 74).
2. In *Brains of the Nation*, his magisterial study of the neglected but once-influential Filipino intellectuals Pedro Paterno, Isabelo de los Reyes, and Pardo de Tavera, the scholar Resil Mojares writes an even-handed portrait of "Pardo," as Rizal and others called him. The introduction includes a necessary summation of Pardo de Tavera's current reputation. "An independent-minded creole, he spent years as an expatriate in Paris and had an uneasy relationship with power. The relationship remained testy even when, after the fall of Spain, he became the most highly placed Filipino in the land as the senior Filipino member of the U.S. Philippine Commission, the country's law-making body. Discarded by the Americans and maligned by Filipinos, his political career was brief. In nationalist constructions of the nation's birth, he is usually cast in a villain's role. In the strongest statement of this historiography, Teodoro Agoncillo remarks: 'Pardo de Tavera should have been shot for his betrayal of the Revolution' " (Mojares 2006: 121).
It is characteristic of Mojares' turn of mind, and yet more proof of Rizal's pervasive influence on Philippine thought, that the title of his indispensable book is from a quote of Rizal's, from the second part of "The Philippines a Century Hence," published on 31 October 1889: "if today the enlightened class constitutes the brains of the nation, within a few years it will constitute its entire nervous system and manifest its existence in all its acts." (See Rizal 2007: 140)
3. Coates writes of Rizal's break with Regidor: "It was an extreme reaction, for

Regidor had not in fact declined assistance; he had not even seriously prevaricated. Del Pilar was at a loss to understand it, even wondering if Rizal's motive was a racial one — Regidor was half-Spanish — an idea of which Rizal quickly disabused him" (Coates 1968: 176). But in fact del Pilar thought it was Regidor who was being racist. On 18 May 1889, he wrote Rizal: "God grant that the reason for his incomprehensible behaviour is not what I fear and suspect, though it seems obvious — his racial prejudice" (Del Pilar 2006: 119). The break was neither total nor prolonged. By July Rizal was back to giving propaganda advice to Regidor (Rizal 1963b: 364).

4. Rizal was enthusiastic about Multatuli's *Max Havelaar*, which he read in London, on his second sojourn in Europe. See Chapter IV, especially pages 104–107.

5. Coates writes: "Within [the Indios Bravos], however, was a secret inner group which, beneath the concealment of the code letters Rd.L.M., was pledged to the liberation of the Malay peoples from colonial rule, a pledge to be made good first in the Philippines, later to be extended to the inhabitants of Borneo, Indonesia and Malaya" (1968, 175). Salazar, quoting this passage, improves on it by blithely spelling out the initials to mean *Redencion de los Malayos* (1998: 120). E. San Juan simply assumes the meaning as a given.

Schumacher confesses that he had been "unable to determine the meaning of these initials. If it is to be supposed that the organization was Masonic ... the "L.M." could well stand for "Logia Masonica," as it is not uncommon in Masonic documents" (1997: 237). He continues to hold the same view, but in an email to me, he vouched for Lopez-Rizal's historiographical rigour.

6. Ramon Guillermo's *Translation and Revolution: A Study of Jose Rizal's Guillermo Tell* is a comprehensive analysis of Rizal's 1886 translation of Schiller's 1804 play, and a fitting companion to Nilo Ocampo's work.

7. I am preparing a volume of the complete Tagalog correspondence of Rizal, del Pilar, and Ponce, with annotations and an accompanying English translation.

2

"The Very Soul of This Rebellion"

A hundred fifty years after his birth, and a hundred and fifteen since his execution, it is difficult to appreciate the subversive nature of Rizal's reputation when he emerged on the political scene. Much of what he dedicated himself to, much of what he served as symbol of, is now simply assumed in the Philippines: civil liberties, the right to education, political representation of the people and a free press, above all freedom of conscience. His martyrdom is so familiar, such a common point of reference, that his willing embrace of it is taken for granted. His appeal to non-violence, to study and the civic virtues, continues to be seen as difficult, but no longer radical.

We can get an inkling of Rizal's significance for his time from his mother's extreme reaction to the so-called *brindis* or toast of 25 June 1884, which is when Rizal began to assume the mantle of leadership of the Filipino community in Spain.

She had fallen seriously ill for a week, and in a letter to Rizal dated 5 November 1884, Paciano explained why:

> You are the cause of her sickness and I'll tell you why. About that time the talk here was the speech you delivered at the banquet in honour of the Filipino painters [Juan Luna and Felix Resurreccion Hidalgo, whose top prizes at the Madrid exposition occasioned Rizal's soon-controversial toast to the equality of the Spanish and Filipino peoples] and commenting on it, there was one who asserted that you would not be able to come back, some that it would be desirable for you to remain there; others that you have made

enemies; in short, there was not even wanting one who asserted that you have lost friends; but all are unanimous in saying that it was not convenient for you to return here. These gratuitous suppositions were the ones that afflicted very much our mother and made her sick. [Rizal 1963a: 149–50]

After the *Noli Me Tangere* circulated, Rizal became the subject of even more suppositions, gratuitous or otherwise. He was, one might argue, the first Filipino celebrity.[1]

In 1888, the Augustinian priest Jose Rodriguez wrote a series of eight pamphlets, all published in Guadalupe, in what is now the central business district of Makati City, condemning Rizal's first novel and other anti-Spanish writings. The Tagalog version of the best-known of the series bore the title *Caingat Cayo!* and the subtitle *Sa manga masasamang librot, casulatan* — "Beware! Of evil books and writings."

The pamphlet listed seven "*utos na paraang pagcacaquilanlan*" or mandatory ways of discernment (mandated, that is, by the Catholic Church). Rizal and the *Noli* are first mentioned only in the sixth directive, but as the response of Del Pilar suggests (he wrote a satirical rejoinder the same year, titled *Caiigat Cayo*, meaning roughly "Be Slippery as an Eel"), the pamphlet was aimed squarely at Rizal's sudden fame.

For precisely that reason, the pamphlet gives us a glimpse of Rizal's reputation in the Philippines as a Spanish friar saw it, a mere year or so after the *Noli* came off the press.[2]

First, in relating the moral law at stake in reading the *Noli*, it accepts the popularity of the novel as a given. The *Noli*, Rodriguez wrote, was "*pinupuri,t, binabasang ualang agam-agam nang maraming natuturang cristiano, baga ma,t, sa pagbasang ito,i, nagcacamit sila nang casalanang daquila* — praised and read without reflection by many who are called Christians, even though, in reading it, they are committing a great sin."

And second, in castigating Rizal for his unheard-of wickedness, the pamphlet describes Rizal's popularity as a fact.

> Tingni, mañga guiniguilio cong tagalog, tingni,t, masdan itong caauaaua capoua ninyong tagalog, na pinupuri nang marami sa inyo na parang ualang capara sa carunuñgan; ualang dao ga sino si RIZAL; di umano,i, capurihan dao nang lahi ninyong tagalog, na sucat ninyong ipagparañgalan. ¡Ay sa aba co! At lalong catampatang sabihin, na sucat inyong ipagmamacahiya ang gayong cahabag-habag na bulag na loob; sapagca,t, siyang CAUNAUNAHANG tagalog na cusang gumamit nang caniyang camay sa pagsulat nang mangfia catacot-tacot na catampalasanan sa Dios, sa ating santa Religión cristiana, at sa mañga sinasampalatayanan natin. [Rodriguez 1888; emphasis in the original]

> See, my beloved Tagalogs, see and observe your pitiful fellow Tagalog, being praised by many of you as though without equal in learning; Rizal is said to be without peer and even said to be the glory of your Tagalog race, whom you should honour fully. Ah, poor me! It is even more fitting to say, that you should be wholly ashamed for his miserable inner blindness; because he is the VERY FIRST Tagalog to willingly use his hand in writing these terrible acts of wickedness against God, our holy Christian religion, and those [articles of faith] we believe in.

The hostility can scarcely be contained, but at least it is channelled through a Scholastic attitude (if not quite with Scholastic rigour). Rodriguez seeks to dispute the strongest possible argument, and in Rizal's celebrity he found it. Nothing less than the glory of the race!

Rodriguez begins with the fact of Rizal's fame, and proceeds to attack it: instead of honour, Rizal deserves shame; instead of praising him for his insight, he should be condemned for his interior blindness; instead of being an example to follow, he was a person to be shunned.

The attack recognizes two of the three defining qualities of Rizal which, while commending him to the countrymen of his time, alerted unsympathetic Spaniards to the possibility of danger: his great learning, and his role as a pioneer. He was not only a medical doctor educated in the capitals of Europe, but was (in the friar's view) the very first Filipino to wage a frontal assault on the religious orders which in reality administered the Spanish colony. He was certainly among the first to ridicule them, and under his own name.

The Spaniards who were unsympathetic to Rizal in his last decade (his years of fame, beginning with the publication of the *Noli* in 1887) may be grouped into two. The first considered Rizal's advanced education as earned and his many talents as genuine; the second denigrated both as a reflection of the Filipino native's inferior status. In this view, he was hailed as learned and peerless only because the natives, the ignorant rabble, didn't know any better.

The Jesuit priest Pablo Pastells, a professor of Rizal's at the Ateneo Municipal and perhaps even his spiritual director in those days, exemplified the first type. He praised Rizal for his genuine gifts. But he went beyond Rodriguez and called out Rizal on his separatism — the third defining quality.

In a letter dated 12 October 1892, part of a nine-letter exchange that best reflects Rizal's mature thought on religion, the Spanish missionary told his former student "to stop being stubborn and to give up this desire of emancipating the Filipinos from the gentle yoke of the Catholic religion and the Spanish nation by supporting and propagating among them the spurious doctrines of reformism and separatism ..." (Bonoan 1994: 128).

Father Rodriguez belonged, firmly, to the second class. His pamphlet excoriated Rizal for being "FOOLISH about many things, because if the writing of the said book is analysed, you would think it was not the hand of a sane person but the foot of an ignoramus who wrote it"[3] (Rodriguez 1888; emphasis in the original).

It was a line of attack that would be used again and again by other Spaniards in the years to come, notably by Wenceslao Retana before he changed his mind about Rizal (and even then he did not manage to erase all traces of condescension) and also by the Spanish lawyers prosecuting Rizal for rebellion and illegal association.[4]

In fact, we can establish a direct connection between Retana's charges against Rizal and the prosecution's case — and see for ourselves whether Retana, as an ex-minister had argued in the Spanish Cortes, had truly "stirred up hysteria in Spain and Manila by his inflammatory and inaccurate writings."[5]

In the 30 September 1896 issue of *La Politica de España en Filipinas*, the newspaper in Spain put up by allies of the religious orders in the Philippines to answer *La Solidaridad* broadside for broadside, Retana wrote a hostile story on Rizal, headed "*Un Separatista Filipino* — A Filipino Separatist." (The excerpts that follow are from Rodrigue Levesque's translation.)

The story is a condescending profile of Rizal ("we are going to do him the favor of dedicating him a full article") written only a month after Bonifacio launched the Revolution, and as a consequence it is impressed with the hysteria of the crisis. Its histrionic tone can best be heard in the last paragraph, which reads:

> Rizal, on accout [sic] of his writings, on account of his antecedents and for many other reasons, is the best propagandist that the Filipino filibusterism has ever had; there lie upon his conscience a great many of the evils that are presently going [on] in that country… He hates Spaniards with a passion. The Government — we end this the way that bureaucratic reports end — shall decide regarding that filibuster detainee as it deems most appropriate. [Levesque 6]

The chilling recourse to bureaucratic language, the kind that is damned by a studied ambiguity that allows political decisions with fatal consequences to be made with a clean conscience, makes of Retana a Pontius Pilate; he is deliberately washing his hands of whatever course of action would be considered "most appropriate." And yet at least two errors in this article, and at least two missing arguments, show that the prosecution in Rizal's trial less than three months after the story saw print borrowed significantly from Retana, and that — not to put too fine a point on it — there is blood on his hands.

Retana is the **first** to assert that a youthful poem of Rizal's, submitted to a contest in 1879, exhibited dangerous nationalistic sentiments. "In truth, the work of a 19-year-old Indian should have produced a shock-wave, because he dedicated his composition — something unusual among those of his race — *to the Filipino youth*" (Levesque 1). In fact, Rizal was only 18 when he wrote "*A la Juventud Filipina.*"

But the telltale error emerges out of the fifth paragraph of the prosecution's brief, dated 21 December 1896. "In 1879, when he was barely nineteen years old, Rizal catches the public eye for the first time by taking part in a literary contest held in this capital city. He won first prize with an ode in which, even then, his views on the colonial question might be discerned" (De la Costa 1996: 121).

Curious, the way Rizal's age is described. His prosecutors had an advantage over the Retana who wrote the *La Politica* story; they knew exactly when Rizal was born. They knew that, in 1879, Rizal could only have been 18 at the most. (The poem was written on 22 November.) They could have simply said Rizal was 18 when he wrote the poem, and that would have been both factual and succinct. To phrase his age, however, as "barely nineteen years old" betrays the influence (perhaps unconscious) of the Retana article.

It is no small thing. Retana's point was to show that, even before he went to study in Europe, Rizal at a young age had already revealed himself "to have certain tendencies for stimulating his *countrymen* to raise their foreheads, as if he saw them as having been humiliated or in a similar situation" (Levesque 2). This is an insight of Retana's that the prosecutors seized and then elaborated on: "From this time forth [that is, from the writing of the poem] he has not ceased to labour for the destruction of Spanish sovereignty in the Philippines" (De la Costa 1996: 121).

(Leon Ma. Guerrero, ever the diplomat, adopts in his biography a on-the-one-hand-this, on-the-other-hand-that approach to Retana's reading of Rizal's phrase "*patria mia*" — an unprecedented reference to the Philippines as a country separate from Spain. Perhaps the very notion was due to youthful exuberance? It ought to be mentioned, however, that the same first five lines[6] that Retana quoted in his article as proof of Rizal's emerging separatism were used by Rizal again nine years after he wrote them, in an exhortatory New Year's Eve letter to his *"Paisanos Amigos"* in Barcelona, in 1888. By then he was already 27, and the famous author of the *Noli*.)

Retana describes Rizal's **second** voyage out of the Philippines in the following manner: "After he had arranged his affairs, he left for Japan in February 1888, and from there returned to Europe, settling in Paris, and later in London" (Levesque 3). In fact, it was the other way around. Rizal settled in London first, and only later transferred to Paris (and still later, to Madrid). The mistake is repeated in the prosecution's brief: "In 1888 the accused left Manila for Japan; from there he proceeded to Madrid, then to Paris, and afterwards to London, with the principal object of continuing the revolutionary propaganda in all these places" (De la Costa 1996: 122).

The echo is certainly strong, but does the sound carry any meaning? I think it does, because it is one of many reminders that the Spanish-centric view of both Retana and the prosecution runs very deep indeed.[7] Again, this is no small thing; placing Madrid at the head of the list seems innocuous enough, may almost be a given, but in fact it reinforces the context for Rizal's *ingratitude* and, therefore, treasonous disloyalty. It harks back to the prosecution's opening argument: "Dr Jose Rizal Mercado, *who owes all that he is to Spain*, since it was in the halls of her universities that he learned the profession of medicine, is one of the principal if not *the* principal figure in the present uprising" (De la Costa 1996: 121; first emphasis supplied).

Repeating Retana's second factual error also alerts us to the prosecutors' rhetorical strategy in the first part of their brief. The first part is an account of Rizal's life, and on inspection we find that it is based almost entirely on Retana's profile; there is hardly anything there that we can trace to the seized evidence or the prosecutors' interrogations.(The information from these other sources comes into use in the second and third parts of the prosecution's brief.)

The pattern of presentation in Retana's article flows according to the following sequence:

1. A summary of Rizal's career with his license in medicine as the highlight
2. The youthful poem of the Motherland
3. His studies in Europe
4. His first novel, and its "disastrous effect" on Filipinos
5. The return to Manila
6. His second book, the Morga
7. His second novel, dedicated to the memory of the three martyrs of 1872
8. The work in *La Solidaridad*
9. An analysis of his writings
10. His relations with the Governor-General Despujol
11. His deportation

The first part of the prosecutors' brief follows a similar pattern:

1. A summary of Rizal's career with his license in medicine as the highlight
2. The youthful poem on "the colonial question"
3. His first novel, and its "evil effects" on the people
4. His return from Manila to Europe
5. His second novel, "dedicated to enhance the memory of the three native priests"
6. His relations with Despujol

Both sequences are essentially chronological, it is true. And the treatment of each number varies greatly; the one on the *Fili*, for example, gets four highly detailed paragraphs in Retana and only one summary paragraph in the prosecutors' brief. But the absence of some numbers from Retana's article in the prosecutors' case suggests some interesting judgment calls. Two missing arguments, in particular, seem to me to be particularly telling.

The writing of the annotated Morga gets no mention in the brief — but then even Retana downplays its legal or criminal significance: it is only "the work that has given him a certain fame among learned people" (Levesque 3). In other words, it is merely scholarly. Rizal's work in the *Soli* is also scanted in the brief — but Retana minimized its importance too: only "a few articles that were really violent ... in addition to a few small articles on various subjects, among the best can be found a study on *Tagalog orthography*" (Levesque 3). In other words, both merely scholarly and entirely negligible. One would have thought that Rizal's frank discussion in various articles published in the *Soli* of the certainty that Spain would lose her colonies if she failed to institute reforms would have engaged the prosecutors' attention; indeed, the dossier prepared by the Governor-General's office and entered into the trial records on 22 December makes precisely that point: "he starts the separatist periodical *La Solidaridad* ... he makes use of its columns to spread the anti-Spanish and antireligious views with which he has infected his country" (De la Costa 1996: 134). Why do the prosecutors fail even to mention the newspaper's name? Because in this first part of their brief they relied largely on Retana.

On 21 December 1896, the prosecution summed up the case against Rizal in almost mystical terms: "Honourable Judges, we can see in Rizal nothing less than the very soul of this rebellion" (De la Costa 1996: 128).

This is a direct echo of the main conclusion the investigating officer Rafael Dominguez reached on 5 December:

"It appears that the accused Jose Rizal Mercado is the principal organizer and the very soul of the Philippine insurrection; the author of associations, periodicals and books dedicated to the cultivation and dissemination of ideas instigating the people to rebellion and sedition; and supreme head of the national revolutionary movement." [De la Costa 1996: 108–109]

The dossier prepared by the Governor-General's office and signed by Enrique Abella on 22 December offered a detailed, more nuanced summary.

> Dr Rizal, through the publication of his works *Noli Me Tangere*, *Annotations to the History of the Philippines by Morga*, and *El Filibusterismo*, and through an endless series of pamphlets, manifestos and printed materials of all sorts attacking religion, the friars, and the Spanish government, is gradually impressing upon the people of the Philippines the idea of expelling the religious orders from the Islands as a means to the further though unexpressed purpose of securing the independence of this country. [137–138]

In legal terms, Rizal stood accused of two crimes. The brief for the prosecution, signed by Enrique de Alcocer on 21 December, "charges Señor Rizal Mercado on two counts, the evidence for which is conclusive in this case. First, that of having founded an illegal association, the Liga Filipina, which had for its single aim to perpetrate the crime of rebellion. The second of the punishable acts for which the Prosecution claims the accused answerable is that of having promoted and brought about, by the incessant activities previously described in this brief, the rebellion itself" (129).

These excerpts tell us, in only a few lines, the Spanish colony's considered opinion on Rizal. Such a sketchy survey of summaries, however, fails to depict the full scale of the resentment mixed with fear with which Rizal's fame and influence were seen by the Spaniards. It is surely one of history's many ironies that, to find the full picture of the Spanish image of Rizal, we need to repair to Rizal's own defence brief.

On Christmas Day, Rizal's counsel Luis Taviel de Andrade (the brother, as it happens, of Jose, the Spanish officer assigned to Rizal's detail when he returned to the Philippines in 1887) began his defence of the man on the dock by taking on the elephant in the room.

For many years now the name of Rizal has had overtones of rebel cries and his person has been regarded as the symbol of Philippine revolutionary sentiment. On what grounds? Has Jose Rizal perchance made any public act or solemn profession of separatism? Has he at any time openly and clearly proclaimed before our beloved Spanish fatherland that he abhors its dominion over these territories and that he intends to wage war upon it until it is no more? No. But Rizal has written two books, *Noli Me Tangere* and *El Filibusterismo*, in which less than due respect is given to the Spanish name, and to the religious orders which are considered, and justly considered, to constitute the indestructible bond of union between the Mother Country and the Philippine Islands. And these books, along with other writings of his in which he criticizes the colonial administration of these Islands, along with his campaign to secure for his country certain rights which would serve as stepping stones to autonomous government and eventually to independent status, and along with the unquestioned ascendancy which he has acquired over his fellow countrymen — an ascendancy due not only to these bold and daring proposals which none of them had hitherto conceived, but also to the undeniable and exceptional superiority of intellect which he has managed to achieve — all these in combination have served to imbue all good Spaniards, both those who were personally acquainted with his works as well as those who knew them only by hearsay, a perfectly natural and understandable attitude of resentment towards Rizal, and of apprehension as to what he might be plotting against Spain. [De la Costa 1996: 141–142]

In short: Rizal is a victim of his reputation. Indeed, towards the end of his brief Taviel de Andrade appeals to the court to judge his client's guilt or innocence on the basis of the evidence, not his reputation: "all that remains to his disadvantage is his past life, his books, and his writings" (150). There is, we have to admit, some deliberate fudging of the facts here. For instance, while Rizal did not "openly and clearly" proclaim separatism, he did not offer any outright denial either. (And any government would consider secret advocacy as at least equally dangerous.) But Taviel de Andrade does confront the real case against Rizal, and in doing so he throws the three defining qualities of Rizal's public image — his superior learning, his trailblazing, his reputation as a separatist — into sharp relief. It is an image perceived, indeed shared, by Spanish colonial and Filipino revolutionist alike.

It is true, however, that Rizal rejected the revolution. Like Apolinario Mabini, who later served in Aguinaldo's revolutionary government; like Antonio Luna, who later distinguished himself as a general in the revolutionary army; like Pio Valenzuela, the doctor who served as Bonifacio's emissary to Rizal in Dapitan and later emerged a hero after the revolution — Rizal renounced the uprisings that began in August 1896.

His most private thoughts may be gauged from the following diary entry, written on 2 September 1896, the night before he left for Spain for the third time:

> Dios quiera que esta noche no haya mas disturbios. Desgraciados paisanos que se lanzan tan locamente a la muerte. — Dicen que Imus fue atacado. [Rizal 1953: 56]
>
> May God will that tonight there be no more disturbances. Unfortunate countrymen who are launched so madly into death. — They say *Imus* was attacked.

Two days later, a Jesuit on board the ship said other passengers were avoiding him because they believed he was the cause of the uprising. His silent response, noted in his diary, said volumes. "*Me rio de la candidez e inocencia de esta gente* — I laugh at the naivete and innocence of these people" (Rizal 1953: 57). In fact, the case can be made that it was Rizal, after four years in relative isolation from the political struggle, who was naive. He was so focused on his personal conduct, unimpeachably honourable in his view, that he failed to realize how, by other definitions of the word "cause," Spaniards and Filipinos alike could well believe he really was "*el causante de los disturbios de Manila.*"

We hear the same alarm over gullibility and disgrace in Rizal's proposed *Manifiesto a Algunos Filipinos*, or Manifesto to Certain

Filipinos, written on 15 December 1896 in an attempt to prove his good faith to the Spanish court-martial trying him for rebellion and illegal association.

> It may be that persons continue to use my name in good or in bad faith; if so, wishing to put a stop to this abuse and to undeceive the gullible, I hasten to address these lines to you that the truth may be known. From the very beginning, when I first received information of what was being planned, I opposed it, I fought against it, and I made clear that it was absolutely impossible. This is the truth, and they are still alive who can bear witness to my words. I was convinced that the very idea was wholly absurd; worse than absurd, it was disastrous. [De la Costa 1996: 118]

The second paragraph of the short statement is even more categorical. It includes not merely a renunciation but a condemnation of the uprising. "Thoroughly imbued with these ideas, I cannot do less than condemn, as I do condemn, this ridiculous and barbarous uprising, plotted behind my back, which both dishonors us Filipinos and discredits those who might have taken our part" (119).

But the manifesto was not published. Nicolas de la Peña, the judge advocate general, recommended against publication because, in a word, Rizal's statement did not condemn separatism at all.

> Your Excellency: The attached exhortation which Dr Rizal intends to address to his fellow countrymen is devoid of that patriotic indignation against all separatist demonstrations and tendencies which should be conspicuous in every loyal son of Spain. Consistent with his published opinions, Dr Jose Rizal limits himself to criticizing the present insurrectionary movement as premature, and because he believes its success to be impossible at the present time. But he suggests pretty clearly that the independence they dream of can be achieved by means less dishonourable than those currently being employed by the rebels; that is to say, when the cultural level of the people shall have been raised to the point where it will be a decisive factor in the struggle and a guarantee of success. As far as Rizal is concerned, the whole question is one of opportunity, not of

principles or objectives. This manifesto can be summarized in these words: Faced with a clear prospect of defeat, my fellow countrymen, lay down your arms; later on, I myself will lead you to the land of promise. A message of this sort, far from promoting peace, is likely to stimulate for the future the spirit of rebellion. This being so the publication of the projected manifesto is inopportune. It is recommended that its publication be forbidden … [De la Costa 1996: 119–120; the recommendation to the Governor General was dated 19 December 1896]

Was the Spanish lawyer over-reading? Rizal does speak of having "given many proofs that I desire as much as the next man liberties for our country. I continue to desire them." He does speak of "the education of the people" as a "prerequisite" — for what? That condition when we "become worthy of such liberties." He does speak of both redemption and reform. And he does fail to condemn the very idea of a future for the Philippines separate from that of Spain.

Eight days later, Judge Advocate General de la Peña endorsed the court-martial's death sentence by returning to the principal issue. "He disapproved of the uprising, certainly; but he did so not because it was a crime but because it was untimely and uncertain of success owing to the lack of the necessary means to guarantee victory" (159).

I am reminded of Rizal's tack in dealing with previous accusations of separatism.

To Pastells' assertion that his ideas were reformist and separatist, Rizal, then in exile in Dapitan, did not offer an outright denial but instead noted that real political discussion needed "wide open spaces where freedom reigns" (Bonoan 1994: 138). To Pastells' expressed hope that he would like "to develop further arguments to refute your separatist ideas. You believe yourself as one sent by God to work for the triumph of these ideas," Rizal replied by refuting the notion … that he was sent by God (144–145). Even his last counter-argument — "And besides who tells you that the good of my country, which is all that I pursue, can be found only in separatism?" — seems merely rhetorical. He does not even bother to expand on it.

About a year before his trial, he took issue with a Spanish official, Benito Francia, whose previous letter had offended him for the same reason.

> I will not conclude this letter, however, without begging you to permit me to express to you the deep resentment that your phrase, "the unfortunate separatist ideas of Rizal" has caused me. Said by another I would have shrugged my shoulders; but said by Your Lordship, the Inspector General of Welfare and Health, a physician and a colleague, it deserves to be rectified. I reject therefore such an opinion and I do not believe that Your Lordship or anybody else worthy of my consideration has a right to qualify my ideas as such. I have not been tried yet nor have I been allowed to make my defense. [Rizal 1963e: 332]

This sounds, to use that Watergate-era phrase, like a non-denial denial.

I do not wish to minimize the genuinely problematic nature of Rizal's conduct during his trial. Despite the wary Spanish reception, the proposed manifesto of 15 December remains a disconcerting read. But a look at the transcripts of the proceedings, as recorded by Retana, suggests that Rizal did not always favour his Spanish interrogators with the truth.

He denied founding the Liga — the first of the two charges lodged against him. He limited his role to the drafting of the association's statutes and by-laws (De la Costa 1996: 94–95); in fact, he *was* the founder. It was his idea, and he had called the organizational meeting. There would have been no Liga Filipina without him.

In his recollection of the meeting with Valenzuela in Dapitan, he omitted his recommendation that someone like Antonio Luna be recruited into the Katipunan. While Valenzuela's various testimonies are problematic for various reasons, this particular detail is confirmed by the memoirs of another revolutionary general, Jose Alejandrino. "Moises Salvador and Mamerto Natividad who initiated me in the Katipunan, knowing the friendship which I had with Luna, requested me to transmit to him the recommendation of Rizal, but Luna refused on that occasion to join the revolutionary movement because he believed it was still premature" (Alejandrino 1949: 4).

Rizal also denied any plan to found a Filipino colony in Sandakan, in North Borneo; he said he had wanted "simply to take his family to settle in that British colony." As his letters about the "new Kalamba" prove, this ingenuous claim was an outright falsehood.

There is even this curious exchange during the interrogation:

> Q. Does he know Andres Bonifacio, president of the Supreme Council of the *Katipunan*, and has he had any dealings with said person?
>
> A. He does not know this person by name, and in fact this is the first time he hears of him. Nor does he know him by sight, although he [Bonifacio] might have been present at the meeting in the house of Doroteo Ong-junco, where he [the prisoner] was introduced to many persons whose names and appearances he no longer remembers. [De la Costa 1996: 98]

Why curious? Because in two days of questioning, he had denied knowing several personalities (Mabini among them) by using the same, simple formula (recorded in the third person) again and again: "He does not know him either personally or by name." And yet the question about Bonifacio elicited a circuitous reply. Why did he say that Bonifacio might have been at that 1892 meeting that launched the Liga? He could have said the same thing about many others but didn't. Why did he say it was his first time to hear the name? He could have said the same thing about Martin Constantino Lozano, Aguedo del Rosario, Jose Reyes Tolentino, Domingo Franco, Irineo Francisco, Ambrosio Flores, Teodoro Plata, Francisco Cordero or Apolinario Mabini — but didn't. I think the gentleman may have protested too much.

Whatever his legal strategy was, the Spanish authorities proved completely unsympathetic. His proposed manifesto of 15 December, and the "Additions to My Defense" he submitted on the day the court rendered judgment, left them not only unmoved but convinced of the opposite. Making special mention of Rizal's damning phrase, that the revolution had been plotted "behind my back," the judge advocate general confirmed the death sentence. All of Rizal's statements, he said (De la Costa 1996: 159), "are an implicit admission of the fact that he is the supreme head of the enemies of Spain."

Notes
1. The poet-novelist Lope K. Santos, the *Paham* or Laureate of the Tagalog language, has a recollection of youthful fandom. "*Madalas naming inaabangan sa daan ang kanyang karwahe kung nababalita naming magdaraan siya mula sa Sta. Ana sa Paco, patungong Ermita* — Often we waited on the road for his carriage when we got news that he was on his way from Sta. Ana in Paco, towards Ermita" (Aspillera 1972: 13, but the interview was recorded in 1959, when Santos was around 80). The passage is not unproblematic. Born in 1879, Santos was only eight years old when the now-famous Rizal returned in 1887 and stayed for half a year. When Rizal returned a second time in 1892, Santos was just 12, and Rizal enjoyed only a week of freedom before being deported. But that Santos, as much a political activist as he was a Tagalog advocate, remembered his early youth in Rizal's glow is telling in itself.
2. Retana, having severed his ties with the Spanish friars who subsidized his earlier writings, observes slyly that it was the wide circulation of these pamphlets, and the "sacred oratory" against Rizal thundering down from the pulpits, which contributed to Rizal's extraordinary fame. "*Los frailes eran sus mas eficaces propagandistas* — The friars were its most effective propagandists" (Retana 1907: 161).
3. Writing to Ponce on 30 September 1888 about Rodriguez and Salvador Font, another Augustinian friar who condemned his first novel, Rizal gave as good as he got: "I have the great pleasure to see that even *writing with the feet* I can do them a terrible harm; what if I should get to write with the hand ..." (Rizal 1963b: 201; emphasis in the original). He did not keep his thoughts private; his satires, *La Vision de Father Rodriguez* and *Por Telefono* (the second a response to Font), were also widely circulated.
4. The clearest expression may be found in the judge advocate general's endorsement of Rizal's conviction. "Rizal is neither a competent writer nor a profound thinker. The products of his pen which are included in this file

betray a most imperfect command of the language and give little evidence of intellectual ability. And yet Rizal became the Word Incarnate of Revolution, the most intelligent leader of the separatist movement, the idol, in short, of the ignorant rabble and even of more important but equally uncultured individuals who saw in this professional agitator a superhuman being worthy to be called the *Supremo*" (De la Costa 1996: 158).

5. From Schumacher 1991: 145. The sentence in its entirety reads: "After the execution of Rizal, Francisco Roxas, and others in December 1896 and January 1897, the Spanish Conservative ex-Minister, Francisco Romero Robledo, would accuse Retana in the Cortes of having stirred up hysteria in Spain and in Manila by his inflammatory and inaccurate writings, and of being responsible for unjust executions." Schumacher's source is a letter of Blumentritt's to A. B. Meyer, dated 17 June 1897.

6. As it appeared in *La Politica de España en Filipinas*:

Alza tu tersa frente
juventud Filipina, en este dia!
Luce resplandeciente
tu rica gallardia
bella esperanza de la patria mia!

The following translation by Nick Joaquin, the late Philippine National Artist for Literature, is of the kind that seeks to improve on the original, but it seems to me that the music rings true (and the first and last lines are fairly faithful).

Hold high the brow serene
O youth, where now you stand;
Let the bright sheen
Of your grace be seen,
Fair hope of my fatherland!

7. Elizabeth Medina notes that Retana, in his biography, made it a point to correct the prosecution's reconstituted itinerary: "No Sir — he went to the United States and later to England" (Medina 1998: 143). This strikes me as yet another example of Retana's intellectual dishonesty; he seems to have conveniently forgotten his own reconstruction of Rizal's second sojourn in Europe, as written down in *La Politica*.

3

Doctor Rizal

The revolutionaries, those who actually took to the battlefield, held Rizal in great esteem. An unusual token of this abiding respect may be found in the instructively erroneous first paragraph of General Artemio Ricarte's memoirs, written some twenty years after the end of hostilities.

> Start of the Insurrection. — The insurrection of the members of the Katipunan began on the day Dr Jose Rizal was cast into prison in Fort Santiago, Intramuros. [Ricarte 1992: 3]

The facts are less congenial. Rizal returned to Manila from his exile in Dapitan on 6 August 1896. He spent almost an entire month, "*detenido pero no preso* — detained but not a prisoner" (Rizal 1953: 55), on board the Spanish cruiser *Castilla*. He left for Spain on board the *Isla de Panay* on 4 September. He arrived in Barcelona on 3 October, but did not disembark until 6 October, when he was escorted to the notorious Montjuich prison. (By then, as he noted in his diary, he had gone 64 days without touching land.) He spent several hours in cell Number 11, before being presented to the ranking official, Eulogio Despujol (as it happens, the same man who banished him to Dapitan), and then was marched off to the *Colon* on the same day, to be taken back to Manila as a prisoner. He arrived on 3 November, and it was only then that he was "cast into prison" in Fort Santiago.

The revolution, on the other hand, began on 29 August.[1]

Ricarte, a brigadier general of the Magdiwang Council of the Katipunan in Cavite and afterwards captain-general of the new revolutionary government, earned fame for his bravery and fighting skill. His nom de guerre was the fearsome and fitting "*Vibora*," or Viper. Opposed to the American occupation until his death in 1945, he was the first ranking revolutionary general to publish his memoirs — in serial form beginning in 1922, in book form in 1927.

His account of the Revolution, *Himagsikan Nang Manga Pilipino Laban sa Kastila*, or Revolution of the Filipinos Against the Spanish, began with a familiar device. In the same way that early chroniclers of the Katipunan linked Bonifacio's founding of the revolutionary organization to the day Rizal was arrested in 1892, Ricarte began his chronicle by linking the start of the Revolution to the day Rizal was (said to have been) imprisoned in 1896. In his account, he dates the "*unang titis ng Panghihimagsik* — the first spark of Revolt" to 23 August, and the first major attack on a Spanish garrison to 29 August. All throughout August, however, Rizal was confined to the *Castilla*.

Did Ricarte make it all up? It may be that he actually thought Rizal was already imprisoned in Fort Santiago at the time; the fog of revolution exists too. Or it may be that he only wanted to vest the somewhat improvised beginning of the revolution with an additional layer of meaning, by draping it with the mantle of the man known as "*Laong Laan*," or Preordained; the coincidences of destiny are real too.

Or, and this seems more likely to me, it may be that he only meant to say that Rizal's fate was intimately, intricately, connected with the revolution.

The presence of Rizal in Manila at the very time the Katipunan rose in revolt was potent with meaning. It certainly came as a shock to the Spaniards in Manila. Luis Taviel de Andrade did not merely allude to this sense of disruption, of apprehension, in his brief for the defence; he described it at length.

DOCTOR RIZAL 89

> With regard to the opinion of which I also spoke, that which makes Rizal out to be the very head, soul and life of the present uprising, that opinion has been crystallized not only by these very prejudices but by the particular circumstance which became public knowledge in Manila that when the said uprising was discovered Rizal was no longer in Dapitan but inside this harbour on board the cruiser *Castilla*. This circumstance was completely accidental and unpremeditated. There is not a shred of evidence to the contrary. Nevertheless, it served to convert the presumption against Rizal into a deep-rooted and unalterable conviction, a conviction encrusted as it were on the public mind as the pearl in its shell, that Rizal was directly involved in the conspiracy. For although it later came to be known that his presence here was in answer to his request that he be allowed to go to Cuba to serve as a military surgeon, they were few indeed who did not interpret that request as a mere subterfuge on Rizal's part to be allowed to come to Manila in order that he might be here when the uprising broke out and thus be able to put himself at its head without delay. (De la Costa 1996: 143)

A key passage is worth repeating: "when the said uprising was discovered Rizal was no longer in Dapitan but inside this harbour." If Spanish Manila felt a shudder of fear at the "public knowledge" that Rizal had returned to the capital, could restive Cavite, where the revolution found Ricarte, not feel instead a sense of possibility?

I understand Ricarte's rhetorical strategy at the beginning of his memoirs as an attempt to locate the revolution within the Rizal narrative. By the 1920s, memories of the revolution had dimmed, but the so-called cult of Rizal, aided and abetted by American colonial authorities, had acquired greater lustre; it made sense for a chronicler of the revolution to make Rizal a point of reference.

Ricarte himself wrote [Ricarte 1992: 6]:

> The circulation of Dr Rizal's "Noli Me Tangere" and "El Filibusterismo" among the educated people, and of the paper Kalayaan among the lower classes, stirred the minds of the Filipinos against Spanish rule in the islands, and as a result, the Katipunan spread to the farthest corners of the archipelago, and more especially in the provinces around Manila, with admirable rapidity.[2]

But it must also be said that the sense of continuity that the revolutionists felt with the Propagandists led by Rizal was shared widely. Ricarte's first paragraph and the passage above effectively connect the work of the Propaganda with the outbreak of the revolution, but the intransigent ex-general was not alone in presenting the revolution as a continuation, the natural result, of what Rizal and others had started.

Isabelo de los Reyes, who shared prison time with Katipunan rebels and was the first to write an account of the revolutionary organization (and the first to mischaracterize it as purely plebeian), shared the common perception of a movement inspired by Rizal's persecution. By forcing Rizal into exile, he wrote in 1901, Despujol "pushed the plebeian followers of his famous victim to rise into arms and found the Kataas-taasan, Kagalang-galangang Katipunan ng mga Anak ng Bayan whose main objective was to redeem the Philippines from her tyrants" (De los Reyes 2002: 242).

Mabini, whose writings offer a tempered view of Rizal's role in history (a fact not generally known, even in the Philippines), still carefully integrated Rizal's novels, the articles in *La Solidaridad*, and the founding of the Liga Filipina into his narrative of the revolution. Of Rizal's execution, he wrote (in his self-taught English): "Such cruelties could not but provoke the general indignation: than to suffer them the insurgents would rather die fighting, though they had but *bolos* for arms" (Mabini 1998: 231).

Antonino Guevara y Mendoza, code-named *Matatag* or Firm, was an officer of the Katipunan who served under Paciano Rizal, among others, during the revolution. In his *History of One of the Initiators of the Filipino Revolution*, written in 1899, he offered a tribute to Rizal — one of the most stirring in the literature — that renders the continuity between Rizal and the revolution both explicit and inevitable. Strolling at the Luneta in January 1898, during the phony peace between the first and second phases of the revolution, he pointed out Rizal's place of execution to his companions and said:

"There, my friends, is the place where our hero fell, irrigating that soil with his precious blood in defense of our beloved fatherland. May his life serve as a model for us. Let us pray for his eternal rest, and let us beseech God to give us many Doctors such as Sr. [Señor] Jose Rizal whenever we find ourselves wanting, in order that we shall gain our coveted independence." [Matatag 1988: 21–22]

An even more moving acknowledgement of the revolution's debt of gratitude to the work of the Propaganda is found towards the end of Matatag's memoirs: a memorial page listing ten Filipinos who had "died gloriously, the first seven during the war of our independence, the last three before them" (1988: 42). The list begins with "Doctor Jose Rizal," includes a revolutionary who had also studied in Europe (Edilberto Evangelista), and embraces three writers of *La Solidaridad*: del Pilar, Lopez Jaena, and Jose Ma. Panganiban. "The last three" died, of natural causes, before the revolution broke out: a penurious del Pilar in Madrid, in July 1896; Lopez Jaena in Barcelona, in January 1896; and Panganiban, also in Barcelona, in August 1890 — before the Katipunan was even founded. That a revolutionist with unimpeachable credentials included them in his memorial to those who had died a glorious (that is, a patriotic and useful) death, while the Philippine-American war still raged in the background, is the best proof of continuity: those like Matatag who took part in the fighting saw no difference between revolutionist and Propagandist.

It must be said that Emilio Aguinaldo, who assumed leadership of the revolution in early 1897 and two years later became the first president of the first Asian republic, was considerably less enthused about Rizal than his generals or his men. His *Reseña Veridica de la Revolucion Filipina*, or True Version of the Philippine Revolution, written originally in Tagalog and published in 1899, does not mention Rizal at all. His memoirs, written in Tagalog between 1928 and 1946 (Aguinaldo 1967: xii) and published in 1967, make up for that lack, but I do not think it is uncharitable to say that, in this book, the Rizal story was subordinated to the purposes of the Aguinaldo narrative.

But in his official acts, Aguinaldo was not remiss in honouring Rizal. On the eve of Rizal's first death anniversary, Aguinaldo and other leaders of the revolution exiled to Hong Kong after the peace treaty of Biak-na-bato held a commemorative programme — the first — to mark Rizal's martyrdom (Esteban de Ocampo, reprinted in Zaide 2008: 278).

On 15 September 1898, he convened the Malolos Congress (a constitution-making assembly) by invoking (first in Tagalog, then in Spanish] the recent glorious dead. Rizal is first among them.

> Illustrious spirits of Rizal, of Lopez Jaena, of [Marcelo] Hilario del Pilar! August shades of Burgos, Pelaez and Panganiban! Warlike geniuses of Aguinaldo [his brother Crispulo] and Tirona, of Natividad and Evangelista! Arise a moment from your unknown graves! See how history has passed by right of heredity from your hands to ours ... [Agoncillo 1997: 227]

Not least, on 20 December 1898 — 10 days after Spain ceded the Philippines to the United States for $20 million and less than two months before American troops began the Philippine-American War — Aguinaldo issued a proclamation declaring 30 December "Rizal Day." Flags were ordered flown at half mast "from 12:00 noon on 29 December to 12:00 noon on 30 December 1898" and "all offices of the government" were ordered closed on 30 December, Rizal's second death anniversary (Zaide 2008: 278). At least two eyewitness accounts of that first Rizal Day exist.

Matatag happened to arrive in Lukban, Tayabas, in what is now Quezon province, on the day itself.

> It was 10 o'clock in the forenoon when I arrived in the pueblo of Lukban. The town was in mourning, with a flag at half mast at each house. I learned later that it was in commemoration of the anniversary of the iniquitous and tragic killing of the eminent Doctor Jose Rizal at the hands of the Spaniards in the execution ground of Bagumbayan. [Matatag 1988: 34]

Intending to proceed with his journey, he was prevailed on to stay. "However, Lieutenant Colonel Eustacio Maloles asked me to stay, with an invitation to attend a soiree with him that evening, to be held in honour of the unforgettable [*el inolvidable*] Doctor Rizal" (35). He listened to the speeches and the music ("There was a band at the gate of the house, playing pleasing harmonies") but was "disgusted to discover that there was to be dancing" afterwards.

In 1937, Elias Ataviado wrote down a personal recollection of that first Rizal Day, observed this time in Legaspi, in Albay province. Like the rest of the prosperous Bicol region, a cluster of provinces in southern Luzon, Albay had joined the revolution late; its people, Ataviado wrote, had been unaware of the work of Rizal and the other Propagandists. But by 30 December 1898, the province had made up for lost time:

> On the 30th, under the auspices of the revolutionary government, the whole province celebrated the second anniversary of the death of Rizal. It was the first time that in Albay a public act was performed in memory of the Great Martyr. ... A lifesized portrait of the National Hero was placed over the catafalque raised up in the middle of the church.
>
> It was not until then that the people of Albay were able to see the likeness of the Great Martyr. At the same time they began to learn of his life, his struggles and his martyrdom, as also of his pre-eminence in the history of the country. And it was also from that occasion that the people understood clearly the sacrifices and the merits of our martyrs and departed heroes — of Fathers Burgos, Gomez, Zamora and of the others implicated in the Cavite uprising of 1872... [Ataviado 1999: 177]

The Rizal scholar Floro Quibuyen has written an exhaustive analysis of the American appropriation of Rizal Day; contrary to what two generations of scholars and students educated under the Agoncillo/ Constantino school of history may have been led to expect, the task of absorbing Rizal into the American story did not prove easy.

> *It was a stroke of genius, therefore, on the part of the American regime to have seized the symbol of Rizal to further their own colonial agenda. However, during the early years of the new regime, the American appropriation of Rizal was resisted.* [Quibuyen 2008: 291; italics all his).

One reason for that early resistance was the subversive nature of Rizal's biography. It was a quality that the revolutionaries strongly responded to. Even Aguinaldo's guerrilla government, pursued by American forces from November 1899 to March 1901, paused to remember his martyrdom. On 30 December 1900, the entry in the diary of Simeon Villa, Aguinaldo's faithful aide, read:

> At 8 o'clock in the morning a solemn funeral ceremony in memory of the grand Rizal was celebrated in the church, all the field and line officers who could be spared from duty having participated in the same, as well as the people of the town [Palanan, in Isabela]. Señor Barcelona delivered an oration touching upon the biography of the illustrious dead man. [Villa 1969: 199]

Harassed by hunger, often at the mercy of the elements while hiding in the mountains, increasingly desperate, and only infrequently restored to health and a sense of hope when visiting the few towns in northern Luzon still unoccupied by American forces, Aguinaldo and his men nevertheless found the time to honour Rizal, with a memorial.

THE RIZAL STORY intersects with the narrative of the revolution at several points; three intersections, in particular, show the depth of the revolutionaries' debt to Rizal.

Pio Valenzuela's Dapitan assignment, which the Spanish court-martial made much of, grew out of a pivotal Katipunan assembly in 1896. The historian Teodoro Agoncillo dates this to Friday, 1 May, based on Valenzuela's own recollection; Aguinaldo remembers it as Saturday, 9 May. Santiago Alvarez, the general known as *Apoy* or Fire, says it began on Sunday, 3 May, and ended the following day; in my view, the number and the specificity of Alvarez's details, which are distinctive qualities of his memoirs as a whole, render his account persuasive.³ All three, however, are agreed on the reason for the assembly: Bonifacio had convened it to discuss the necessity of rising in revolt, after news spread that the secret organization had been betrayed.

Alvarez, the captain-general of the Magdiwang faction of the Katipunan in Cavite, describes the secret assembly held in Pasig and reconstitutes the statements made in it at length. In his telling, it was he who reminded the assembly of Rizal's situation in exile, and it was Aguinaldo who then suggested that Rizal be consulted about the Katipunan's plan.

After Bonifacio called for a recess, the members clustered in groups. Alvarez surveys the scene with the wide-angled lens of memory:

> Some smoked, while others chewed betel; some sat on chairs, while others sat on their haunches on the floor; some were joking and laughing; others were sad and deep in thought. But everywhere, the whispered consensus was that Dr Rizal must first be consulted about the matters discussed before any final decision and concrete action be taken. Others were asserting that if Dr Rizal were to favour a revolution, they could count on his many influential friends abroad. [Alvarez 1992: 12–13]

The break over, Bonifacio raised the question again, whether it was time to rise in arms. The assembly gave a clear answer. "*Ang lahat ay nag-aagawan sa pagsagot na: 'isangguni muna kay Dr Jose Rizal, bago pagtibayin ang paglaban* — Everyone scrambled to reply: consult first with Dr Jose Rizal, before resolving to fight" (Alvarez 1992: 248).

Aguinaldo has a more picturesque recollection of the assembly, as a meeting held in several *bancas* (canoes) clustered together on the Gahet river, also in what was then known as Morong province. "In the middle banca was the Supremo who presided over the meeting." But the outcome is the same. It was agreed "That a messenger be sent to Dapitan to ask Dr Jose Rizal for his opinion regarding the Revolution.

It must be remembered that Jose Rizal was the honorary head of the Katipunan" (Aguinaldo 1967: 34).

The crown of honour was placed on his head without his knowing it. Rizal would later make a point, during his trial, of asking what kind of leader was one who did not know what his members were doing. But that the Katipunan, already then coming under surveillance by the authorities, would invest two months in a bid to consult Rizal shows that the honour it accorded him was for real. That is exactly what Nicolas de la Peña concluded: the evidence showed that Rizal conducted himself, and was treated, as "the supreme head of the enemies of Spain."

Why did the enemies of Spain want to consult him? Alvarez's detailed recollection of the talk at the assembly gives us three possibilities. They saw the novelist-polemicist as an expert analyst of politics, and wanted his opinion on the assembly's common concerns: their lack of arms and general preparation, their fear of being manipulated by the friars, above all their prospects of victory. But they also saw the internationally known scholar as an ally; they hoped "they could count on his many influential friends abroad." Not least, they saw the self-sacrificing patriot as a kindred spirit; in a word, they sought his blessing, like a child seeks his father's.

Valenzuela, a doctor like Rizal, was deputized to speak to the exile. It was a time-consuming task. He and his companions could not leave for Dapitan until the middle of June, and he didn't get to consult Rizal until 21 June (in Agoncillo's reckoning) or 1 July (in Rizal's recollection, as he testified during his trial). But there is no argument that Valenzuela did meet Rizal.[4]

But after Valenzuela returned from his mission to Dapitan, both he and Bonifacio said nothing.

> *Ang nangasa panganib na kalagayan ng di matigil at balisang Katipunan, ay may malaking pagmimithing makaalam ng naging kapasyahan ni Dr Jose Rizal, kung umaayon o hindi sa panghihimagsik; at kung hindi, ano ang dapat gawin upang mailagan ang kapahamakang banta ng mga kaaway ...?* [Alvarez 1992: 249]

The riskiness of the situation of the constantly worried Katipunan [gave it] a big desire to know the decision of Dr Jose Rizal, if [he] agreed or not with rising in arms; and if not, what needed to be done to avoid the threat of harm by the enemies."

But the silence of Bonifacio and Valenzuela "gave meaning to the belief of everyone that Dr Rizal did not agree with rising in arms. Because of this, the Katipunan returned to a state of anxiety [*nasauli sa balisa*]..." (249).

Despite the rebuff — or, perhaps, the receipt of a calibrated response contingent on many conditions, which would amount to the same thing — the Katipunan planned at least three times to rescue Rizal: the first in Dapitan; the second when he was on board the *Castilla*, detained but not a prisoner; and the third time in his final days. Any one of the three can serve as more proof of the revolutionaries' debt of gratitude.

On 29 December 1896, the day Rizal's death sentence was announced, the two revolutionary councils in Cavite met at the friars' estate house in Imus, Cavite. One item on the meeting's agenda was the fate of the famous doctor. "*Napag-usapan din at binalak na mailigtas si Dr Jose Rizal* — It was also discussed and planned to rescue Dr Jose Rizal," Alvarez wrote. He added: "*ipinangako ng Heneral Apoy ang pagpapadala ng mga kawal na sandatahan ng baraw sa buong magdamag ng gabing iyon, sa Maynila, na ihahalo sa mga magsisipanood ng pagbaril at tutugon sa biglaang sisiran ng pakikihalo* — General Apoy [Alvarez himself] pledged to send troops armed with knives to Manila throughout the night, who will mix with those watching the execution and respond to a sudden signal to intervene" (Alvarez 1992: 306).

As many of Rizal's biographers note, talk was rife on the day of the execution that rebels from Cavite would make an attempt. But the rescue didn't happen.

Rizal's older brother Paciano (whose name Alvarez misspelled as Ponciano) had arrived at the Imus assembly. "And he said his brother Dr Rizal would agree to be rescued, if only one life were to be risked ["*kung isa lamang buhay ang pupuhunanin*"], because that would be equal to his own in service; but if two lives were to be risked, then don't even think it because he could not agree, since two lives in service to the nation ["*sa pangangailangan ng Bayan*"] could never be equal to one."

Aguinaldo has a somewhat different version. His chapter on the planned rescue is given the title, "My Plan to Save Rizal," and the plan itself is hatched more than a day before the execution.

> When I learned of the decision of the Council of War that Rizal would be shot to death at six o'clock on the morning of 30 December 1896, I went to the Supremo to request his assistance in my plan to save Rizal. I told the Supremo that Rizal was a patriot and a learned man who was needed by our country, and that all efforts should be exerted to save him from the enemy. [Aguinaldo 1967: 110]

Aguinaldo's plan was less specific than Alvarez's, and from our vantage point less likely to have succeeded. It called for the Katipuneros in Manila and its suburbs (not the rebels from Cavite, as Alavarez had remembered proposing) to congregate near the place of execution, and then for them to "kidnap" Rizal "while on his way to Bagumbayan." But the next morning Aguinaldo spoke with Paciano, who talked him out of it. "But he refused obstinately, repeating emphatically, 'Do not dare save my brother if you want to avoid bloodshed' " (Aguinaldo 1967: 111).

Aguinaldo said he heeded Paciano's stern advice. "I therefore reluctantly gave up my plan to save Rizal. God surely saved us from bloodshed and sure death" (Aguinaldo 1967: 111). A bold streak of self-serving recollection is apparent here; unlike Alvarez's version, where Rizal's rescue was discussed collectively, Aguinaldo's plan is a personal initiative: "I learned of the decision"; "I went to the Supremo"; "I told the Supremo"; "I outlined my plan"; "My plan follows." At the same time, he manages to make Bonifacio look petty, or at least not as solicitous about the wellbeing of the "learned man who was needed by our country."

We should note that, on many details, the memoirs of the three revolutionary generals agree. On the dramatic intervention of Paciano, the three may even be said to be synoptic accounts. Both Alvarez and Aguinaldo write of Paciano objecting to the rescue; both Aguinaldo and Ricarte agree that Paciano left Manila for rebel-controlled territory before execution day; both Alvarez and Ricarte describe a general assembly in Imus, in liberated Cavite. All three speak of Paciano as presenting himself in Imus, either the day before Rizal's execution or in the afternoon of the day itself.

Both Alvarez and Ricarte also relate the arrival in the rebel stronghold of Rizal's wife Josephine Bracken, together with Paciano (although details like date and place differ greatly). Only Alvarez, however, remembers the scene with some exactitude:

Ika-30 ng Disyembre, 1896. Umaga nang barilin si Dr Jose Rizal sa Bagung-Bayan ng Maynila, at nang mahigit na ika-1 oras n. t., si Josefina at si Trining, balo at kapatid ni Dr Rizal, ay dumating sa Malabon, kasama si G. Ponciano [sic] Rizal, nagtuloy at nakipagkita sa Supremo Bonifacio sa bahay ni Ginang Estefania Potente; dala ang dalawang maliliit na tiklop na papel, na nang katapusang pagdalaw nila kay Dr Rizal sa bilangguan, ay nakuha sa ilalim ng kusinilyang inilabas. Maliliit na maliliit ang sulat; ang isa'y wikang kastila, na siyang "Ultimo Adios," at sa himanhik ng Supremo Bonifacio ay naiwan muna sa kanya at siya ang unang tumagalog ... [Alvarez 1992: 306-207]

30 December 1896. It was morning when Dr Jose Rizal was shot in Bagung-Bayan in Manila, and past one o'clock in the afternoon, Josephine and Trining, widow and sister of Dr Rizal, arrived in [San Francisco de] Malabon, together with Mr Paciano Rizal, went and met with the Supremo Bonifacio in the house of Mrs. Estefania Potente; carrying two small pieces of folded paper, which on their final visit to Dr Rizal in prison, they took from the bottom of an alcohol burner they brought out. The handwriting was very, very small; one was in Spanish, which was the "Ultimo Adios," and on the request of the Supremo Bonifacio was left temporarily with him and which he was the first to translate into Tagalog ...

Bonifacio's authorship of the translation now widely known as "*Pahimakas ni Dr Jose Rizal*" remains controversial to this day. Even Jaime de Veyra's definitive survey of the farewell poem's various translations can only source the Supremo's translation this way: "To Andres Bonifacio is attributed the first Tagalog version of the Adios" (De Veyra 1946: 107). But that the founder of the Katipunan thought it was important to render the poem in Tagalog, and necessary to be seen as its translator — a circumstance we can deduce from the fact that those who do not accept his authorship still acknowledge that the translation was circulated *as attributed to Bonifacio* (that is, the real translators did not claim it in their own name) — suggests that even after Rizal's death Bonifacio continued to see him as central to the revolutionary cause. Bonifacio's attempt to translate Rizal's final words into his native tongue, then, constitutes a third and final proof of the revolutionaries' debt to Rizal.

The post-execution scene described by Alvarez, an ally of Bonifacio's but also a friend of Aguinaldo's, is thick with meaning: in it we see the farewell poem passed from Rizal to Josephine and Trinidad and then to Bonifacio — a direct line of succession that recalls Aguinaldo's own words at the inauguration of the Malolos Congress: "See how history has passed by right of heredity from your hands to ours."

Ricarte does not mention this incident. He writes, instead, of Josephine joining the revolution, who then "gave genuine proof of her support of the cause of the country for which her husband gladly gave a life full of vigor and hope, by rendering much service to the insurrection and suffering much want and misfortune" (Ricarte 1992: 27). But in 1913, while in Hong Kong, temporarily out of reach of the American colonial government, Ricarte offers Rizal his own, extraordinary tribute.

He writes nothing less than a charter for a new nation: a "Constitution of the Revolutionary Government in the Rizaline Islands Which Are to be Erected Into a Nation With the Name of

Rizaline Republic." A preamble to the charter that he wrote a year and a half later, from "Mindoro, R. I." — that is, Mindoro, Rizaline Islands — sounds Rizal's trumpet again, calling Filipinos, now under American control, to the field of battle anew, to wage a new revolution (Ricarte 1992: 137–156).

> ... it is now time for you to rise, to make effort to go without support and to demonstrate on the field of battle the purest honor, justifying by acts that the precious doctrines, which at the cost of his life and his blood, Dr Jose Rizal left us as a legacy, live and thrive in your hearts.

Notes

1. The actual date that the Philippine Revolution is reckoned to start is shrouded in some confusion. Alvarez, whose lead I follow, dates the start to 9 o'clock in the evening of 29 August, which coincided with the "UNANG SIGAW — First Cry" of the Katipunan (Alvarez 1992: 262). Ricarte, representing what I think is the still-popular view, dates the so-called Cry of Balintawak to 23 August; Agoncillo categorically denies that any battle took place on 26 August, or indeed ever, in Balintawak, then a barrio in Caloocan, in the province of Manila. Instead, he dates the first Cry to 23 August, but in Pugadlawin (Agoncillo 2002: 346; 150). Borromeo-Buehler (1998) proves convincingly, however, that Agoncillo was wrong to base his version on the testimony of Pio Valenzuela, who was **not** in Balintawak. The first skirmish, then, took place in Balintawak. But after that clash, the Katipunan spread the word that the uprising would officially begin on 29 August; in Cavite, the rebellion broke out the following day.
2. The 1963 translation of Ricarte's memoirs by Armando Malay is standard, and deservedly so. But in this paragraph, we might note some problematic improvements in the text. The original reads: "*Ang pagkalat ng "Noli Me Tangere" at ng "Filibusterismo" ni Dr Rizal na nagkapasalin-salin sa kamay ng mga Pilipinong mulat, at ng pahayagang "Kalayaan" sa kamay naman ng mga kasamang mamamayan, ay siyang nagpasiklab sa damdamin ng lahat ng mga Pilipino laban sa kapangyarihang kastila sa Kapuluan, at sa gayo'y mabilis na lumaganap ang Katipunan sa lahat ng sulok ng Pilipinas, lubha pa sa mga bayan at pook na kalapit ng Maynila*" (Ricarte 1927: 6). This can be translated as: The circulation of "Noli Me Tangere" and of "El Filibusterismo" by Dr Rizal that were passed from hand to hand by aware Filipinos, and of

the newspaper "Kalayaan" in the hands of residents in the country [or perhaps *mga kasamang mamamayan* = farmer-citizens], was what inflamed the feelings of all Filipinos against Spanish rule in the Islands, and thus the Katipunan spread quickly in all corners of the Philippines, especially in the towns and districts neighbouring Manila. This version avoids the "educated" vs. "lower classes" dichotomy that, in my view, is unnecessarily, perhaps subconsciously, introduced into the passage — as well as the obvious editorializing of "admirable rapidity."

3. Through *The Katipunan and the Revolution*, Paula Carolina Malay — as it happens the wife of the translator of Ricarte's memoirs — has allowed General Alvarez's memoirs to reach a much wider audience. (In my view, the work of Alvarez is the most detailed and the most even-handed of that narrow genre of personal accounts of the Philippine revolution.) Her English translation, however, is quite problematic. Instead of the "simple, straightforward English" she promises in her Translator's Note, we often get unconsciously academic, intrusively explanatory, language: "*sa anyaya ng Magdalo*" becomes "on the initiative of the Magdalo faction" — instead of the simple, straightforward "on Magdalo's invitation." "*Napag-usapan ang pagsasanib ng Magdalo at Magdiwang nang maging isang Pamunuan na lamang*" becomes "They explored the possibilities of a merger between the Magdalo and Magdiwang so that there would be a unified leadership" — instead of "The merging of Magdalo and Magdiwang to form just one Leadership [or Government] was discussed."

4. Excluding the interview he granted to Agoncillo in 1947, Valenzuela made at least four other statements regarding the meeting with Rizal; the first two, extracted in 1896 while Valenzuela was in Spanish prison, conflict with the latter two, his 1914 memoirs and his 1917 court testimony. Quibuyen marshals the evidence and concludes that the two post-prison statements, which show Rizal supporting the revolution, can be trusted (Quibuyen 2008: 45–56). I cannot agree completely — but then there is no need to; Valenzuela can safely be set aside, and we can still make sense of Rizal's final months.

4

"Halfbloed"

It is an intriguing possibility. On his first voyage to Europe, Rizal struck up a friendship onboard the French steamship *Djemnah* with two sets of Dutch sisters from the Netherlands Indies. After disembarking in Marseilles, he found to his great pleasure that the girls were staying at the same hotel, the Hotel Noailles.

> Once back in the hotel with my luggage, I looked for a companion, but all the Spaniards had gone out. I hear a young voice speaking Dutch and I go out and I meet Celiene Mulder going down the stairs. I greeted her affectionately, for our conversations did not go beyond that; she does not speak anything else but Dutch. She answered me in her charming and innocent manner, and how sorry I was to see her go down and disappear. When I raised my eyes I saw the two sisters, the friends of Mulder, and I talked with them. They were on the second floor. The older, Sientje, told me that they were leaving the following day for The Hague and would live with their grandmother, but they preferred Batavia, their native country. I replied: "I too love my native land and no matter how beautiful Europe may be, I like to return to the Philippines." [Rizal 1953a]

Rizal kept a diary, on and off, for many years. In each of his major trips, he used the diary (and several well-chosen letters) to document his impressions, to keep a record of the journey. His six-week voyage to Europe in 1882, the first time he travelled outside the Philippines, was particularly well-documented; to the boundless enthusiasm of the eager tourist was joined the pre-ironic introspection of the earnest student. The day after disembarking in Marseilles, he chanced upon the family of the younger Dutch girls preparing to leave the hotel. As he later noted in his diary, his emotional vulnerability made him hesitate.

> Upon our return [from lunch], I saw the preparations of the Dutch for their departure. I wished then to bid my little friends goodbye. I hesitated whether to see them or not, fearful that I might make a display of my emotions. But, at last, my affection prevailed and I waited for them in the corridor or vestibule. They came from the dining room, Mr Kolffne asked for the name and address of the Governor and he gave me his so that I could give them to Mr Salazar. My little friends bade me farewell repeatedly. I lost sight of them when their coach turned around the corner. One affection less and more pain. [Rizal 1953a]

Rizal was almost 21, but both to the Dutch and in his own view he was less than fully adult; that in parting Mr Kolffne asked for the particulars of Mr Salazar, the elderly gentleman who had served as governor of Antique province in the Philippines and had travelled with them on the *Djemnah*, seems to me telling. But the possibility that he could have begun a correspondence with the girls, especially if they had somehow managed to return to Batavia (present-day Jakarta), is of more than passing albeit counterfactual interest. He was a dutiful correspondent; perhaps one of the Dutch girls would have turned out to be a Miriam de la Croix, Minke's conscientious letter-writing friend in Pramoedya Ananta Toer's Buru Quartet.[1]

If Rizal and the Kolffnes had kept in touch, perhaps Rizal would have taken a greater or earlier interest in the Dutch East Indies. It was not until six years later, when he was residing in London, all but chased out of the Philippines on account of the notoriety of the *Noli*, that he paid sustained attention, at least for a time, to his country's southern neighbour. He had discovered Multatuli.

Eduard Douwes Dekker had served in the Dutch East Indies civil service for 18 years, before resigning in 1856 on a matter of principle.

In 1860, he published *Max Havelaar, Or the Coffee Auctions of a Dutch Trading Company*, in Amsterdam. The groundbreaking anti-colonial novel that exposed systematic Dutch injustice in Java caused a sensation; "It sent a shiver through the country," a member of the Dutch parliament said shortly after it came out (Multatuli 1987: 12). Multatuli, Dekker's pseudonym, was deliberately evocative of his travails in the colonial civil service; it meant "I have endured much." By the time he died in 1887, at least three translations of *Max Havelaar*, in English, German, and French, were already available in Europe.[2]

On 6 December 1888, in a newsy letter to Blumentritt, Rizal retailed his discovery: He had found a novel that anticipated the *Noli* by an entire generation. "Multatuli's book, which I shall send you as soon as I receive it, is extraordinarily interesting. Without doubt it is much superior to mine. But, as the author himself is Dutch, his attacks are not as violent as mine are. He is finer and more artistic, though he shows only one phase of the life of the Dutch in Java" (Rizal 1963c: 219). Perhaps sensing the excitement in Rizal's tone, Blumentritt replied on 10 December by postcard (Rizal 1963c: 221). "I do not know the book of Multatuli ... I shall be very glad to know it because I want to go after the enemies of *Noli Me Tangere*. Then, I could probably use that book." (He signed off in English, with the Americanism "All right.")

On Christmas Day, fresh from a 12-day trip to Spain, Rizal wrote Blumentritt again from London (Rizal 1963c: 224). "The Multatuli is unobtainable. May God keep it! It was so beautiful! I am going to order it in Dutch, for you also understand this language and in case it cannot be obtained, I shall write to Paris as there might be a translation of this book there. Be patient!"

It is probable that Rizal read Multatuli in London in the 1868 English translation by Baron Alphonse Nahuijs, and then ordered a copy of the 1875 German translation for his friend in Leitmeritz; this proved, unfortunately, to be out of stock. Given Rizal's own eagerness to have his estimate of an extraordinary find validated by his esteemed friend, it seems to me that that appeal for patience was probably directed not so much at Blumentritt but at himself.

Sometime early in January, Rizal finally sent off a copy of the Dutch original. On 14 January, after surprising Blumentritt with the offer of the presidency of the *Association Internationale des Philippinistes*, an international congress of scholars on the Philippines he had formed, he also wrote: "Last week I sent you Max Havelaar. As you understand Dutch, I am sure the book will be of interest to you" (Rizal 1963c: 230; the book's title was not underscored).

Rizal's find is of interest to us today for at least two reasons. His observation that *Max Havelaar* was "finer and more artistic" reflected a continuing concern of his about his own novel-writing; his other letters suggest that he thought he was sacrificing his artistic standards for political or polemical objectives.[3] This was a source of dissatisfaction that nagged at him, even after completing *El Filibusterismo*; it led him, on 31 January 1892, to say a second time to Blumentritt (Rizal 1963d: 434): "I want to write a novel in the modern sense of the term — an artistic and literary novel. This time I want to sacrifice politics and everything for art." (This sentiment was a symptom of a larger malaise: Rizal believed his entire political career had been forced on him by circumstances, at the expense of his art.)

The novel in the modern sense: perhaps that is what Rizal meant when he described Multatuli's first book as "so beautiful." Benedict Anderson, referencing Paul Vincent, has written on the possible appropriation in the *Fili* of rhetorical strategies found in *Max Havelaar*.[4] But — our second reason — the letter of 6 December was also the first time in almost two years that Rizal discussed a "regional" theme, that is, something to do with the Philippines' neighbouring countries or its Malay heritage.

The correspondence with Blumentritt began in July 1886 with an exchange of books, and very early on a mutual interest in and appeal to that Malay world was evident. "By telling me about universities and professors you have awakened my eagerness," Rizal writes in his third letter. He adds, "I will study Dutch also, because the Dutch are our neighbours [of course, only in the East Indies!] and they have written much about us" (Rizal 1963c: 12).

On 9 March 1887, he writes from Berlin (Rizal 1963c: 53): "I'll soon leave Berlin because I don't feel well here. Since my arrival I have been sick several times, which never happened to me before. I don't know yet where I'll go. I have in my blood the *wanderungslust* of the Malays. I always have it. Humour and opportunity for this!" He certainly travelled. In May he visited Blumentritt in Leitmeritz, meeting him and his family for the first and as it turned out the only time. He toured Prague, Munich, Vienna, Geneva, Florence, Rome. He was back in the Philippines by August, and out again by February 1888. He spent a couple of weeks in Hong Kong, over a month in Japan, three weeks traversing the United States, before pulling up stakes in London. He was busy studying at the British Museum — "I read assiduously all the old sources of the history of the Philippines. I do not think of leaving London until I shall have read all the books and manuscripts which bear on the Philippines" (Rizal 1963c: 203) — when he discovered Multatuli.

A letter from A. B. Meyer, the eminent naturalist in Dresden, must have helped deepen his renewed interest in the Malay world. Shortly after he read *Max Havelaar*, Rizal was asked for his scholarly view on the location of Tawalisi, an island mentioned in the chronicles of an intrepid Malay voyager named Ibn Batuta. (His response, a very lengthy and detailed letter dated 7 January 1889, identified Tawalisi as in all likelihood Luzon, the largest Philippine island.)

Rizal's renewed consciousness of himself as a member of the Malay race is evident again in his 14 January letter to Blumentritt; in listing the members of the steering committee of the *Association Internationale des Philippinistes*, he identifies Antonio Ma. Regidor as mestizo Filipino ("*Metis philippinais*") and himself as Malay-Tagalog ("*Malais-Tagale*"). In a matter of months, this greater self-awareness would lead to the founding of that secret society hidden under the initials "Rd. L. M."

Two days after Rizal's execution on 30 December 1896, the news appeared in Amsterdam. On page 11 of the 1 January 1897 issue of *Het Nieuws van den Dag*,[5] a small item in the foreign news round-up dated 31 December read: "Madrid has received notice that the most popular leader of the rebellion in the Philippines, Dr Rizal — the title indicating a European education — sentenced to death by court martial, was shot yesterday." On the same day, the *Nieuwe Rotterdamsche Courant* reported the execution, with an emphasis on the "highly romantic" angle of Rizal's last hours: "And then Rizal, upon his explicit wish, was united in pardon in matrimony with his mistress, a woman from Canada" (Muijzenberg 1998: 391). Both stories misidentify Josephine Bracken as Canadian, an error in detail suggesting a common source.

Other Dutch newspapers, on other dates, carried the news too; as reflected in the overseas columns of newspapers around the world[6], the revolution that broke out in August 1896 (although it was never referred to as such, but only as an insurrection or a rebellion) was very much a part, albeit a small part, of the prevailing international situation. Rizal's execution was news in precisely that context. (Blumentritt wrote Retana on 29 January 1897, saying he had already gathered seventy-three news clippings in the month since Rizal's execution — Medina 1998: 189.)

Otto van den Muijzenberg's helpful, context-setting study of news coverage of the Philippine revolution in Dutch and Dutch East Indies newspapers reinforces this view; the four representative newspapers in his sample "usually had one foreign news page, where events in European countries and their colonies were presented in the order of their perceived importance: in general, west and central European countries received most of the space" (Muijzenberg 1998: 394). In the 1 January 1897 issue of *Het Nieuws van den Dag*, the news on Rizal's execution, part of a two-paragraph report sourced from Spain, appears in the middle of the column, after items about peace efforts in Cuba, the legal case of a French citizen in Venezuela, a continuing "landslide" in Ireland, a meeting of the Indian National Congress in India, and a murder trial in Bulgaria, and before news items about a government appointment in Turkey, the return of Sir Cecil Rhodes to Cape Town in South Africa, a government initiative in Brazil, and a hurricane in Australia.

The news reached Batavia only on 16 January 1897. On that date, "... the news of his execution on 30 December 1896 was printed on the front page of the newspaper *Bataviaasch Nieuwsblad*, [for] this was probably the only paper to have a correspondent in Manila" (Bosma and Raben 2008: 303; that the report came out more than a fortnight after the event suggests that the newspaper did not in fact have a correspondent in Manila). On the same day, the *Java Bode*, more or less the establishment paper in the colony, ran the news too, but with a similar stress on the romantic angle: Rizal "married one and a half hours before his execution with an English girl from Hongkong, who had come to the doctor with her foster father, who was treated at length by the doctor for his eyes. After the death of that foster father she had stayed on with the doctor" (Muijzenberg 1998: 391).

These citations, and the many others on the Philippine revolution and its aftermath that Muijzenberg (and the Indonesian historian Adrian Lapian a year earlier) found in the course of research, show that in fact news about Rizal and the Philippines did reach the Netherlands Indies. The great Indonesian novelist Pramoedya Ananta Toer was mistaken in asserting otherwise, in the second volume of his Buru Quartet.[7] This is of some importance, not because it bears on the uses of history in fiction, but because it reveals the outer limits of Pramoedya's storied research into Indonesian history.

In fact, even before Rizal's execution, a telling article had already seen print in *Java Bode*. On 19 December 1896 (while the rebellion was in full swing, and Rizal was in jail), an article raised the possibility that Philippine independence, if attained, would be vulnerable to Japanese expansionism. It cited a three-month-old assertion by Blumentritt that "the Filipinos' fight for independence was a direct consequence of the Japanese victory in the war against China" (this paraphrase of Blumentritt's "claim" is from Lapian 1998: 91–92). The fear of Japan was apparently widely shared among the Dutch; it appeared repeatedly in Muijzenberg's sample of newspapers.

"More remarkable were suggestions that the Japanese government was behind the uprising," Muijzenberg wrote. "This fit in with a trend in the foreign-affairs debate in the Netherlands. Only two years earlier, a well-known professor of Japanese had addressed the Royal Netherlands Academy of Sciences with a lecture outlining a long-term plan of the Japanese empire to expand southward" (Muijzenberg 1998: 395). This geopolitical concern (there were others; Muijzenberg tracks down references to Germany, Britain, and the United States) made particular sense in light of the notion that Filipinos reportedly viewed the Japanese as their elder brothers. "The idea of the Japanese as 'elder brothers' was said to have been fostered by Spanish ethnologists who reiterated that the Japanese were of the same Malay stock as the peoples of Southeast Asia — an idea which was 'readily accepted by the inhabitants of the Philippines, because the Tagalogs who formed a principal part of the population had intermarried with Chinese and were thus in appearance similar to the Japanese' " (Lapian 1998: 92, quoting J. G. Doorman's "De Philippijnen," 1896).

By and large, however, news about the Philippine revolution or Rizal was desultory in the Dutch-language press in Indonesia and — except for one 1899 reference in North Sulawesi that Lapian and his researchers traced, a false story on Emilio Aguinaldo's surrender (premature, as it turned out, by over a year and a half)[8] — seemingly non-existent in the Malay press.

A QUARTER-CENTURY AFTER RIZAL DISCOVERED MULTATULI, Multatuli's grandnephew discovered Rizal. It is difficult to say exactly when the discovery took place, but one thing is certain: In April 1913, E. F. E. Douwes Dekker prepared to undertake a tour of the Philippines, "to study the fast-developing political situation in the American colony" (Van der Veur 2006: 247). As part of his preparations, the Eurasian pioneer of Indonesian independence read up on the available literature, paying particular attention to the Englishman John Foreman's standard reference, *The Philippine Islands*.

The first result of his intellectual combat — he said he was "surrounded by books on the Philippines" (Douwes Dekker 1913: 575) — was an essay titled "Rizal," written for the 15 May issue of the scholarly journal he had himself founded in 1911, *Het Tijdschrift* (The Magazine). It was written in Singapore, on the first leg of his journey to Manila.

Reflecting the philosophical turn of mind that would characterize much of Douwes Dekker's writing, it began with four closely reasoned paragraphs on the definition, or rather the recognition, of greatness, navigating a middle path between Aristotle (*"De grieksche denker was hierin wel ultra-behoudend —* The Greek thinker was ultra-conservative in this") and Nietzsche (*"Wij zijn in onze democratische denkbeelden, ondanks Nietzsche's anathema tegen Demos —* We are democratic in our ideas, despite Nietzsche's anathema against Demos"). For DD, as the ex-prisoner-of-war-turned-journalist was better known, the proper ideal of greatness was nobility of spirit in the struggle for liberty. *"Zoo dus zien wij de nobele figuren in de historie der menschheid als helden strijden voor de Vrijheid —* So therefore we see the noble characters in the history of mankind fighting as heroes for freedom." In this history, he privileged such *nobele figuren* as Galileo Galilei and Giordano Bruno, who wrestled with the demons of obscurantism in the established (Roman Catholic) church. And in this history he saw Rizal taking his rightful place. *"Dr Jose Rizal y Mercado was een uit de heldenrij —* Dr Jose Rizal y Mercado was one of this line of heroes."

He described Rizal as *"prachtigen patriot, dezen halfbloed, die met opgeheven hoofde en fieren blik zijn leven gaf als life offer aan de vrijheid van zijn vaderland*" — In van der Veur's translation: "A courageous, magnificent patriot, this half-blood, who with uplifted head and proud look gave his life as a costly sacrifice to the freedom of his fatherland" (Douwes Dekker 1913: 570; Van der Veur 2006: 250). He pronounced Rizal's martyrdom "an enviable fate," because with it he bought "*verdrijving der onderdrukkers uit zijn vaderland en de zekerheid der eindelijke vrijheid van dit vaderland* — the expulsion of the oppressors from his fatherland and the certainty of ultimate freedom of this fatherland" (Douwes Dekker 1913: 574; Van der Veur 2006: 250, but with slight changes).

The details of Rizal's life and life-giving death come straight from Foreman, on whom DD depended for his Philippine-related articles "frequently to the point of verbatim translation" (Van der Veur 2006: 250). Thus the main details from Foreman's eight dense pages on Rizal (out of a total of 692 pages, excluding photographic plates, in the third or 1906 edition of the influential reference work) leap out from the columns of *Het Tijdschrift*: the basic chronology, the three major books, the Mindanao exile, the role of the friar Mariano Gil in the conspiracy to assure Rizal's death, the use of the first and last stanzas from the farewell poem, and, after the execution, Josephine Bracken's stirring progress through rebel lines. There is also Foreman's mention of Rizal's "oft-quoted saying, 'What is death to me? I have sown the seed; others are left to reap.'" By the same token, Foreman's telltale errors are repeated: six in the morning as Rizal's time of death (instead of three minutes past seven[9]), 1893 as the year he came back from Hong Kong and was sent off to exile (instead of 1892), the name of Rizal's older brother spelled as Pasciano (instead of Paciano) — an error, as an Indonesian magazine article published 50 years later proves, with a long memory.

Foreman's work suffers from major flaws; its over-dependence on highly placed sources (including officials of the American occupation he criticised) seems obvious, even markedly naive, a hundred years removed. Its account of Josephine's heroism, while welcome, could have done with a little more scepticism; it seems to be based primarily on the report of "a friend of mine who interviewed her" — Edwin Wildman, I would guess, the author of the controversial *Aguinaldo: A Narrative of Filipino Ambitions*, who wrote down an interview with Josephine that is marred by serious chronological and other issues, and that was designed to show both Aguinaldo's ineptitude and Filipino ingratitude! (Wildman 1901: 27–39, especially 37 and 38) The American historian James LeRoy attacked Foreman's work in the *Boston Evening Transcript* as "Malicious and Untrustworthy" (Kramer 2005: 75).

But even today *The Philippine Islands* ("John Foreman's great history," the *New York Times* declared on 15 September 1906) remains a readable yarn; its pages on Rizal are especially compelling, because Foreman seemed to know both Rizal and his family at the precise time the Rizal reputation was being formed. At least three encounters with Rizal are recorded:

> On his return to the Islands, a year after the publication of this work [the *Noli*], we met at the house of a mutual friend and conversed on the subject of "Noli me tangere," a copy of which he lent to me. [Foreman 1985: 382]

> At length prudence dictated a return to Europe. I often recall the farewell lunch we had together at the Restaurant de Paris, in the *Escolta*. [382]

> Not a few of us who saw the vessel leave [Rizal was on his way to Barcelona, to serve in Cuba] wished him "God speed." But the clerical party were eager for his extermination. [385]

But to Foreman's narrative Douwes Dekker added his own distinctive touch. Where Foreman had written, "Deeds in Europe, almost amounting to miracles, were attributed to his genius, and became current talk among the natives when they spoke *sotto voce* of Rizal's power and influence. He was looked up to as the future regenerator of his race…," DD paraphrased as follows (Douwes Dekker 1913:

571–572): "*Half-bloed en inboorling begonnen hem te zien als de redder, de regenerator van 't Vaderland* — Half-blood and native began to see him as the saviour, the regenerator of the Fatherland."

Douwes Dekker, the son of a Dutch father and a German-Javanese mother, a half-blood or "Indo" in other words, had managed to insert himself into Rizal's story. Only a few months previously, he had become the first nationalist in Indonesia to advocate independence (Van der Veur 1958: 556). He had co-founded the first pro-independence organization in the islands, the Indische Partij, on 25 December 1912; four months after writing on Rizal, he would be sent into a long exile. At this point in DD's evolution as "the evangelist of Indonesian political nationalism," however, he believed the Eurasians had a unique leadership role to play. "We really form the beginning of our own nation," he said once (Van der Veur 1958: 551; 558). Thus his characterization of Rizal as "*dezen halfbloed*," his inclusion of "*halfbloed*" in his description of the Philippine population, his notion of mestizo leadership, betrayed his own, initial understanding of Indonesian independence as a movement to be led by Indos like him.

It is worth noting that before founding the Indische Partij, DD had at first sought to restructure a mutual aid organization that may have been inspired by events in the Philippines into a movement for "political action." His plan to reorganize was rejected by the executive committee of the Indische Bond, the pioneering union for Europeans in the Indies, as a virtual *coup d'etat* (Van der Veur 1958: 553-555). But the nature, or even the fact, of that inspiration is somewhat in dispute. Bosma and Raben have outlined the debate: "Contemporaries, and indeed historians, have suggested that the birth of this organization, with its economic nationalist rhetoric, may have been inspired by the rebellion in the Philippines. However, [the planter-turned-journalist George Albertus] Andriesse's propaganda had already started in 1895, a good year before the revolution broke out in the Philippines. The man who inspired this revolution, the ophthalmologist Jose Rizal, a descendant of a Chinese-Mestizo planter's family from the sugar-growing district of Laguna, near Manila, was virtually unknown in the Dutch East Indies" (Bosma and Raben 2008: 303). But they also noted that the colonial government was on guard precisely against contamination by ideas inspired by the Philippine revolt.

> The government of the Indies viewed the emergence of the Indische Bond as a dangerous symptom of social unrest. Unemployment among the European residents and the downhill effect this had on wages for those not highly educated would, they feared, almost certainly lead to radicalism of the Indische Bond. In this context what they most feared — remarkably enough — was not so much the influence of the Dutch Labour Party, the SDAP, as the flames of revolution that might wing their way from the Philippines. [Bosma and Raben 2008: 309]

Douwes Dekker missed the heyday of the Indische Bond; at the turn of the century, having volunteered to fight the British in the Boer War in South Africa, DD found himself a prisoner of war, detained in Sri Lanka. He did not return to the Dutch East Indies until 1903. "He was then fortunate in receiving a thorough journalistic training on the editorial staffs of the *Soerabaiaasch Handelsblad*, the Semarang *Locomotief*, and the *Bataviaasch Nieuwsblad*" (Van der Veur 1958: 551). He joined the last newspaper the same year he helped found Budi Utomo, in 1908 (Bosma and Raben 2008).

His training made it only natural for him to try and forge a link between the present situation in the Indies and whatever it was he was writing about. In "Rizal," he writes of the *parallel de historie* between "the, fortunately terminated, Spanish colonial rule" and the domination of his fatherland "by another people" (that is to say, his own Dutch forebears). He ends the essay with an expression of hope in Indonesia's own heroes:

> *Ik ben getroost. Als eenmaal onze Rizal's, onze Josefine's, onze Pasciano's, onze Aguinaldo's, onze Maximo Paterno's, onze Burgos',*

onze Zamora's, onze Gomez' noodig zijn — wat 't Lot verhoede — dan zullen zij er zijn! [Douwes Dekker 1913: 575]

I am comforted. *If* our Rizals, our Josefines, our Pascianos, our Aguinaldos, our Maximo Paternos, our Burgoses, our Zamoras, our Gomezes would be needed — Fate forbid — they — *will* be there! [Van der Veur 2006: 250, but revised; his list of names is incomplete]

We may find Douwes Dekker's fervent belief that when the time comes the heroes of the Indies will step forward rather sentimental (when he wrote the essay he was almost the same age as Rizal on the day of his execution), but the idealism, the impetuosity even, was characteristic. His "Open Letter" to the Governor-General in 1912 strikes the same "inflammatory" note, down to the same notion of an intervening fate: "But Excellency, I tell you, *if* one day our fist clutches a weapon — may fate forbid — it will *not* be our fault. Then you Governor-General of the *Netherlands Indies*, you and your associates, will be responsible ..." (Van der Veur 1958: 555, quoting the 15 October 1912 issue of *Het Tijdschrift*).

He ends the essay on Rizal with a resounding last line, harking back to the quote from Rizal that Foreman had carefully preserved: "*Anderen zullen oogsten, rijkelijk, wat eerderen zaaiden* — Others will reap, richly, what forerunners had sown."

E.F.E. Douwes Dekker never made it to the Philippines. While he was in Hong Kong, on the final leg to Manila, he received an important cable. The parliament in the Netherlands had unexpectedly resolved to discuss the future of the Indische Partij, and the news upset his plans; he was told to proceed to the Netherlands. Characteristically, he chose the longer, cheaper route — which is why in May 1913, Douwes Dekker found himself travelling from Harbin in northeastern China to St. Petersburg, Russia on the Trans-Siberian Railway, a journey that lasted eight days. On those eight days, the Philippines was very much on his mind.

[L]ittle could have been reported during the days that the train chugged through the Siberian steppes. But DD was bent over his Corona typewriter. What was he doing? At the start of his trip from the harbor of Tanjung Priok [in present-day Jakarta], thinking that he would proceed to the Philippines, DD had surrounded himself with manuals on that country. While reading this material he claimed to have been struck by the similarities between 'the, fortunately terminated, Spanish colonial rule' and the rule in his own fatherland 'by another people' ....

Now, moving through the plains of Siberia, DD in his train compartment began a series of fourteen articles on the Philippine Revolution of 1896–1898 ....

DD's contribution, although hardly an original one, was important in that it presented material in Dutch concerning what had happened in the neighboring colony to an audience which had been kept in the dark as to events which had taken place. There was, moreover, the usual DD addition: the repeated drawing of parallels with conditions in the Netherlands Indies ... [For instance:] The Philippine mestizo had led the revolution that had resulted in Spain's losing its colony. This was a lesson which should fill one 'with profound satisfaction'. [Van der Veur 2006: 250–251]

The articles saw print in *De Expres*, the newspaper he founded, between 30 June and 26 July 1913. "DD was pleased with his description of the Philippine Revolution. Dutch colonial officials, annoyed by the frequent and to them dangerous comparisons with the Netherlands Indies, were far less appreciative" (Van der Veur 2006: 251).

By the time he returned to Batavia on 1 August 1913, the colonial government's patience was at an end. He learned that his two co-leaders in the Insulinde movement, Tjipto Mangoenkoesoemo and Soewardi Soerjaningrat, had been arrested two days earlier. Straightaway, he wrote an impassioned defence of his colleagues, calling them "our heroes," and deploying, yet again, his argument from inevitability: "these sacrifices [of Tjipto and Soewardi] — and the many still to be made — [are] the seeds of the great national movement that is to come and of which we do not yet fathom the consequences" (Van der Veur 2006: 261). That lead article in the 5 August 1913 issue of *De Expres* led to his immediate detention (Van der Veur 1958: 559).

The last paragraph of the last article in Douwes Dekker's 14-part series on the Philippine revolution, which appeared in *De Expres* less than a week before his return from Europe, had reminded his influential readers why studying recent Philippine history was vital: it was "a lesson of enormous importance for other colonies and other motherlands" (Van der Veur 2006: 291). His 5 August defence of his colleagues, those "martyrs" to a great cause, showed he had taken the lesson to heart.

In Van der Veur's precis of DD's defence, it is possible to catch glimpses of the Philippine historical experience that Douwes Dekker had only recently studied. "History had taught other things as well such as that abuse of power always leads to eclipse of power; that the blood of martyrs is the seed of progress; that no advance is possible without the making of great sacrifices; and that there always will be courageous men and women willing to make them. When one day great things would happen in 'our Fatherland', people would think back to these days of July and August 1913" (Van der Veur 2006: 261). Classic, irrepressible DD, writing of the future as if it were already documented fact.

On 18 August, the order to send all three leaders to exile was announced; permitted to leave the colony instead if they wished, all of them took advantage of the official offer. Douwes Dekker would not return to Indonesia until 1918, but he had already made his signal contributions to the emerging Indonesia: He had played a key role in founding Budi Utomo, he was the first to openly advocate independence for the islands, and, in Takashi Shiraishi's words, he had "brought home the idea of rally and organized the first rally ever held in the Indies." This last achievement would have fateful consequences: The Sarekat Islam leader Tjokroaminoto "learned its power from the [Indische Partij] rally [organised by Douwes Dekker] and turned the form into a powerful weapon for the SI" (Shiraishi 1990: 340).

Prior to DD's return, a secret report by the chief of the Political Information Service was prepared for the Governor-General. Excerpted in Van der Veur's 1958 paper, it offers both a document of acute historical insight and a prefiguring of the analytical reports the Native inspector Pangemanann wrote on nationalist leaders, Douwes Dekker included, in Pramoedya's *House of Glass*.

> As the development of the political life in this country proceeds, however, the inner contradictions in Douwes Dekker's nationalism will become more obvious. Five years ago the Eurasian group had not experienced as strongly as at present the competition of the increasing number of native intellectuals. Year after year this competition will make itself more strongly felt. The Eurasians, at the moment still partially indifferent and for that matter divided into several groups, will be driven together to make a united front against the surging native flood. [Van der Veur 1958: 561, quoting the "Secret Report" of W. Muurling dated 16 February 1918]

Three decades after this report was written, when DD had taken his new name of Danu Dirdjo Setiabuddhi and converted to Islam, the native intellectual at the head of that surging, triumphant flood paid Douwes Dekker high tribute.

"In the name of our people I also want to express the people's gratitude for your services to land and nation," President Sukarno said in ceremonies marking the occasion of Douwes Dekker's 70th birthday, in 1949 (Van der Veur 1958: 556). "I consider you one of the Fathers of political nationalism in Indonesia."

Notes

1. Rizal's influence on the historical novels of Pramoedya Ananta Toer is discussed at length in Chapter 10. Despite repeated references to the Dutch children from Java in his diary, Rizal did not mention any of them in his letters home, at least in those that have survived. Unlike his letters or indeed

anything else he wrote, the diaries he kept on and off for many years were not meant to be seen by other eyes.
2. The memory of the influential writer is well-served by the Multatuli Museum; I accessed much pertinent information from the museum's website, available at <www.multatuli-museum.nl>.
3. See, for instance, his letter of 5 March 1887, written in French and presumed to have been addressed to the painter Felix Resurreccion Hidalgo in Paris, discussing the just-published *Noli*: "My book may have — and it has — defects from the artistic or aesthetic point of view. I don't deny it; but what cannot be questioned is the impartiality of my narration" (Rizal 1963b: 84). Or his letter to Blumentritt of 22 September 1891, several months after the *Fili* came off the press: "I am thinking of writing a third novel, a novel in the modern meaning of the word. But this time politics will not occupy much space in it" (Rizal 1963d: 415).
4. See Anderson 2005 and Anderson 2006. There may be something to the idea (2005: 108–109) that the extraordinary burst, not merely of realism but of current events, at the end of Chapter 10, when the *Fili*'s author directly addresses the reader about the outrages in Calamba, may have been inspired by a similar apostrophe in the last chapter of *Max Havelaar*. But Don Quixote, in which Rizal's generation was steeped, and from which Rizal quoted in his other writings, was full of similar fact-bursting-out-of-fiction authorial play too.
5. The page was accessed through the immensely useful website of the Royal Library of the Netherlands, available at <http://kranten.kb.nl>.
6. See, for instance, the newspapers researched by the indefatigable Paz Policarpio Mendez (1978: 162–170), including the 30 December 1896 issues of *Le Figaro, Allgmeine Zeitung, The Times of London*, and the *New York Times*, and the 2 January 1897 issue of *The New York Herald*. Closer to home, I have read news items on the execution in the *Singapore Free Press* and *Mercantile Advertiser* of 31 December, the *China Mail* of 6 January, 1897, the *Hong Kong Telegraph* of 4 and 27 January — as well as in the pages of *Het Nieuws van den Dag* and *Nieuwe Tilsburgsche Courant*.
7. There are at least three references to the supposed absence of news in *Child of All Nations* (Pramoedya 1991: 88–89; 92; 263); as well as at least two references to an official ban ordered by the Dutch colonial government on news about the Philippine rebellion in *House of Glass* (Pramoedya 1992). The uses of Philippine history in Pramoedya's narrative of the Indonesian awakening are discussed in Chapter 10.
8. "In a small item the *Tjahaja Sijang* announced in its issue of 7 August 1899 (page 4) that Aguinaldo had surrendered" (Lapian 1998: 92). In fact

Aguinaldo was captured by pursuing American troops and their Filipino scouts in Palanan, Isabela province, in northern Luzon, on 23 March 1901.

9. Retana bases this estimate on Felipe Calderon's moving personal account. Calderon was in his home in Ermita, very near the place of execution, when he heard the gunshots that killed Rizal; he happened to look at the clock at that very moment. Next door, another Filipino family had been busy praying for Rizal since dawn. (Retana 1907: 432).

5

"No Marx or Lenin"

In 1921, an official holiday to mark the birthday of the Philippine revolutionary supremo Andres Bonifacio was celebrated in the Philippines for the first time; it came a generation after his execution. As labour leader Hermenegildo Cruz was to later recall, the day before the new holiday his school-aged children asked him, "*Sino ba iyan si Bonifacio?* — Who is that [man] Bonifacio?"

The pioneer labour organizer and nationalist writer was stunned. "*Wari ako'y natubigan ...* — I felt like I had been doused." After he recovered, he began to tell his children about Bonifacio and the Katipunan:

> Sa maiikling pangungusap, ay aking ipinatanto sa mga anak ko ang buong kabuhayan ni Andres Bonifacio at ang sanhi't katwiran kung bakit siya'y ibinubunyi ng ating lahi't Pamahalaan. Akin ding ipinakilala sa kanila ang mga aral ng "Katipunan"; at isinaysay ang kapakinabangang natamo ng Bayang Pilipino sa paghihimagsik na pinamatnugutan ng kapisanang yaong itinatag at pinanguluhan ni Andres Bonifacio. [Cruz 1922: 9]
>
> In simple words, I made my children understand the whole life story of Andres Bonifacio and the roots and reasons why he was being honoured by our race and government. I also introduced to them the principles of the Katipunan; and narrated the benefits gained by the Philippine nation through the revolution directed by that society founded and headed by Andres Bonifacio.

That teaching moment led Cruz to write *Kartilyang Makabayan* or Patriotic Primer, a revealing catechism (it follows a question-and-answer format) about Bonifacio and the Katipunan "*na nagturo at nagakay sa Bayang Pilipino sa Paghihimagsik laban sa kapangyarihang dayo* — which taught and guided the Philippine nation in the Revolution against foreign powers," as the latter half of the volume's kilometric subtitle put it.

The *Kartilyang Makabayan* is revealing not only for what it suggests about Cruz's own biography (the dig at foreign powers seems to me calculated; Cruz was director of the Bureau of Labour in the American regime at the time he wrote the book), but also and mainly because it catches the evolution of the labour movement's understanding of Rizal a quarter-century after his execution. The same labour movement was the hydraulic force behind the elevation of Bonifacio into the national pantheon, and much later would help catapult the nationalist school of history-writing to ascendancy. At its peak, that school would portray Rizal as deeply compromised and ultimately undeserving of his preeminent place in Philippine history. But in the 1920s, midway through the American period, the country's workers continued to see Rizal as the epitome of the heroic. Rizal, in a word, remained the benchmark. Despite some of his own arguments in the primer, Cruz subscribed to the same view too.

Kartilyang Makabayan is a testament to Bonifacio's greatness, and while it does without documentation or often even the courtesy of attribution, the primer does not seem to strain after effect. In a few instances, the contemporary reader with access to more information might think that Cruz has tried to stretch the point, but all told, the primer is that rare thing, the reasonable paean, the measured praise.

Its principal objective can be glimpsed in Question No. 11.

Ano't idinadakila ng Bayang Pilipino si Andres Bonifacio at siya'y ipinalalagay na dakilang Bayani sa piling ni Rizal? Sapagka't siya ang nagtayo at nahalal na pangulo ng "Kataastaasan, Kagalanggalang Katipunan ng mga Anak ng Bayan," na pinagkautangan ng Bayang Pilipino ng kabayanihan sa pagusig sa kanyang ikalalaya. "Maypagasa" ang sagisag niya na "nangyari" bago siya mamatay. [Cruz 1922: 13]

> Why does the Philippine nation honour Andres Bonifacio and seek to place him as a noble hero beside Rizal? Because he founded and was elected head of the Highest, Most Honourable Society of the Sons of the People [the Katipunan], to whom the Philippine nation owes the heroism of its struggle to be free. "There-is-hope" was his pseudonym, which "happened" before he died.

To honour Bonifacio in full is to place him "*sa piling ni Rizal*," which means not only "on the side of," but "in the same rank as," Rizal. In 1922, the year Cruz published his primer, that meant accomplishing two tasks: locate Bonifacio in the Rizal story, and then distance the supremo of the Katipunan from the martyr of Bagumbayan.

Cruz traces the founding of the Katipunan to Rizal's arrest after his return from Hong Kong. "*Nang maalaman ito ni Andres Bonifacio ay nagalab ang kanyang loob* — When Andres Bonifacio came to know of it, his heart was inflamed." He then gathered Ladislao Diwa, Valentin Diaz, Ildefonso Laurel, and Deodato Arellano (other accounts include other names) in a house on Azcarraga street, and together they founded the Katipunan (14).

Cruz attributes the Katipunan's sluggish growth in its early years to Bonifacio's deferential decision to give way to Rizal's Liga.

> *Nang mga sumusunod na buwan ng pagkakatatag ay di nagpamalas ng kanyang pagsulong, pagkat ang nais ni Bonifacio ay huwag makapinsala sa pagpapalaganap ng "Liga Filipina," na itinatag ni Rizal at mga litaw na kababayan, karamihan ay mason, bago sumilang ang "Katipunan."* [22]

> In the months following its founding, it [the Katipunan] did not show any progress, because it was Bonifacio's wish not to impede the growth of the Liga Filipina, which Rizal and other prominent countrymen, many of them Masons, founded before the Katipunan was born.

In my view, this is the single weakest item in the entire primer; plainly put, it does not make sense. Why start a revolutionary organization and then wait for another group to succeed? It seems to me the attempt to locate Bonifacio in the Rizal saga is at its most apparent here. But even the esteemed Teodoro M. Kalaw, in his 1925 classic *The Philippine Revolution*, makes the same irrational assertion (1969: 12; also 307).

Cruz also details the attempt of the Katipunan to consult Rizal about the planned revolution, which Rizal rejected as inopportune; and its attempt to free Rizal from the Spanish cruiser where he was detained, which Rizal rejected as unnecessary (Cruz 1922: 32; 42). These moments are recapitulated at the end of the book, which lists dates mentioned in the telling. Thus, the list includes Dr Pio Valenzuela's consultation with Rizal in May 1896, and Rizal's return to Manila from his Dapitan exile in August 1896, and Emilio Jacinto's attempt, on the same day, to convince Rizal to escape.

> 1896. – *Buwan ng Mayo, sinugo ni Bonifacio si Dr Valenzuela kay Rizal*
>
> ....
>
> 1896. – *Ika-5 ng Agosto, paglunsad ni Rizal sa Maynila buhat sa Dapitan.*
>
> 1896. – *Ika-5 ng Agosto, tinangka ng mga "Katipunan" na iligtas si Rizal.* [63]

What makes this select chronology interesting to the contemporary reader is that it is very selective indeed. It leaves out the date of Rizal's execution. In fact, in the entire primer, there is only one passing mention of the killing of Rizal — and only as one of many Masons executed by the Spanish colonial government.

Here we see Cruz at work on the second task, of distancing Bonifacio from Rizal. The primer *is* Bonifacio's narrative, and in the book crucial distinctions between the two are made.

The contrast between Bonifacio's conviction that the time for an armed revolt had come and Rizal's punctilious regard for peaceful means is sharpened by several anecdotes, embodied in the answers to the questions in Cruz's catechism. Indeed, a survey of the questions themselves is already telling. No. 34: "In other words, the Masons and the wealthy Filipinos were not in agreement with the Katipunan?" No. 36: "What did the Masons do to Bonifacio and the Katipunan?" No. 37: "Was Rizal in agreement with the revolution started by the Katipunan?" No. 39: "What did Bonifacio do in the face of the opposition of Rizal and others to the revolution?" (Cruz 1922: 29–34)

The contrast between the methodical patience of the wealthy and the ready fatalism of the poor is also heightened, with Cruz's waxing eloquent in defence of the poor's come-what-may attitude.

> ... ang mga dukha, manggagawa, mga maralita, na mga hamak na taong bayan, dito sa atin at saan pa man, ay kapag niyakap ang isang gawain at napagkilalang kailangang gawin sa ikasusunod ng isang dakilang layunin, ay di na nagtutumigil ng pagiisip at karakaraka'y ginagampanan sa pamamagitan ng salitang "Bahala na!". Ang "bahala" nang ito, ay makikita natin na siyang nagligtas sa bayaning pilipino ng mga panahong yaon at naghatid sa atin sa tagumpay. [33]
>
> ... the poor, workers, the destitute, the lowly people, here [in the Philippines] and wherever else, when they embrace a deed they realize needs to be done to meet a noble objective, do not tarry in thought and act immediately, by means of the words "*Bahala na* [Come what may]!" We will see that this "*bahala*" is what saved the Filipino people in those times and led us to victory.

One more thing. After describing the three grades of Katipunan membership — *Katipunan*,[1] *Kawal, Bayani* — Cruz explains the password for the third and highest level in these terms: " '*Rizal*' *ang hudyat na salita, bilang pagtutol sa walang katwirang pakakapabilanggo sa kanya* — 'Rizal' was the password, in protest against his unjust imprisonment" (23). This seems to be standard, even boilerplate, praise of Rizal and his role in the national awakening; on closer look, however, its narrowness of purpose suggests a much more limited role for Rizal. In Cruz's view, the password is not an expression of the

Katipunan's deepest ideology as shaped in large part by Rizal, but merely a symbolic protest, against a specific injustice. Cruz's phrasing even makes it sound merely tactical.

But despite all this, Cruz — organizer of one of the first labour strikes during the revolutionary era, co-founder of the first labor federation in the Philippines, first president of the biggest labour group of the period, and lifelong nationalist and rabble-rousing orator[2] — still shared the common assumption of his time and of the labour movement he helped shape, that Rizal was the heroic standard. This sense breaks the surface of the primer every now and then, but it emerges for all to see in the last question of Cruz's catechism.

> *Nguni't ang lalong pinakamahalaga, bukod sa palatuntunan at mga aral ng "Katipunan," at ang "Katungkulang gagawin ng mga Anag [sic] ng Bayan," ay ang "Huling Paalam" ni Rizal, na kanyang isinatagalog sa gitna ng pagdadagundong ng Paghihimagsik, na siyang inaawit ng ating mga kawal ng sila'y nakikipaglaban sa Kastila.*
> [Cruz 1922: 58; with Bonifacio's translation following on 59–61]

> But the most important [of Bonifacio's writings], aside from the program and the principles of the Katipunan, and his "Duties of the Sons of the People," is the "Mi Ultimo Adios" of Rizal, which he translated into Tagalog in the middle of the tumult of the Revolution, and which our soldiers sang as they fought the Spaniards.

If we compare this assertion with the landmark study by Bienvenido Lumbera on Tagalog poetry, completed in 1966 but first published only in 1986, we can gauge how far the nationalist school that emerged out of the labour movement begun by Isabelo de los Reyes and Hermenegildo Cruz and their allies had succeeded in placing Bonifacio in the pantheon of heroes: in this reckoning, he had quite literally displaced Rizal.

Lumbera's study has a classic postscript on "Poetry and the Revolution (1882–1898)," which privileges the poetic achievement, if not quite the poetic genius, of Bonifacio (Lumbera 1986: 138–149). This reading, however, is marked by a curious absence: Nowhere is

Rizal's "Mi Ultimo Adios," surely the most consequential poem in Philippine history, even mentioned. (There are two brief references to Rizal, unrelated to revolutionary poetry.) To be sure, the poem was written in Spanish, and the scope of the groundbreaking study was poetry in Tagalog. But wouldn't Bonifacio's widely available translation have qualified it for discussion?

The translation is not without complications. Some historians have argued that in fact it was not Bonifacio who translated the poem, but the writer-revolutionary Diego Mojica; the first printing of the translation only carried Bonifacio's name (Medina 2001: 91). For our purposes, however, it does not really matter. Bonifacio and his closest allies made a concerted effort to establish the Katipunan supremo as the translator. The revolutionary general Santiago Alvarez, for instance, narrated the circumstances in which Bonifacio was said to have received a copy of the poem from Rizal's own sister, brother, and widow (Alvarez 1992: 306–307; his memoirs were first published in 1927). In other words, Bonifacio thought Rizal's farewell poem was both potent and important enough to be translated without delay, and that it was good for him to be seen as translating it.

For an ardent nationalist like Lumbera to scant the poem in a survey of revolutionary poetry — the kind that rebel troops would read or remember in the trenches, as Cruz suggested — can only mean that by the 1960s, the re-visioning of Philippine history begun by labour organizers and developed in full by nationalist historians like Teodoro Agoncillo was complete. Rizal had been ousted.

"A REVOLUTIONARY VETERAN WHO KNEW HIM told me that the father of the revolution, Andres Bonifacio, was an indigenous Indonesian from Tondo on the outskirts of Manila."

No one else but the Indonesian Marxist revolutionary Tan Malaka could have written that warmly assertive, wonderfully complicated recollection-cum-description (Tan Malaka 1991: 118). He had spent a couple of years in the Philippines between July 1925 and August

1927. (To be more precise, the "chief Comintern representative for Southeast Asia" had based himself in the Philippines between those dates, partly for health reasons). During his stay, he had befriended both high officials (including Senate President Manuel Quezon, the highest-ranking Filipino in the American colonial government) and ordinary citizens; and met Emilio Aguinaldo and other veterans of the Philippine revolution (it had only been a quarter-century since Aguinaldo's surrender). Above all, he had immersed himself in the working-class movement (Saulo 1990: 11–12).

It is this rootedness in the Philippine labour movement, from which the first communist organizers in the country emerged, that gives colour and life to Sutan Ibrahim gelar Datuk Tan Malaka's description of Philippine society in his 1948 autobiography *Dari Pendjara ke Pendjara*. (I am using Helen Jarvis's English translation, *From Jail to Jail*, published in 1991.)

Tan Malaka calls his pages on the Philippines a mere "lightning sketch" (Tan Malaka 1991: 117), an incomplete portrait "drawn from my impressions of some twenty years ago, when I was fortunate enough to obtain information from young and old. But it is clear that the picture does not have its *finishing touch*, has many weaknesses, and could be improved here and there" (133).

It is precisely those "weaknesses," however, that recommend Tan Malaka's chapter on the Philippines to the modern reader. By this I mean his selection of Philippine historical facts, which strike us now as very much a reflection, a palimpsest, of the time.

In one of her many generous footnotes, Jarvis quotes a comment from a letter of the Filipino scholar Reynaldo Ileto that allows us to make better sense of Tan Malaka's insights, thus: "The comments on Rizal and Bonifacio [Day] tell us a bit about Tan Malaka's informants. To my knowledge, to the peasantry Bonifacio does not signify a more radical stance than Rizal. 'Courage' and 'struggle' can equally be represented in a quiet, penetrating manner. It was labour organizers from the first decade of this [twentieth] century on who saw Bonifacio and his raised bolo (equivalent of the clenched fist) as a fitting representation of the working class struggle. Just as Americans were reshaping Rizal, the radical nationalists were reshaping Bonifacio" (Tan Malaka 1991: 258).

The interesting thing about Tan Malaka's description of Bonifacio, then, is not the inclusion of the Philippines in an expansive understanding of Indonesia, but what he says before and after he calls Bonifacio Indonesian. To be sure, the way he begins the chapter on the Philippines may give the Filipino reader an attack of vertigo: "What were the Philippines like after 450 years of separation from South Indonesia? This is the obvious question to arise in the heart of a lover of history who confronts the history of the whole of Indonesia" (117). As Jarvis notes, Tan Malaka is indulging his concept of Indonesia as "including the whole Malay or Indonesian archipelago," which fell into disunion only after European colonisers arrived in the sixteenth century (246).

It is difficult to imagine any veteran of the Revolution describing Bonifacio as "an indigenous *Indonesian* from Tondo on the outskirts of Manila" — the Indonesian label must have been Tan Malaka's own gloss. But the location of Tondo, the working-class district outside the city of Manila with which Tan Malaka would have been familiar, and the description of Bonifacio as indigenous, that is to say, not mestizo, were part of the Bonifacio narrative even while the Katipunan supremo was still alive. He *was* a non-mestizo from Tondo.

But in Tan Malaka's telling these indices of identity become freighted with extra meaning. In contrast with the Netherlands Indies in which he grew up, in the Philippines the mestizo was a term of approval, not insult. "Up to the time I was there (1927) the mestizos were not a class apart, distrusted and hated by the indigenous Filipino. On the contrary, the word "mestizo" was not pejorative, but a symbol of a privileged group in Filipino society" (119). This Minangkabau (West Sumatran) native had reached the same, initial conclusion as the "Indo" E. F. E. Douwes Dekker. To him, however, mestizo pre-eminence in Philippine society was not something to be emulated. "We can say that the higher we go on the political, social, economic, and cultural ladder, the more we see of yellow and even white skin .... [But] The high position held by the mestizos was a result of the political revolution in the Philippines, which, viewed even from the political angle, let alone the economic one, was a failure" (118).

A result of the political revolution: For Tan Malaka, the divide between the mestizo and the indigenous was not merely a matter of skin colour or body type, or even of unequal power relations, but ultimately of revolutionary credentials.

"Almost 100 per cent of the *Veterano*, the former revolutionary fighters of 1898–1901 who struggled first against the Spanish and then against the Americans, consisted of indigenous Indonesians," he notes. He identifies Bonifacio, Aguinaldo, "the famous minister of foreign affairs, Mabini," and Rizal, "the father of the Philippines," as "all indigenous Indonesians who had little if any mixed blood." In sum, the Revolution "was a revolution of the workers and peasants under the leadership of a truly revolutionary section of the intelligentsia" (118).

In contrast, "it was in the main they [the Spanish mestizos and Chinese mestizos) who were used by American imperialism to 'develop the Philippines.' Thus, nearly all Philippine administrative offices were staffed by mestizos who became American subjects and willingly cooperated with American imperialism" (119).

And again: "Since they shared language and religion and action during the revolution, it is not surprising that the mestizos in the time of American imperialism entered the administrative offices and even the legislature without opposition from the common people" (120).

The reference to Tondo, repeated twice more in the chapter, together with mentions of Bonifacio's interrupted schooling and his status as a "lowly clerk" (123) — all this is meant to draw attention to Bonifacio's working-class origins. In fact, some historians have disputed this plebeian portrait of the supremo (Richardson and Fast 1979, especially 67–74; Richardson 2007). Bonifacio was no mere clerk in a store, but a worker with increasing responsibilities at a British and then a German firm, in an era when foreign (especially British) enterprises dominated Philippine commerce (Richardson and Fast 1979: 51–52). John Foreman, writing at the end of the nineteenth century, noted that, "In Manila, the fathers of many of the half-castes and pure natives who at this day figure as men of position and standing, commenced their careers as messengers, warehouse-keepers, clerks, etc., of the foreign houses" (Foreman 1985: 258).

Richardson's excellent website on the Katipunan contains many papers that convincingly demonstrate the falsity of the sweeping generalization of the secret society as composed of "the unlettered masses" (Agoncillo 2002: 111). His "Notes on the Katipunan in Manila 1892–96," for instance, draws on Katipunan documents in Spanish military archives to draw a profile of over 200 men (and some women) active in the revolutionary organisation.[3]

But by the 1920s the "reshaping" of Bonifacio was well under way, and Tan Malaka's account reflects the influence of the working-class movement engaged in that earnest enterprise.

On Rizal, Tan Malaka is nothing if not sympathetic. Despite a diligent attempt to "place" Rizal in the revolutionary struggle and point to his limitations, the Indonesian revolutionary evinces genuine admiration for the Filipino propagandist. It may be that his years in the Philippines, and especially the overwhelming support he received from Filipinos when the American colonial government sought to deport him in 1927, may have suffused his account with the glow of remembered good will, but Rudolf Mrazek's review of the Jarvis translation suggests that this warmth, this quality of fellow-feeling we sense, truly marks the man.[4]

He is not above trading in the gossip that Rizal's last years gave rise to, the kind we've seen printed in American and Dutch and Chinese and Dutch East Indies newspapers.

When he was in exile in Dapitan, Mindanao, he was visited by the French consul in Hong Kong, accompanied by his daughter. The consul had an eye disease which many different doctors had failed to cure. He had been unable to see for some time and had to be led everywhere by his daughter. In Dapitan his eyesight was restored, but he lost his only child. His daughter became the admirer and lover of the quiet, exiled doctor and, on receiving her father's permission, became his life-long companion, joining the guerrilla struggle after her husband had been executed. This is a popular tale in the Philippines. [Tan Malaka 1991: 122]

But he also describes Rizal's international reputation. He lists his familiar qualities: his medical career, his scientific research, his civic spirit, his gift for languages, his art. And he insightfully summarizes Rizal's work as a writer in terms of both prophecy and legacy. "As a writer of two novels, *Noli me tangere* and *El filibusterismo*, he is regarded as a prophet of the revolution by his people, but as a deadly enemy by the priestly caste. The poem he wrote only hours before his execution is still regarded as a priceless inheritance by the appreciative masses" (122).

Not least, Tan Malaka sees a direct connection between Rizal's work and the revolution. "Inseparable from this revolution," he writes, "is the name 'La Liga Filipina' (the Philippine League) and that of its founder, Dr Jose Rizal" (121). He makes the connection explicit by promoting Bonifacio to "secretary" of the Liga (instead of mere member), and describes Rizal's short-lived association as Bonifacio's "school for learning about organization" (124). He is careful to write, after narrating Bonifacio's well-known outburst over Rizal's rejection of the revolution, that: "His remark did not ... imply loss of respect and love for the person he regarded as his teacher in everything, as we shall see later in this story" (124–125).

At six pages, all told, Tan Malaka's account of Rizal's story makes up the longest section in the 22-page chapter.

I do not know if Tan Malaka ever met Hermenegildo Cruz; I cannot find any reference to any encounter. (According to McInerney

2007, at about the time Cruz completed the writing of *Kartilyang Makabayan*, Tan Malaka was still in Moscow, attending meetings of the Executive Committee of the Communist International.)

And yet it is evident that, in Manila, the Indonesian exile moved in the same milieu as Cruz: he was, for instance, a close collaborator of Crisanto Evangelista, the labour organizer who would found the first communist party in the Philippines, but who had also served with Cruz in the Congreso Obrero de Filipinas (the Workers' Congress of the Philippines, for a long time the largest labour group in the country). Tan Malaka's links with Filipino labour leaders were forged even before he stepped foot in the Philippines; a delegation of workers' representatives from the Philippines, meeting Tan Malaka in Canton (present-day Guangzhou), was so moved by his "sad plight" that they invited the "sincere nationalist" to take refuge from Dutch spies by relocating to Manila (Saulo 1990: 11).

Like Cruz, Tan Malaka held views on Rizal that were both admiring and critical. Tellingly, he compares Rizal to Dr Sutomo, "the late Pak Tom." In Indonesian history, the moderate Sutomo is credited, among others, with the founding of Budi Utomo, from which date Sukarno traces the start of the national awakening; Tan Malaka thought Sukarno's views on history were fundamentally in error, however, and it is no surprise that Budi Utomo gets short shrift in Tan Malaka's account. The comparison with Sutomo is only to emphasise Rizal's reformist agenda. "To begin with, La Liga Filipina, founded by Dr Rizal in 1894 [sic] after his return from Europe, was a *Party of Reforms* and cooperation" (Tan Malaka 1991: 121; emphasis in the original).

After worrying the comparison, Tan Malaka works his way to a final judgment on Rizal. It is severe, but not harsh:

> "But measured on the revolutionary scale, Dr Rizal was no Marx or Lenin, nor even comparable to his colleague on the banks of the Pearl River, Dr Sun Yat-sen. A man of great intellect in many fields, a writer able to penetrate the consciousness of the masses, he

nevertheless did not turn his powers to the situation, character, aims, and forces of the revolutionary movement. For Dr Rizal, independence was contingent on the number of intellectuals and literates in the Philippines, on the strength of the colony's industry, agriculture, and trade, and above all on the arms held by the masses for the seizure of power. It was beyond his ken that the dynamic of the revolution could give rise to unimagined forces, could confront arms superior in number and power, and could generate a real spirit everywhere, provided that the force of the masses had previously been gauged, awakened, and coordinated by an honest, aware, and disciplined leadership. His lack of contact with the masses (caused partly by the fact that he was always watched carefully by the government and the Spanish priests) means that experience did not open his eyes to these possibilities. Dr Rizal remained an intellectual in relative isolation from the masses." [Tan Malaka 1991: 123]

In other words, Rizal was no revolutionary. His rejection of Bonifacio's planned revolution, and the offer to lead it, is his true measure. With the practiced hand of a revolutionary organiser, Tan Malaka picks apart Rizal's "most important objection to the plan ... the masses' lack of arms":

In fact, this weakness is one shared by all rebellious oppressed nations and classes from the time of Moses to the present day, including the French Revolution, the Russian Revolution, and the present Indonesian revolution of 17 August 1945. There has never been an oppressed and exploited nation or caste whose arms have exceeded or even equalled those of the caste that oppressed it. You do not have to have an intellect of international calibre to see this. If a nation or caste could equal, let alone exceed, its enemy in possession of arms then it would not be oppressed. Neither equality nor superiority can be attained before the revolution, but only during or after it, if it is a real social and economic or national revolution organized in a disciplined fashion. [Tan Malaka 1991: 124]

I find all this very interesting, not because he (illogically) equates Rizal's concern about a lack of arms with "equality" or "superiority" in weaponry, but because Tan Malaka has been accused of exactly the same thing: rejecting an armed uprising for lack of preparation. In fact, the last five pages of the chapter on the Philippines detail his reasons why the so-called Prambanan decision of the Partai Komunis Indonesia in December 1925 to launch an armed insurrection the following year was fatally premature.[5]

He enumerates the reasons in schematic fashion (Tan Malaka 1991: 134):

1. It was taken hurriedly, without careful consideration.
2. It resulted from provocation by our enemies and did not correspond to our own strength.
3. It could not be defended either to the masses or to the Comintern.
4. It did not correspond to communist strategy and tactics, that is, mass action.
5. It would result in great harm being done to the movement in Indonesia.

Except for the reference to the Comintern and to communist strategy and tactics, this list tallies closely enough with Rizal's own reasons for calling Bonifacio's planned revolution "foolhardy."

There are several versions of the meeting in Dapitan between Rizal and Bonifacio's emissary, Pio Valenzuela (like Rizal also a medical doctor). If we use Rizal's own testimony during his trial, and force-fit his recollection of the answer he gave Valenzuela into the same schema, we get this:

"The prisoner told him that it was hardly the time to embark on such foolhardy ventures,

1. as there was no unity among the various classes of Filipinos,
2. nor did they have arms,
3. nor ships,
4. nor education,
5. nor any of the other requirements for a resistance movement."
[De la Costa 1996: 93]

I do not wish to belabour the point, but the case can be made that Rizal's reading of the political situation when Valenzuela consulted him in May 1896 and when the Revolution broke out the following August corresponds to all but one of Tan Malaka's indicators of a premature uprising. His second and third reasons agree with Tan Malaka's first and second (that the discovery of the Katipunan precipitated the revolt only sharpened Rizal's worries about the lack of arms and materiel). His first coincides in part with Tan Malaka's third (one reason for the lack of unity was precisely the lack of agreement on the how and why of revolution). And his fourth and fifth align with Tan Malaka's last: Without adequate preparation, including instruction that will make the people "worthy of such liberties" (De la Costa 1996: 118), a spontaneous rising or a protracted guerrilla war would only result in great harm to the cause.

The one exception is the "communist" reliance on the motive force of mass action, something that Rizal, it must be conceded, evidently did not understand. His view of political change, contained within the limits of the controversial manifesto of 15 December 1896, placed the burden of history on a people's leaders, not the people themselves. "I have also written (and my words have been repeated by others) that reforms, if they are to bear fruit, must come *from above*, for reforms that come *from below* are upheavals both violent and transitory" (De la Costa 1996: 118–119).

Tan Malaka was surely right, when he described Rizal as living in "relative isolation" from the very people he had stirred into thought and action; Rizal did not seem to be aware, for instance, of the existence of Aguinaldo and the rebel leadership in Cavite, the province whose resistance weakened the Spanish colonial government the most. Tan Malaka may have been right too, when he described Rizal as lacking the revolutionary imagination: "It was beyond his ken that the dynamic of the revolution could give rise to unimagined forces …" By revolution, of course, he meant a social upheaval, class-based and unavoidably violent, and understood in Marxist terms.

For Rizal the true revolution was moral. But then he was no Marx, or Lenin.

BY THE LATE 1920s, the labour sector in the Philippines was languishing in the shadow of a looming split. Leaders of the Congreso Obrero de Filipinas workers' federation had been busy with work of a different nature. "Federation officials became more involved in political activities than in strengthening the federation's organizational structure," Melinda Tria Kerkvliet writes in a summing up of the pre-war era (1992: 111), and this political involvement began to peak at the end of the decade. The leaders' politics, however, did not converge.

A former believer in the Nacionalista Party and its campaign for independence, Evangelista had converted to a less gradualist faith and started a third labour party in 1925, together with Antonino de Ora (it was Ora's third attempt). The date, 30 November, Bonifacio Day, was chosen for its working-class significance. "The June election results that year may have convinced them of the futility of working within the framework of the traditional political parties," Kerkvliet notes (73). "It is also possible that Tan Malaka, an Indonesian nationalist and communist who was then in Manila, inspired them to form a political party advocating a different ideology." (In one of her many brimming footnotes, Kerkvliet references Jim Richardson's argument for Tan Malaka's direct influence on the Partido Obrero.)

In the account of Jose Ma. Sison, the founder of the Communist Party of the Philippines, the Partido Obrero was a way station on the communist road:

> In most of the 1920s, Evangelista and other progressive leaders of the working class movement preoccupied themselves with striving to unite the trade unions and labor federations in the Congreso Obrero de Filipinas (COF). It was only in 1925 that they established the Partido Obrero (Workers' Party) on the basis of the trade union movement and the peasant movement. It became the occasion for the patriotic and progressive labor leaders, who were in the majority in the COF, to distinguish themselves from the yellow labor leaders. But the Partido Obrero was not yet a Marxist vanguard of the working class. [Sison 2006]

The division of the labour sector into "reds" and "yellows," "revolutionary" and "reformist," "progressive" and "reactionary," sharpened. (The language would prove to be extraordinarily influential; today the same pairs of opposites are still in heavy use in Philippine political discourse — and in Rizal studies.) Other labour leaders (the yellows) sought to strengthen their ties to Quezon and the dominant Nacionalista political party. Evangelista and his associates (the reds) severed theirs.

In 1927, Evangelista as COF secretary presented a proposal to reinvigorate the federation, including a plan to change the ideological orientation of the labour group from class collaboration to class struggle. Soon after, Evangelista and Jacinto Manahan came under the spell of Soviet Russia, travelling there in 1928. The following year, a contentious annual convention of the COF and manipulated election results led Evangelista's faction to bolt and form the country's third labour federation, the Katipunan ng Mga Anak-Pawis sa Pilipinas (generally better known in English as the Proletarian Labor Congress of the Philippines). And on 7 November 1930, on the 13th anniversary of the founding of the Soviet Republic, KAP leaders launched the Partido Komunista sa Pilipinas, or PKP (Kerkvliet 1992: 73–79).

I do not wish to overemphasize the communist role in the evolution of the Philippine labour movement. Kerkvliet makes the case for a more nuanced appreciation of the communist movement's contributions to the critical sector (110–113). But the first revision of the image and understanding of Rizal emerged in the first three decades of the twentieth century, through the increasing radicalisation of the labour sector.

Rizal was still in the front rank of the country's heroes; he continued to be seen as revolutionary, not merely reformist; but he was no longer the primary hero. Bonifacio shared that honour with him.

The pages of *Ang Manggagawa* (The Worker), a monthly publication that billed itself as "*tagapagtanggol ng katwiran at karapatan ng mga Anak-Pawis* — defender of the justice and rights of the Sons of Sweat" (that is, the proletariat), reflect this image of Rizal. The title had served as a forum for the debates that had riven the labour sector, and the 30 December 1929 issue was no exception. It gave generous play, for instance, to Manahan's stories written (glowingly) from his second visit to Russia. But the cover of the magazine was devoted to a Tagalog version of Rizal's letter to his countrymen, written from Hong Kong in the expectation that he was returning to certain death in the Philippines. And one of the paper's editorials argued that the working class had a special responsibility to continue what Rizal had started:

> Sa hanay nang mga unang magigiting na anak ng ating bayan, si Dr. Rizal, sa larangan ng kanyang mga gawaing mapanghimagsik laban sa isang pamahalaan at sa isang religiyong mapangalipin, ay siyang unang naghandog ng buhay upang ang dugong titigis sa kanyang kamahalmahalang katawa'y maging hudyat ng isang mainapoy at kakilakilabot na himagsikan. Ang bagay na ito'y natupad gaya ng pagkaputi ng katakotakot na buhay. Sa pagtupad ng mga anak ng bayan sa kanyang Dakilang Halimbawa, ang himagsikang ibinangon ni Andres Bonifacio'y ipinagpatuloy hanggang sa sumapit sa dalawang yugto (sa Kastila't Amerikano), at humangga sa dati ring kalagayan, sa kalagayang alipin din ng kapwa bayan. [8]

> In the ranks of the first courageous sons of our nation, Dr. Rizal, in view of his revolutionary works against a government and a religion that was oppressive, was the first to offer his life so that the blood that would flow from his revered body will become the sign of a fiery and terrible revolution. This [sacrifice] was achieved, like the fearsome taking of so many lives. Through the sons of the people following his Noble Example, the revolution raised by Andres Bonifacio was continued until the second act (against the Spaniards and Americans), and ended up in the same situation as before, a situation [where we remain] oppressed by both countries.

Indeed, it was not only Rizal who was seen as exemplary. Even the first Philippine Republic, in later years the subject of so much nationalist scorn, was held up as a noble ideal: *"ikaw lamang ang tanging magpapasiya sa paraang dapat gawin upang manumbalik ang naglahong larawan nang Republika sa Malolos* — only you [the worker] will decide on what must be done to recover the vanished portrait of the Republic at Malolos."

Notes

1. Agoncillo's standard text, *The Revolt of the Masses*, labelled the first grade, more reasonably, as *Katipon* — member. Isabelo de los Reyes' "The Religion of the Katipunan," published in 1901, gave the first grade the name of *Katipuri*, or pioneers. In both texts, however, the second and third grades are the same as in Cruz's account: *Kawal* — soldier and *Bayani* — patriot (Agoncillo 2002: 52–53; De los Reyes 2002: 243–244). Agoncillo, however, found no use for Cruz's 1922 primer; it isn't cited in his text.
2. Ileto has an unusual portrait of Cruz as militant public speaker (in Ileto 1998: 135–163), unusual in that other references to Cruz (for instance, Saulo 1990: 6; Sibal 2004: 30; and especially the very useful Kerkvliet (1992) are about his pioneering work in labour organizing, first as union leader and then eventually as the second director of the labour bureau. *Talambuhay ni Hermenegildo Cruz* (1955), published by Alejandro de Jesus, compiles several biographical accounts, notably including that by Lope K. Santos.
3. "Most commonly and typically, therefore, the Katipunan activists were clerks, employees, agents, tobacco workers, printers and service personnel. They were indubitably proletarians in the Marxist sense, because they did not own any means of production and had to sell their labour in order to earn a living. Nevertheless, it is clear that Isabelo de los Reyes, Teodoro Agoncillo and others were wrong to classify them as collectively belonging to 'the lowest stratum of society'. Their wages or salaries were either around or above the median for the city in the mid-1890s. Clerks were generally paid about 25 pesos a month, but those who reached senior positions, as did Roman Basa (Bonifacio's predecessor as KKK president) at the Comandancia de Marina, earned over twice that amount. *Dependientes* and *personeros* would mostly earn between 15 and 20 pesos monthly, and the wages of skilled workers in the tobacco and printing industries were in much the same range. Andres Bonifacio was paid 20 pesos a month for his labours as a bodeguero, and supplemented his income by making stylish walking canes and paper fans and by employing his talent for calligraphy". Lower-paid occupations, by contrast, are conspicuously absent, or at least

under-represented, in the cohort. Only one KKK activist in the city is listed as a labourer (*jornalero*), and yet labourers comprised one sixth of Manila's working population. There is not a single servant, nor a single sailor, launderer, seamstress or coachman, and yet these modes of employment each occupied thousands. These were the people who truly had to scrape by on the most meagre wages, and these were the people, together with the unfortunates who had no regular means of livelihood, who truly belonged to 'the lowest stratum'. Women who worked as seamstresses or *lavanderas* made as little as 20 centavos a day, equivalent to about 5 pesos a month. Servants, male as well as female, got between 5 and 10 pesos monthly. Labourers got about 10. Sailors and coachmen were slightly better off, earning perhaps 12 pesos a month, but even that was less than half the "standard salary of an *escribiente*" (Richardson 2007).

I am greatly indebted to Jim Richardson for pointing me in the right direction. The website is available at <http://kasaysayan-kkk.info>.

4. Mrazek called Tan Malaka's autobiography "the warmest statement by and about Indonesia during the first fifty years of the twentieth century, and maybe the warmest statement by and about the Asian revolution during the same period" (Mrazek 1992: 65). This fellow-feeling embraced not only Filipinos but the Chinese too, among whom Tan Malaka lived for many years. Anderson notes: "In reading his autobiography one is struck by how warm Tan Malaka's personal relationships with Chinese of virtually all social classes were" (Anderson 1972: 274). The W-word again.

5. The uprisings in West Java in November 1926 and West Sumatra in January 1927 were catastrophic failures. Consulting *The Communist Uprisings of 1926–27 in Indonesia: Key Documents*, by Harry J. Benda and Ruth T. McVey, was somewhat outside the scope of my research, but I have profited from Audrey Kahin's reappraisal of one uprising (Kahin 1996: 19–36) as well as the treatment of Tan Malaka's dissent in Kahin (1952: 80–85) and Anderson (1972: 272–273). I have also learned from consulting Ingleson (1979: 31–32) and Shiraishi (1990: 336–338).

6

Under the Southern Sun

The notice took up a mere column inch of premium newspaper space.

"Memperingati Jose Rizal"

Pada hari Sabtoe, tanggal 30 Des. moelai poekoel 8 10 malam oleh radio Djakarta akan disiarkan pidato oen toek memperingati hari wafatnja Dr Jose Rizal, poedjangga patriot Filipina. Pembitjara: toean Rosihan Anwar.

The announcement, a "commemoration of Jose Rizal," ran at the top of the back page of the 29 December 1944 issue of *Asia Raya*. Like other newspapers allowed to publish by the Gunseikanbu, the Japanese military administration, the Indonesian-language Jakarta daily was limited on most days to two pages.

On Saturday, 30 December, from 8 to 10 o'clock in the evening, Jakarta radio will broadcast a speech to commemorate the death of Dr Jose Rizal, Filipino poet [and] patriot. Speaker: Mr Rosihan Anwar.

The notice was inserted in between a three-column reconstruction of a speech by Mohammad Hatta, the prominent nationalist who would in eight months' time co-proclaim the independence of Indonesia, and a two-column feature on "religious space." Hatta's speech sought to explain how education could help achieve Indonesian independence, and included a useful sectoral analysis of Indonesian society at the end of 1944 (Dahm 1969: 285). The religious feature, prompted by the prospect of reciprocal visits between Christian pastors and leaders of the "Masjoemi" Muslim association, carried the headline "The basics of working together."

The leftmost column was occupied by news briefs running under the heading "Mata Hari" — a sort of intelligence round-up, aptly named. The first item defined what was at stake in the ongoing war in the Philippines, two months after the American general Douglas MacArthur kept his famous promise and landed in Leyte: "our destiny as nations of Greater East Asia, at any time, depends on whether or not our soldiers who fight for their life in the Philippines are victorious."

But in the last days of 1944, the hope of Japanese victory, whether in the Philippine campaign or in the Pacific as a whole, had already grown faint. The stories on the front pages of the *Asia Raya* were a mixture of desperation and bombast. The main, four-column headline of the 29 December issue read: "Over half a million Americans die in A. T. R. war," the initials standing for *Asia Timoer Raja* — Greater East Asia, the Japanese imperial project. The story, quoting senior Japanese generals, was datelined Tokyo. But beside it was a one-column article about the "kamikaze spirit" infusing every house in Burma, a conquered territory that, like the Philippines under Japanese occupation, had been granted independence the previous year. The kamikaze or divine wind suicide tactic, however, had been invented only after the tide of war turned decisively against Japan, to counter the American forces' overwhelming superiority in men and materiel. In short, relying on the kamikaze spirit was a defensive strategy.

The front page also prominently featured a reflective piece entitled "Impressions from the battlefields around Leyte Gulf," the first of a series written by a Japanese correspondent. And the main story "below the fold" was about the ongoing battle for Mindoro, another major island in the Philippines.

The mix of stories betrayed a preoccupation with Indonesia's northern neighbour, for obvious reasons. Japanese soldier and

Indonesian nationalist alike sensed that, when the Americans finally drive the Japanese out of the Philippines (in December, key officials of Jose P. Laurel's wartime cabinet had already been flown to the mountain resort town of Baguio, as a safety precaution), Allied forces would be that much closer to retaking Indonesia.

The radio announcement must have been an accommodation; toean H. Rosihan Anwar (the honorific, *tuan* in the modern spelling, is Malay for master or sir) had been an *Asia Raya* reporter since April 1943.[1] The strategic placement of the notice, top and centre, looked different from other announcements about radio programs the newspaper had previously carried, which were often stuck somewhere in the middle of the page. (See, for instance, the radio programming schedule published on 30 April 1943; or the announcement about Sukarno's radio address after the Koiso Declaration, on 9 September 1944.) In perhaps the same way, the radio programme itself was by special arrangement too. "I made an arrangement, with my friend, [an] Indonesian friend, who worked at the radio station, where everything was supposed to be supervised by the Japanese," Rosihan recalled (2010b). "He gave me a chance to read it, which I did ..."

"It" was Rosihan's translation, the first ever in Bahasa Indonesia, of Rizal's farewell poem. Originally untitled, the 14-stanza poem written during Rizal's last days in jail and completed before his execution in 1896 has come to be known, rather redundantly, as "Mi Ultimo Adios." An artful restatement of his deepest convictions and at the same time a moving farewell to family and country, it marries the public and the private, the political and the personal, with the finality of poetry.

Rosihan had heard of Rizal before, in lessons taught around 1940 by his history teacher in senior high school in Yogyakarta, the Dutch H. J. Van den Berg. His classes discussed "Rizal, Mahatma Gandhi, that sort of thing" (Rosihan 2010b); "he did not follow ... the textbooks. He used a technique called '*capita selecta*'," or selected chapters (Rosihan 2010c). But late in 1944, while browsing through the volumes of the Jakarta Museum (now the Central Library of the National Museum) where he was a frequent visitor, he found a book — a potpourri, he described it later, whose title or author he could no longer remember (Rosihan 2010c) — which bore a photograph of Rizal and a description of his martyrdom. He then saw the poem in its original Spanish, and a translation in English.

Quickened by a sudden impulse, Rosihan decided then and there to render the poem in Indonesian. He translated from the English (Spanish was not one of the five languages he had learned in school). Afterwards, he submitted the translation to the censors; it was headed by a first lieutenant of the Japanese army, who in late 1944 increasingly depended on the assessments of his Indonesian assistants (Rosihan 2010b). When the censors approved it, Rosihan told his friend at the radio station.

Radio was the indispensable cog in the Japanese propaganda machine. "[D]irected not towards the intellectuals but towards the boys and girls between the ages of ten and twenty, and to the illiterate masses of Indonesia" (Wehl 1948: 2), the wartime propaganda campaign was relentless. While in David Wehl's ranking radio came behind stage and school in order of importance (the press was a distant fourth), it in fact played an outsized role. It was the first target of the conquering Japanese army, who "sealed" all radio sets it could find — only certain frequencies could be used to listen to "official domestic broadcasts," under the censor's baleful watch (Rosihan 2010a).

At the same time, the Japanese expanded the reach of radio as a mass medium with its "singing trees" — "Large public address systems linked to the radio network ... set up at important points throughout the cities," in George Kahin's classic description (1952: 108). A passage in *Out of Exile*, a collection of letters and reflections by Sutan Sjahrir, the Rizal-like intellectual nationalist who became Indonesia's first prime minister, serves to sum up an entire era of propaganda:

... the air was filled with the palaver of the Japanese propaganda machine. Public radio sets were set up in the remotest villages, and the propaganda squads came with their films and equipment. [Sjahrir 1949: 250]

But the propaganda network the Gunseikanbu put in place was a two-edged sword; it cut both ways. A nationalist movement the Japanese had initially underestimated learned to use the propaganda machine for its own purposes. The best example was Sukarno, the foremost Indonesian nationalist, who had mastered the difficult art of anti-imperialist double talk. John Legge's explanation is succinct:

> The use for propaganda purposes of prominent figures, including Sukarno himself, was intended to reduce opposition to Japanese authority. In fact, it gave such leaders a vantage point from which radical nationalist consciousness could be developed among the masses of the population. [Legge 1964: 131–132]

In other words, enterprising Indonesian nationalists were able to use the very forms of propaganda the Japanese deployed to smuggle hidden messages of their own. Rosihan's translation of Rizal's eve-of-execution valedictory was a modest part of this tradition of nation-making enterprise.

> *Selamat tinggal, Tanah koepoedja*
> *Daerah pilihan, soerja Selatan*
>
> Goodbye, land I adore
> Region chosen in the Southern sun

I note the use of "*Daerah ... Selatan*." Japanese leaders indifferent or actively hostile to Indonesian independence aspirations, such as Prime Minister Hideki Tojo or General Moichiro Yamamoto of the Java district, and official statements beginning in 1943 (Dahm 1969: 223–224), did not use "Indonesia" or the "East Indies" to refer to the islands. Either they pointedly used Java, one of the three districts into which the former Dutch East Indies had been sectioned by the Japanese military, or they preferred the politically freighted term

"Daerah Selatan," meaning "southern regions" — south, that is, of an expansive Japan.

The word "region" is found in Rizal's original, but the notion of "South" is almost unique among the hundred-odd translations of Rizal's poem. There may be only one other version where the land-caressing sun is located in the South: The truncated version that appears in the introduction to *An Eagle Flight* (1900: xii–xiii), the first English translation or adaptation of *Noli Me Tangere*. "Land I adore, farewell! thou land of the southern sun's choosing!" Like the adaptation itself, however, the poem in English is by an unknown hand. In 1902, Congressman Henry Cooper recited this version in the U.S. House of Representatives to win approval of key legislation for the new American colony of the Philippines. A copy of *his* version, itself missing other lines, appears in *The Hero of the Filipinos* (296–298), the 1923 biography co-authored by Charles Edward Russell, the American "prince of muckrakers," and E. B. Rodriguez. As far as I can tell, "South" was a creative gloss on the part of the unknown translator; if Rosihan translated from either the 1900 novel or the 1923 biography, that gloss may have been what got his attention.

Thus: "*Daerah ... Selatan.*" In this view, the first two lines of Rosihan's version are not only a faithful translation of the poem's opening passage; they are a transposition. To knowing or alert Indonesian readers at the end of 1944, the lines conflate Rizal's sun-kissed country with their own.

The Japanese Occupation of Indonesia lasted three and a half years, but historians have identified three distinct periods in the occupation, determined in large part by Japanese military interests and official Japanese policy regarding Indonesian independence (e.g., Dahm 1969; Kahin 1952). Some 40 news stories, more or less, referenced Rizal in Indonesia's censored press between 1942 and 1945, several of them very prominently. But in all likelihood, Rosihan's translation (bearing the title the poem's first Spanish-speaking editors should have given it, "Adios, Patria Adorada") would not have been possible, or wouldn't have made urgent sense to an Indonesian audience, in any period except the third.

Many Indonesians welcomed the Japanese conquest and the startling collapse of the Dutch, their former colonial masters, because the ancient Djajabaja prophecy had already predicted "a year of corn." Borrowing from Bernhard Dahm's instructive classification of Sukarno's phases of engagement with the Japanese, and then extending it, we can speak of three seasons in that yellow year: hope (from February 1942 to 1943); humiliation (from 1943 to 1944); and hunger (from 7 September 1944 to August 1945).

Djajabaja (or, alternately, Djojobojo) was a Javanese king of the fourteenth century (Kahin 1952: 100) whose predictions of a temporary defeat and ultimate triumph were once again on people's lips. Sjahrir, writing in 1947, recalled the mood of the months leading up to the Japanese invasion: There was a sense that fateful things were about to happen. Even in his place of exile, Bandaneira in the remote Moluccas, one of the original Spice Islands, the air seemed to crackle with expectation. "The *Djojobojo* rumors appeared again, and were whispered everywhere."

What, exactly, did the rumours say? Sjahrir again:

> According to the Djojobojo myth, the Dutch would be driven out of Indonesia by a yellow race that would come from the north, and for the ordinary people this meant the Japanese. The idea grew that the liberation of Indonesia would begin with the expulsion of the Dutch by the Japanese. The Japanese would thus be the liberators, or so it was thought. Long before Pearl Harbour it was widely felt that they would invade Indonesia ... among the mass of the Indonesian people the conviction was generally held that war would come to the islands. [Sjahrir 1949: 218]

Dahm records a play on words that became popular in the wake of the September 1940 Japanese trade mission led by Ichizo Kobayashi:

> After the statement by Kobayashi in the autumn of 1940, that should Japan extend its sphere of influence to the East Indian

islands, it would need the help of the native people, the speculations began to be revived again, especially on Java. Soon an acrostic in Indonesian, based on the name Kobayashi, was circulating: "*Koloni Orang Belanda Akan Japan Ambil Seantero Indonesia* (Japan will take the entire Dutch colony of Indonesia)." [Dahm 1969: 217–218]

And when the Japanese military finally prepared to launch the invasion of Indonesia, it sent warplanes to drop pamphlets in Java with the following message:

> We announce to you the arrival of the Japanese Army. The Japanese Army will land in Indonesia in order to fulfill the prophecy of his majesty Djajabaja .... Remember: his majesty Djajabaja said, yellow men will come out of the north to liberate the Indonesian people from the slavery of the Dutch. Look for the yellow skins. [Dahm 1969: 218–219]

The Japanese occupation thus began on a note of hope. The surprising changes the Japanese allowed pushed all other considerations aside: permitting the red-and-white Indonesian flag to be flown and the "Indonesia Raya," the national anthem, to be sung; subjecting the once lordly Dutch colonials to a policy of deliberate degradation, beginning with stripping them of their posts and forcing them to do menial tasks; appointing Indonesians to the positions the Dutch and the "Indos" had been forced to vacate; not least, bringing Sukarno, the most prominent of the Indonesian nationalist leaders, back to the political centre stage.

Soon enough, however, the heavy hand of the military began to be felt. Within two weeks, the display of the Indonesian colours was banned. Within two months, the "suddenly awakened nationalism" (Dahm 1969: 222) of the Indonesians was being forced back to sleep. There *was* scope for Indonesian participation in government, and Sukarno was able to establish a rhetorical perimeter behind which he could praise Japan while pursuing his nationalistic goals, but the reality was, Indonesian nationalism did not coincide with any Japanese objectives while Imperial forces continued to advance in the Pacific.

The second period began when the tide of war seemed in danger of turning. Dahm writes:

> But after the beginning of 1943, when the advance of the Japanese had been checked, they became increasingly interested in Indonesia's natural resources. In addition, by holding onto the Netherlands Indies they intended to secure a valuable pawn for possible peace negotiations. From then on, the notion of future independence was pushed more and more into the background. Whereas preliminary steps toward independence for the Philippines and Burma were taken in January 1943, at a secret meeting in May 1943 Tokyo decided to "incorporate" the Indonesian archipelago into the territory of Japan. [Dahm 1969: 223–224]

In this period Prime Minister Tojo visited the islands twice, and Yamamoto was appointed chief of operations; both steadfastly refused to recognize Indonesian nationalist aspirations, to the point of ritual insult.

The third season began on a specific date: 7 September 1944. As continuing military reverses finally forced Japan to recognize the possibility of total defeat, it suddenly revived its plan to grant independence to the "East Indies." That day, General Kuniaki Koiso, Tojo's successor as Prime Minister of Japan, addressed the Diet to make it policy: "the Japanese empire announces the future independence of all Indonesian peoples, and thus the happiness of the Indonesian peoples may be forever secured."[2]

The Koiso Declaration burst on the darkening Indonesian landscape like a lasting flare. *Asia Raya* covered the news and its implications almost ecstatically: for two days after the announcement, and despite the wartime scarcity of paper, it doubled its pages, from two to four, and filled them with story after hopeful story. The headline of the September 8 issue, a true banner running from one end to the other, declared: *"Indonesia Merdeka!"* And underneath it, in only slightly smaller type, a three-deck subhead that read: "Indonesian independence promised by Imperial Japan."

Borne on the same wave of excitement, Rosihan contributed a poem on the struggle to win independence, calling on "*pemoeda petjinta bangsa*" — the youth who love the nation — to wake the air at dawn with the happy strains of the national anthem. Like the lengthy feature story on Rizal he would write for the 30 December issue, to accompany his translation, Rosihan addressed his post-Koiso poem, published on the fourth page of the 8 September issue, "To Youth" — at that crossroads in Indonesian history the crucial, the most vital, audience.

It is likely that he had specific *pemuda* readers in mind. Kahin (1952) and Anderson (1972) have written classic treatments of the pemuda underground in Jakarta, essentially informal networks of concerned youth, concentrated around particular *asrama* or dormitories.

> The asrama provided a refuge from families, beds for students stranded in the capital or visiting it from the provinces, a forum for intense and reasonably private discussion, and a focus for solidarity. The three main undergrounds that developed in Djakarta drew their style and membership largely from the asrama that served as their institutional bases. [Anderson 1972: 39]

The three main networks in the capital revolved around the Medical Faculty, located in Prapatan 10, in a residential district; the Asrama Angkatan Baru Indonesia (Asrama of the New Generation of Indonesia), located in Menteng 31; and the controversial Asrama Indonesia Merdeka (Free Indonesia Asrama), which was sponsored by Rear Admiral Tadashi Maeda, a Japanese Imperial Navy officer sympathetic to the Indonesian nationalist cause. (Indeed, he played a major role in the dramatic last-minute events that led to the proclamation of Indonesian independence on 17 August 1945.)

While there were other such networks, it is likely that Rosihan had links to the first two: B.M. Diah, senior to Rosihan in *Asia Raya* and with him and in less than a year a co-founder of the *Merdeka* weekly, was a regular of the Menteng 31 circuit; and Sjahrir, the nationalist leader he most identified with, was highly influential among the Medical Faculty members.

A time of debilitating rice shortages, the final season of the "year of corn" was also marked by another kind of gnawing hunger — for freedom, for an independent Indonesia, perhaps above all for the time and chance to fight for merdeka.

The politicized youth were poised, in Ignas Kleden's precise yet evocative description (Rosihan 2010a: 9), between recklessness and uncertainty. By the end of the third period the pemuda had a new slogan, and it was stirring in its stark clarity: "*Merdeka atau mati*." Freedom or death.

ON THE SAME DAY as Rosihan's radio broadcast, Rizal's 48th death anniversary, *Asia Raya* devoted a substantial part of its back page to Rizal. The year before, it had featured Rizal prominently on page one, with a headline story "above the fold." In 1944, it moved its coverage to the back, but considerably expanded it.

The translation received special treatment, with almost half of the editorial space on the second page devoted to Rizal: a photograph of the hero, a two-column feature which served as the main story of the page, a poem entitled "Jose Rizal," and the translation itself, which ran down one column and carried three short paragraphs of explanatory notes. Except for the photograph, Rosihan was responsible for all the pieces — and even the photograph, he recalled later, he borrowed from the book where he found the poem (Rosihan 2010c). But except for his initials at the bottom of his own verses (for some reason, he decided to use H. R.), Rosihan's name was nowhere to be found.

RIZAL, PAHLAWAN KEMERDEKAAN FILIPINA

the all-caps headline of the feature read. "Rizal, Hero of Philippine Independence." Underneath it, the subhead: "*Seorang geni Melajoe* — A Malay genius."

Elsewhere, Rosihan has written about the professionalism of the journalists who worked, despite the constraints of censorship, at

Asia Raya (Abdullah 1997: 43–53). The editing of the Rizal pieces in the 30 December 1944 issue may be cited as proof. The placement of the stories would not look out of place in a modern newspaper: a clearly marked main story accompanied by a sidebar; the lines of text broken up by a visual and the use of headlines inside the package of stories; the photograph at the top of the third column balanced by the commemorative poem at the bottom of the first; the fitting in of the entire suite of stories inside the three columns. But I note the choice of head and subhead too. From the get-go, the reader is alerted to the existence of two layers of meaning: news about the Philippines, the neighbour to the north currently being reoccupied by American forces; and a narrative about independence made possible by Malay genius.

The feature story's lead followed the same tack: it struck a commemorative note, and at the same time pulled familiar, race-based strings. "On this day, 30 December 1896, forty-eight years ago in a corner of East Asia, the Philippines, the pure spirit of a son of the Malay race living in the Philippines was wrongfully killed by the Spanish government."

The story recounts the life of Rizal, paying particular attention to his educational achievements and his travels, his facility with languages (22, according to the story), and, not least, his youth.

The profile narrates the standard account of Rizal's life and martyrdom that was already available in the first decade after his death (which is in all likelihood when the book where Rosihan found Rizal's poem was published). American recognition of Rizal's greatness was part of this account; the *Asia Raya* feature thus includes a reference to the famous debate in the United States Congress on a 1902 autonomy bill, where Congressman Cooper (but unnamed in the story) defended the capacity of Filipinos for self-government against scurrilous attacks from expansionist American officials by reciting Rizal's last poem. (The bill passed.)

The last paragraphs of the profile turn exhortatory, making the connection between the fact of Philippine independence and the promise of Indonesian freedom transparent. "Rizal is the hero of the Philippines, the hero of Malays: so also the hero of Asia, for those who struggle to ennoble the native people. That is something the Indonesian nation, a nation of Malays, must celebrate."

And even more explicitly:

"Indonesians, let us pay our respects to the hero of Philippine independence, as we respect our own national heroes!"

The story ends with an apostrophe, addressing the pemuda who have grown in ambition in the year of the corn. "Youth, in determining the fate of our nation, take an example from this great soul, who is willing to die for his nation and the homeland!"

The translation came with a retinue of endnotes. Because of the bearing they have on the way the poem was eventually received and understood, it is worth quoting them in full.

Dimalam sebeloem Jose Rizal, pahlawan Filipina akan berangkat menghadap Toehannja, sebeloem dia akan ditembak mati oleh bangsa Sepanjol, didalam pendjara dibawah kelipan tjahaja lilin dia menggoebah seboeah sjair sebagai "boeah renoengan terachir". Amanatnja kepada Tanah dan Bangsa Filipina ini dimoelai dengan kalimat yang masjhoer: Adios, Patria adorada...... (Selamat tinggal, Tanah koepoedja).

Sjair ini dimoeat dalam "La Independencia," 25 September 1898 dan telah diterdjemahkan selain dalam segala bahasa daerah di Filipina djoega dalam bahasa Nippon, Tionghoa, Perantjis, Inggeris dan DJerman.

Salinan diatas sangat merdeka, hanjalah beroepakan pertjobaan mendekati arti dan djiwa yang terkandoeng dalam sjair Rizal. Lagi poela jang diambil tjoema beberapa bait sadja. [Asia Raya, 30 December 1944: 2]

On the night before Jose Rizal, the hero of the Philippines, was to meet his Maker, before being shot dead by the Spanish, he composed in prison, under candlelight, a poem that was the last gift of the muse. Addressed to the Philippines, it began with "Adios, Patria adorada."

The poem was published in "La Independencia," on 25 September 1898, and has since been translated in all regions in the Philippines as well as Japanese, Chinese, French, English and German.

This is a very free translation, with the approach simply to capture the significance and spirit contained in the Rizal poem. And it is based on a few verses only.

Those verses would prove to be consequential.

Half a century after they first saw print, Sabam Siagian, an Indonesian journalist-turned-diplomat, remembered his first encounter with Rizal (Sabam 1996): "It must have been sometime in late 1944 or perhaps early 1945 that the name Jose Rizal caught my attention. I was then a student of an elitist junior high school in Jakarta which was under Japanese military occupation ... One day, on the pages of *Asia Raya*, I encountered an article by Rosihan Anwar on Jose Rizal with a translation of the latter's moving poem, 'Mi Ultimo Adios,' his last work that he smuggled out from his confinement before he was executed on 30 December 1896. I am sure you must have experienced the way a poem, article, photograph or a conversation makes such an intense impression that it remains stored in your mind. That was the case with Jose Rizal's poem translated by Rosihan Anwar. It stirred strong feelings in me and inspired me to love my country."[3]

Copies of Rosihan's translation began to circulate; as Rosihan was to remember it 17 years later, the poem "in that early part of the Indonesian Revolution" was "repeatedly published in various newspapers and magazines ... one of those magazines was circulated among the front-line soldiers at Surabaya, a city in East Java famous for its battle against the British-Dutch troops on 10 November 1945" (Rosihan 1961: 301).

The iconic battle of the Indonesian Revolution is commonly thought of as beginning on that day, and indeed the British commenced aerial and naval bombardment on 10 November. But in fact the armed clashes between the British troops at the Allied vanguard and the militant pemuda broke out much earlier. Despite overwhelming Allied superiority, the battle also did not end that day, but an improbable four weeks later.

The image of the fanatical *Arek Suroboyo* (the youth of Surabaya) attacking British tanks armed only with spears is enduring. But while it was true that many of the untrained pemuda fought without firearms, the Republican resistance was not exactly without weapons. "In subsequent fighting the Indonesians deployed twelve tanks, much heavy artillery including anti-aircraft guns, and enough arms to equip a regiment" (Reid 1974: 51) — all these courtesy of the Japanese fleet, which was headquartered in Surabaya and commanded by an admiral sympathetic to the Indonesian cause.

And the romance of resistance, of youthful rebels forging a zone where the people were finally sovereign, survives to this day, celebrated in official rites and also at the Surabaya museum, built on the site of some of the fiercest fighting. The revolutionary image of Bung Tomo, the 25-year-old former reporter who returned to Surabaya on 12 October to set up *Radio Pemberontakan* (Radio of Revolt), is a lasting one: the long-haired rebel calling his brothers to arms over radio,[4] the "pure voice of *perjuangan*" (Reid 1974: 57). But while the tenacity and courage of the pemuda troops cannot be gainsaid, Surabaya was also a civic hell.

Scholars have used *Surabaja*, the classic long short story written after the battle by Idrus, the most influential prose writer of the time, as an alternative measure of the conditions in the city. It makes for disturbing reading; it provides a rankly disillusioned, even vicious view of the iconic battle and its aftermath. (The literary critic M. Balfas, like Idrus a member of the *Angkatan 45* or 1945 generation of writers, has called it "the only satire of the Indonesian revolution.")

> Thousands of human beings lay dead in the streets. The air was filled with thick, black smoke. Lightning flashed repeatedly. Flames licked at buildings and at the soul of Indonesia.... (Idrus 1968: 4)

But to Idrus, the devastation visited on the city was nothing compared to the havoc wrought on the moral life of the Indonesian pemuda ("the cowboys") and the British troops ("the bandits"), on the survivors and the refugees, on the "gods" of usury and the visitors from Jakarta.[5] The episodes from the novelette (indeed, it consists largely of episodes) tell a harrowing story: women killing a fleeing man by dropping stones on his head, a band of pemuda beating a newly married woman almost to death for wearing the wrong clothes (the colours were the red, white, and blue of the Dutch flag), rebels extorting from residents or refugees under the guise of exercising the "people's sovereignty."

It is a necessary reminder of the almost gratuitous viciousness of a society's collapse. And it puts the practical idealism of seat-of-the-pants magazine publishing in some relief.

When the British commenced bombing on 10 November, Rosihan, by then the managing editor of the weekly *Merdeka*, happened to be in Yogyakarta, the de facto capital of the Republican resistance, "together with Sukarno, Hatta, and then-minister, chief of information Amir Sharifuddin, who later became prime minister" (Rosihan 2010b). When they heard the news, at around 11 in the morning, the officials asked Rosihan to go to Surabaya, to size up the situation.

("Okay, I'll do it," he had responded. He spoke "without thinking, in case of what it meant ... I was rather naive. But yes, that was the spirit" — Rosihan 2010b.)

He left that very same day. Together with another reporter from *Merdeka*, he hitched a ride on an ammunition train, "with two wagons crammed with ammunition, sent by the youth, the pemudas, in Yogyakarta, for the youth of Surabaya" (Rosihan 2010b). The train had to travel at night, to avoid British warplanes. But instead of a silent, even stealthy passage, the journey turned out to be loud and public. At every station, a crowd would gather, urging the train on, shouting "Merdeka!"

The train arrived in Wonokromo, the suburb of Surabaya (and the setting, as it happens, of the home of Nyai Ontosoroh, in the Buru Quartet), before dawn. In all, Rosihan spent three days in the smouldering city; he was never at the front line, but he interviewed the rebel soldiers, many of whom were as young as 17 or 18 years old. He surveyed the parts of the city he could still negotiate. Each night he and his colleague slept in an abandoned hut in the middle of a field. And he heard Bung Tomo on the radio — the daily call to battle.

When it was time to go, some of the pemuda showed him copies of a magazine, printed on bad paper. "It [contained] public information, political news, and then also short stories," he remembered later (Rosihan 2010b). Afterwards, he saw another magazine, "and then I saw Jose Rizal."

That is, he saw an excerpt from his translation of Rizal's farewell poem ("they took only a few stanzas"). It had been almost a year since "*Selamat tinggal, Tanah koepoedja*" first saw print, in Jakarta; he was naturally both pleased and surprised. "*Asia Raya* has a big circulation for that time, but [it was] primarily circulated and read in Jakarta."

He mused: "Maybe they heard me talking [on the radio]."

Notes
1. In the first interview I conducted with him, *Pak* Rosihan gave the date as March 1943. But in his "Reminiscences of the Indonesian Press During the Revolution 1945–49," published in *The Heartbeat of Indonesian Revolution* (Abdullah 1997), he wrote April 1943, twice. I have adopted the later date.
2. The date of promised independence is not without controversy; Kahin and Anderson have somewhat contrasting versions. But Koiso's pledge is quoted in the 8 September 1944 issue of *Asia Raya*; I am using Dahm's translation in his political biography of Sukarno (Dahm 1969: 276).
3. Sabam, who later worked together with Rosihan on the volume commemorating Sjahrir's centenary (Rosihan 2010a), may have misremembered reading Rosihan's byline. There was nothing in the 30 December 1944 issue of *Asia Raya* to identify Rosihan as the poem's translator. But the occasion of Sabam's remarks helps explain the vagaries of memory. Invited to speak at the 1996 Kuala Lumpur conference on Jose Rizal and the Asian Renaissance, he did the necessary research — and must have found later references to Rosihan as Rizal's youthful translator. Alternatively,

he may have heard of Rosihan's role when he (Sabam) was still active in journalism.
4. It does not seem likely that Bung Tomo mentioned Rizal in any of his fiery speeches; Rosihan did not think the rebel leader was even aware of Rizal. But Bung Tomo's son, Bambang Sulistomo, proves the contrary. In an email he sent me, he professed a deep admiration for Rizal learned he said from his father, and recalled that "sometimes my father ... [would tell] us the story about the late Jose Rizal, especially his spirit and his struggle for the freedom of his country" (Sulistomo 2010).
5. Aside from a deeply unsympathetic portrait of Bung Tomo, the novelette also includes the following biting sketch of a visiting journalist (Idrus 1968: 6):

> A well-known journalist arrived from Djakarta. He wanted to look into the conditions of the refugees. He had a thin chest and bony buttocks. Everyone who saw him was certain that he had never played any games, but had often played with himself. But he had a sharp mind and now, rather condescendingly, he asked a doctor: "How many refugees were victims of the Allied machine-guns?"
>
> The doctor, who was very busy, was annoyed at being interrupted like this and answered: "I'm not a statistical bureau! Count them yourself!" The journalist felt insulted, and to get rid of the bitter taste of this pill, he turned his gaze towards some pretty female refugees: "Ah, lots of opportunities here! This is real heaven!"
>
> But by the time he returned to Djakarta he had completely forgotten these attractive women. Yet the sharp words of the doctor still rang in his ears, and without thinking he wrote in his newspaper: "The medical care given to the refugees is very bad. Most of the doctors do not realize the seriousness of our struggle."

7

The Hope of Millions in Asia

On 17 January 1946, the first issue of *Bakti*, a small magazine published in Mojokerto, some 40 miles southwest of Surabaya, saw the light of day. In its devotion to the idea of independence, its earnest polemics and exhortatory rhetoric, it was characteristic of the many publications (Rosihan 1997) that flourished during the Indonesian revolution.

Bakti styled itself "*Soeara Rakjat ditengah api perdjoangan* — The Voice of the People Amid the Fire of Struggle." The stirring slogan would appear under the magazine's banner in almost all of its issues. The name of the magazine itself could perhaps be best translated as "Loyalty," and the cover page of the first issue emphasized the point, with a message headlined "*Kebaktian warga Negara* — Loyal Citizens."

It was a revolutionary publication, in that it identified completely with the aims of the revolutionary Republican government then precariously in power. The message on the cover, effectively the magazine's editorial, defined a citizen's loyalty in terms of purity of intention, with a recent quotation from Soerjo, the newly named governor of East Java, setting those terms. "Each of the obligations imposed by the State on all should be done with purity of heart. Each person should feel that he is always witnessed by God in doing his job." The editorial concludes:

Only in this way will the public interest be guaranteed and we will also avoid the false path, those roads marked "public interest" only in name but are in fact "self interest."

For the young journalists behind *Bakti*, part of the true path led through Jose Rizal and the Philippines' own struggle for independence.

The traditional emphasis on "purity of heart" was followed by a quotation on the second page about modernity. Headlined "Public Opinion" (in English and in inverted commas), the set of excerpts from a directive of the Ministry of Information called for "modern tools" to generate more books, magazines, and newspapers. "This is the most important tool to generate public opinion in modern society."

It was this need, the creation of public space where ideas and opinions can be shared, that *Bakti* sought to fill. A lengthy foreword on Page 3 (that is to say, the first page of the magazine, the covers excluded) rooted the publication in the independence struggle. "Independence already exists in our country," the foreword declared, protesting a little too much. "Now we have travelled far, and must continue the journey until the final stop."

In January 1946, the Republican government was four years, three rounds of negotiations, two Dutch military offensives, and one communist-led regional uprising away from full independence.[1] The foreword itself alluded to the provisional, work-in-progress nature of the independence proclaimed on 17 August 1945. "Our president P. J. M. Engineer Soekarno recently revealed the nature of our struggle in the present, which is divided into three parts, thus: defend, attack and build."

The struggle in the present meant resisting the re-occupation of the Netherlands Indies by the Dutch, still assisted in that period by British troops, while at the same time building a truly independent nation. The journalists behind *Bakti* earnestly saw the magazine as proving useful in this struggle, and offered variations on a theme of utility: "we can use the magazine as the voice of struggle of the Indonesian people;" it can be "used for a public pulpit;" it will give "room to the public" to explore "matters in harmony with our struggle during this period" — all of this "in service to Country and Nation."

Extending the metaphor of a journey, *Bakti* saw its mission as, first, forging ahead (no stopping or reversing gears); and second, keeping on course (no detours, no deviating to false paths marked "self-interest").

The earnest foreword ended on a practical note:

> Our first issue is still very simple, one way or another connected with the limited time for preparation. Gradually with the help of readers, we hope our efforts can be improved.

The history of Indonesia's neighbour to the north was not far from the journalists' minds. *Bakti* referenced the Philippines several times in its short life. The first issue already had a few mentions, albeit in the context of Japanese promises of independence to the people of Burma, the Malay peninsula, and the Philippines. In the fifth issue, dated 24 February 1946, two boxes, using up about a third of Page 13, were set aside for the Philippine oath of allegiance, described merely as the "oath of schoolchildren during flag-raising ceremonies in the Philippines."

The first box ran the English version:

> I love the Philippines.
> It is the land of my birth.
> It is the home of my people.
> It protects me and helps me to be strong, happy and useful.
> In return,
> I will heed the cuonsel [sic] of my parents;
> I will obey the rules of my school;
> I will perform the duties of a patriotic law-abiding citizen;
> I will serve my country unselfishly and faithfully;
> I will be a true Filipino in thought, in word, in deed.

The second box carried the Indonesian translation:

> *Akoe tjinta pada Philipina.*
> *Tanah toempah darakhoe.*
> *Tanah air bangsakoe.*

Jang melindoengi dan menolong soepaja akoe tetap koeat, merasa senang dan bergoena.
Sebagai pembalas boedi,
Akoe akan menghormati nasehat orang toea-koe.
Akoe akan menoeroeti atoeran2 sekolah-koe.
Akoe akan memenoehi kewadjibankoe sebagai pendoedoek jang tjinta pada Tanah Air dan toendoek pada hoekoem Negara.
Akoe akan mengabdi pada negerikoe, setia dan dengan tidak mementingkan dirikoe sendiri.
Akoe ingin mendjadi seorang Philipino jang sedjati dalam fikiran, perkataan dan perboeatan.

The oath and its Indonesian version were published without any further explanation; they could have served simply as space-filler, perhaps in the same manner that excerpts from Rosihan's translation of Rizal's "Ultimo Adios" were used in the Surabaya magazines he had seen in November 1945. But even then their use seems revealing, of a mindset that saw the Philippine experience in building a nation, from the classroom and the school yard up, as instructive. (I note also the moving insertion of a second phrase about "love of the homeland" in the eighth line.)

References to the Philippines were made in other numbers, but it was in the two issues for July 1946 that the Philippine experience, its struggle for freedom and Rizal's leading role in it, took centre stage.

On 4 July 1946, the Americans transferred sovereignty over the Philippine Islands to the new government led by Manuel Roxas. The third Republic of the Philippines (after Emilio Aguinaldo's in January 1899 and Jose P. Laurel's in October 1943) was born. The headline on the cover of issue No. 20 read:

Kemerdekaan Pilipina harapan berdjoeta-djoeta bangsa Asia
Philippine Independence, the hope of millions in Asia

"*Penghargaan bangsa Indonesia, sebagai bangsa djoega telah merdeka.*" The tone of the front-page editorial was warm and familiar, one new member of the club of independent nations welcoming another.

"[With] Indonesia's appreciation, as a nation which is also independent."

The editorial is worth quoting in full, for the light it throws on the geopolitics of the immediate post-war period, at a time when American largesse seemed to be the very guarantee of independence.

> On the 4th of the seventh month (1946), the Philippines earned its independence.
>
> This event was welcomed by all the people of Indonesia, which has also been independent since 17 August 1945, with great joy and appreciation.
>
> Gen. Romulo, Philippine representative in Washington, explains that the political decision of the United States (to give independence to the Philippines) is an encouragement to the people of Asia.
>
> With this action, the demand of the people of the Philippines to advance equal rights and obligations has been answered, with no bloodshed.
>
> Philippine Independence has become a symbol of good for all Asian people who seek independence. Independence, is the thing which every nation is entitled to expect ......!

In July 1946, less than a year after the Second World War ended, the Republican government and the revolutionary forces of Indonesia saw the United States as a valuable ally against the Dutch. The fame of Carlos P. Romulo, Pulitzer-prize winning aide to Douglas MacArthur, was not only a source of credibility; it was a touchstone of American goodwill. The fact that the transfer of sovereignty occurred without violence (without additional violence, that is, to the havoc wrought by the war) inspired the Indonesians, or at least the journalists behind *Bakti*, to dream of a similar fate — less than a year before the Dutch launched its first military offensive. The ideological alignments of the Cold War (the debate over American interests, Indonesia's non-aligned positioning, or the iconic role of Romulo himself) were still very much in the future.

Owing perhaps to the press of time, the first issue of July only carried the editorial. But the second issue, No. 21, featured special coverage on the newly independent nation; it reserved six of the first seven pages of the magazine, out of a total of 20, to two essays and a poem on the Philippines.

"Philippine independence," on Page 3, placed the neighbouring country's new status in higher perspective. "The Philippine nation, historically, is derived from our nation" — with such things in common as customs and climate. The third paragraph is key: "Philippine independence is the result of the struggle of her sons, who do not retreat even in the face of mortal danger. For example, Dr Jose [misspelled as Joze] Rizal is a great leader who deserves respect. With a smile he met his end, a death sentence for his unflagging defence of Country and Nation." The paragraph ends with a word about Rizal's poem, his final legacy to "Homeland and Nation beloved."

"*Sekitar Pilipina*," running from Pages 4 to 7, served as a primer on the Philippines, almost like an encyclopaedia entry but with a decidedly political cast. Items on geographical location and historical highlights were followed by sections on Rizal ("*Pahlawan kemerdekaan Pilipina*"), current or recent leaders of the country ("*Beberapa pemimpin Pilipina*"), the Luzon-based guerrilla movement *Hukbo ng Bayan Laban sa Hapon* ("*Hukbalahap*"), and Indonesian-Philippine relations ("*Republik Pilipina, Republik Indonesia*").

The section on Rizal is heavily indebted to Rosihan's feature story in the 30 December 1944 issue of *Asia Raya*. Of the many possible measures of that debt, I note three in particular:

A tell-tale quote, retold. The *Asia Raya* story lifted several quotations from Rizal's writings; one of these came from his letter "*A los Filipinos*," written in June 1892 in the expectation that his second return to the Philippines would be met with a death sentence.

Saja hendak menoendjoekkan pada mereka jang tidak mengakoei patriotisme kita, bahwa kita insaf bagaimana kita haroes mati oentoek kewadjiban dan pendirian. Apakah artinja mati, djika seorang-orang itoe mati oentoek apa jang ditjintainja, oentoek tanah air dan mereka jang dikasihinja?

With the exception of an ellipse added at the end of the passage (before the question mark), *Bakti* uses the exact same quote, a translation from Rosihan's English source, word for word. A much later English translation by Leon Ma. Guerrero in 1963 renders the passage, thus:

> "I also want to show those who deny our patriotism that we know how to die doing our duty and for our convictions. What does death matter if one dies for what one loves, for one's country and loved ones?" [Guerrero 2007: 341]

This passage is from one of Rizal's last two letters from Hong Kong (the other one was addressed to his family). These were vouchsafed with a Portuguese doctor Rizal had befriended, with express instructions that the letters be opened only after his death. He wrote the letters, then, as an explanation why, despite the blissful months he spent in Hong Kong and the partial reunion of his family, he chose the more dangerous path — a final statement, in sum, on the reasonable assumption that the Spanish colonial authorities would punish him for his work by hauling him off to the firing squad.

Incidentally, the same quote, in Rosihan's translation, also appeared in the 20 May 1946 issue of the new newspaper, *Merdeka*, where Rosihan, at 23, was managing editor under the veteran B. M. Diah, all of 28. But the Rizal quotation, printed on the left "ear," was shorter and inexact, as though it had been written down from memory.

A sweeping argument, repeated. The notion that Rizal's heroism was not limited to the Philippines, that he was a hero for other oppressed peoples, was argued forcefully in the *Asia Raya* story.

Rizal adalah pahlawan Filipina, pahlawan Melajoe: djadi djuga pahlawan Asia jang tahoe berdjoeang oentoek meninggikan deradjat bangsa berwarna.

Rizal is the hero of the Philippines, the hero of Malays: so also the hero of Asia, for those who struggle to ennoble the native people.

This argument is repeated, given new currency and at the same time widened in scope, in *Bakti*, in the Philippine report's section on Rizal:

> Rizal adalah pahlawan Pilipina, pahlawan Asia, pahlawan semoea bangsa jang tertindas dan melawan penindas.
>
> Rizal is the hero of the Philippines, the hero of Asia, the hero of all countries under oppression and fighting oppressors.

A makeshift coinage, reused. Of the many quotations from Rizal's writings that fill the *Asia Raya* story, the longest is a passage from Rizal's second letter to his former teacher, the Jesuit Father Pablo Pastells, when he was already several months into his exile in Dapitan, in northern Mindanao. The passage consists of two paragraphs, with the first a repetition of something Pastells, in his first letter, had said. Raul Bonoan SJ, who wrote the definitive study of the Rizal-Pastells correspondence (crucial in Rizal studies for an understanding of Rizal's mature theology), translates the paragraphs thus:

> Your Reverence exclaims on the first page, "What a pity that such an outstanding young man had not lavished his talents on the defence of worthier causes!"
>
> It is possible that there are causes worthier than that which I have embraced, but my cause is a worthy one and that is enough for me. Other causes undoubtedly will bring me more lucre, more renown, more honours, more glory; but the bamboo wood, growing as it does on our soil, is intended to support nipa huts, not the massive structures of European buildings. I am not sorry that my cause is lowly and its returns meagre, but that few are the talents God gave me wherewith to serve my cause. If I were the strong molave instead of the weak bamboo that I am, I would be able to render better service. But he who made things the way they are, sees what the future brings, and does not go wrong in any of his acts — he knows only too well the uses of humble things.

Here, in five well-tempered sentences, is a manifesto for the common man! It is easy to see the appeal of such a declaration of purpose, of the usefulness of even the smallest things. Both the *Asia Raya* story and the Rizal section in *Bakti* ran the entire passage. But how did Rosihan translate *molave*, the Philippine hardwood?

> *Djika saja boekan bamboo, tetapi* kajoe-besi *jang koeat* [emphasis added]

The *Bakti* version, which again reproduces the passage from *Asia Raya* accurately, uses the same made-up term too: iron-wood. (The translation for *nipa* hut, however, was more generic: a shack made of lightweight material.)

There is another proof that the *Bakti* survey on the Philippines, especially in its appreciation of Rizal, was indebted to Rosihan's story. Rosihan's translation of Rizal's final poem which accompanied that story a year and a half previously was published in full, on the second page. Except for one major change — "*Daerah pilihan*," chosen region, was edited to read "*Daerah Pilipina*," the Philippine region — the *Bakti* version is a faithful copy.

It used the title as printed in *Asia Raya*: "*Adios patria adorada*." It followed the line breaks, the order of stanzas, the punctuation. It used Rizal's name as tagline, albeit misspelled: Dr Joze Rizal. The only thing missing was any form of acknowledgement, to either Rosihan or *Asia Raya*.

Fifteen years later, the translator spoke at an international conference of Rizal scholars about the uses of his translation.

Rosihan recalled: "When the independence of the Republic of Indonesia was proclaimed on 17 August 1945 and the revolutionary youth took up the arms against the foreign troops that returned to re-establish their colonial rule and when in the ensuing battles many were killed, quite a number of the youth who participated in the fighting found inspiration and inner strength, perhaps consolation, in Rizal's poem. Particularly the opening line '*Selamat tinggal tanah kupudya*' or in Rizal's words: '*Adios patria adorada*,' must have created a profound impression among these young freedom-fighters. No one would have foreseen — least of all the translator himself — that Rizal's poem could arouse such an impact" (Rosihan 1961: 300-301).

The paper Rosihan prepared for the conference added a footnote to this paragraph: "See the extinct magazine 'Madjalah Bakti,' 1946, Modjokerto."

It would be pleasing to describe the short trajectory traced by the publication of *Bakti* as meteoric, but in fact I cannot find any other references to the magazine aside from Rosihan's. No doubt this is a reflection on the limits of my research, but unlike, say, *Asia Raya*, without which and to name only one illustrious example a book like Bernhard Dahm's *Sukarno and the Struggle for Indonesian Independence* would have been impossible to write, none of the sources I consulted make even one reference to *Bakti*.

It was a small if aggressively earnest magazine, produced by young if decidedly idealistic journalists, aligned explicitly with the Republican government. As far as I can figure it out, the writers used pseudonyms or hid behind official titles: thus, the foreword in the very first issue was signed "Publisher," on behalf of the writers' board; announcements about the business side of the publication were posted under "Administration;" a column on women was bylined "A Woman." But I take the increasing references to the pemuda, especially in the magazine's last months, as an index of the writers' deepest interests, and their youth.

But after the devastation of the Second World War, and during the straitened circumstances of the Republican resistance to the returning Dutch soldiers, it must have been exceedingly difficult to publish a 20-page magazine like *Bakti*.

It began optimistically enough, as a weekly. Indeed, the promise "*Madjallah Minggoean*" continued to appear on its masthead long after it could no longer follow the punishing weekly pace. The fifth issue, dated 24 February, still managed to keep to the weekly schedule. But by the time the special Philippine independence coverage ran in the two July issues, the magazine no longer printed the day of publication, although it still carried the weekly promise. The second Philippine number carried an announcement (from "Administration") that printing problems had forced the magazine to turn fortnightly, and the issue after that was the first to announce the new pace. "*Madjallah tengah Boelanan*," part of the masthead now read. But even under these relatively relaxed conditions it didn't have long to live. Only six more issues came out in the four months between August and November.

Its last issue, dated November 1946, carried a small notice, announcing that because of difficulties with paper and printing the magazine would stop temporarily. The issue was almost entirely dedicated to the first anniversary of the Battle of Surabaya.

Note

1. The Dutch East Indies officially ceased to exist on 27 December 1949. The Linggajati Agreement was signed on 25 March 1947, the Renville Agreement on 17 January 1948, the Round Table Conference at The Hague concluded on 2 November 1949. The first Dutch "police action" was launched in July 1947; the second in December 1948. The Madiun rebellion of 1948 was directed against Sukarno, Hatta and the republican leadership.

8

"His Name is Sweet In our Memory"

On 20 May 1962, on the anniversary of the founding of the Budi Utomo — for Sukarno the true beginning of his country's nationalist movement[1] — the self-styled "Mouthpiece of the Indonesian People" tore into the Dutch, the country's former colonial masters, again. Sukarno criticized the Netherlands for reneging on its promise to resolve the West Irian dispute within a year after recognizing Indonesian sovereignty in 1949. He announced, again, his government's new policy of liberating West Irian ("before the cock crows on the 1st of January 1963"), if diplomacy failed one final time. And he deployed his iconic army of famous trouble-making nation-makers, again.

Jose Rizal, for instance.

> And I also ask the United States of America, is it true if people say for instance, that the independence of the Philippines was the result of the trouble maker Jose Rizal Y Mercado, or Aguinaldo. No!
>
> That movement was not made by Aguinaldo or Jose Rizal Y Mercado, but it was the movement of history [Sukarno 1962: 6; the capitalized "Y" is in the official English translation].

The particular use of Rizal in this speech, or indeed of Aguinaldo and other pioneers of nationalism, is unusual. Instead of direct praise, or a reference to them as inspiration or source or cause of the nationalist movement, as was his usual practice, Sukarno negates their role — in favour of historical forces. It is a subtle change, but in fact the effect is not negative. The listener does not hear the language as a putdown; the leaders remain singular, attention is directed to them, and their purpose, as always, is to serve as a reflection, or a reiteration, of Sukarno. It is Sukarno who has been accused of mischief-making.

Except for this subtle inversion, the speech Sukarno gave at the commemoration of "National Reawakening Day" in 1962 to a mixed audience (mostly local, but with the diplomatic corps in attendance) at the Negara Palace is a characteristic if late example of his powerful oratory.[2] Rosihan Anwar has argued that "one cannot deny the substantial role played by President Sukarno" in popularizing Rizal's name in Indonesia (Rosihan 1961: 298); for that reason, we must take a closer look at Sukarno's influential speechmaking.

The paragraphs before the passage on Rizal are instructive:

> I know, as I have said the other day at Semarang, that the Dutch hate me very much, the person Sukarno, that the Dutch always say: "Hey, Sukarno is the trouble maker." It is he who always makes trouble, makes nuisance, makes chaos.

> Why is it that the Dutch say so? Because the Dutch do not understand history. Because the Dutch do not understand that all the activities of the Indonesian Nation, especially those activities in regard to the achievement of the full freedom of their Fatherland from Sabang to Merauke are not made by one leader but emerge from the hearts of the entire Indonesian Nation.

> I ask, if the Dutch say that I, Sukarno, is [sic] the trouble maker, is it nice and is it proper if I say, "that Prince Willem van Oranje is a trouble maker"? Was the independence movement in Egypt, the United Arab Republic, the sole result of the work of Arabi Pasha, of Mustafa Kamil? No! The independence movement in Egypt at that time, now the United Arab Republic, was the movement of history which emerged from the hearts of the Egyptian Nation.

> I also ask: "Was the freedom movement in India the sole result of the work of Krishna Gokhale, of Mahatma Gandhi only, or

Jawaharlal Nehru only, so that the British could properly say for instance that Gandhi was a trouble maker, that Jawaharlal Nehru was a trouble maker?" No! The movement of India was not made by Gandhi, not made by Jawaharlal Nehru.

And I also ask the United States of America, is it true if people say for instance, that the independence of the Philippines was the result of the trouble maker Jose Rizal Y Mercado, or Aguinaldo. No!

That movement was not made by Aguinaldo or Jose Rizal Y Mercado, but it was the movement of history [Sukarno 1962: 5–6].

Sukarno continues by calling a roll call of "awakened" nations, those who have seen "an outbreak of the Social Conscience of Men." He starts with his own — "If the Indonesian Nation has reawakened, that is the manifestation of the 'Social Conscience of Men' " — and then proceeds to trace the map of the "new emerging forces" of the time, calling on Egypt, India, Vietnam, Korea and Cuba in turn, and saying exactly the same thing. He ends this part of his speech with a bang: "If in this world a big revolution explodes, a 'Revolution of Mankind' I said, that is the outbreak of the Social Conscience of Men."

Only a handful of paragraphs, but we get the authentic Sukarno. That is to say, the turns of thought, the stock phrases, the rhetorical devices, the sense of movement, the basic stance, that have marked his major speeches and writings from the 1920s, on through *Indonesia Accuses*, that masterpiece of rhetoric, through the radio addresses during the Japanese occupation, to the key speeches collected in *Toward Freedom and the Dignity of Man*.

There is the colloquial touch. "Hey, Sukarno is the trouble maker" sounds a familiar note; it is echoed by other instances of deliberate informality throughout the speech. "Hay, Indonesian People! ... don't forget that only a nation who stands on its own strength can become a great nation." The informal touches create an impression of a conversation, or of a small crowd arguing loudly, but familiarly, on a street corner.

There is the comprehensive background, or at least the impression of comprehensiveness. The assertion that "the Dutch do not understand history" is followed and supported by a sweeping view of history and a command of the necessary facts; he casually notes, for instance, that the Dutch foreign minister had just met in Athens with the American secretary of state: "Twice. The first time for $2^1/_2$ hours, the second time for $1^1/_2$ hours, in all 4 hours long." The display of detail is deliberate; it is a demonstration of his intelligence.

There is the community of new nations in which Sukarno always situates his Indonesia. It was a rhetorical device he first used in the 1920s, when Egypt was a protectorate, China but a shadow of its former glory, and India, the Philippines, and Burma still colonies. It was a device he continued to use through the years, in court, in the newspaper columns, in the radio addresses, in the major speeches at Bandung and the U.S. Congress and the United Nations. The references to China and India are almost a constant; those to Egypt and Turkey less frequent; those to the Philippines and other Southeast Asian countries more occasional.

Then there is the corps of nationalist leaders, freedom fighters, pioneers of independence (and on certain occasions influential intellectuals too), without which no Sukarno speech would be complete. On at least two occasions, he spoke of reading as inhabiting a mental world where he communed — his word — with the authors he read.

"In the world of my mind," he says in his autobiography,

> I also communed with Prime Minister Gladstone as well as Sidney and Beatrice Webb; I came face to face with Mazzini, Cavour, and Garibaldi of Italy; Austria's Otto Bauer and Adler; Karl Marx, Friedrich Engels, and Lenin, and I chatted with Jean-Jacques Rousseau, Aristide Briand and Jean Jaures, the grandest orator in French history. I drank in these stories. I lived their lives. I actually was Voltaire. I was the great fighter of the French Revolution, Danton. A thousand times I, myself, in my black room saved France

singlehanded. I became emotionally involved with these statesmen. [Adams 1965: 39]

Howard Jones, ambassador to Indonesia for seven years, also records him in his own memoirs as saying:

> I met with Mazzini, with Garibaldi, with Plekanov, with Trotsky, with Lenin, with Gandhi, with Mustafa Kemal Ataturk, with Ho Chi Minh, with Sun Yat-sen, with Saygo Takamori. I met with Nehru, with Mohammad Ali Jinnah, with Jose Rizal y Mercado, who was shot dead by the Spanish in 1903. I met Thomas Jefferson and Abraham Lincoln. [Translated from the excerpt published in the Suara Merdeka website; Sukarno's list is actually longer].

It is possible to distinguish at least two levels to this elite corps. (While the distinction is not made by Roger Paget in his masterly edition of *Indonesia Accuses* or in his superb introduction, I find myself greatly indebted to his analysis of the influences on Sukarno's oratory.)[3] A couple of statesmen, to use Sukarno's own label, are almost constantly referred to: Mohandas K. Gandhi and Sun Yat-sen. They are joined in the first rank by Sukarno's favourite intellectuals, including the socialists Karl Kautsky and Otto Bauer and the assassinated parliamentarian Jaures, "the grandest orator in French history." Statesmen and authors of the second rank include Mustafa Kemal Ataturk, Karl Marx, Thomas Jefferson, and (occasionally) "Jose Rizal y Mercado."

The use of famous and less famous names is thus not only characteristic of his speaking style; it is characteristic of Sukarno's way of thinking. He saw himself as keeping select company. More to the point, his audience saw him as both impressively educated (the names were a measure of his learning) and world-historical (the names were an index of his ambition).

One characteristic of Sukarno's speech-making is not reflected in the self-reliance speech of 1962: The use of extensive quotations from his wide reading. He had the ability to repeat certain passages, some of them quite involved, from books and documents he had read. (Apparently, once he read something that made an impression on him, he never forgot it.) But there are other rhetorical flourishes in the speech that mark Sukarno's style: the instinctive emphasis on unity (freedom as "emerging from the hearts" of a unified nation); the gift for the organic image ("A sentence I repeatedly state is: come let all of us stream to the sea"); the repetition of emotive phrases, the use of words charged with meaning ("Come let's go to the sea, come let's go to the sea! To the open sea! To the free sea! To the vast sea, to the grand ocean, the grand ocean of freedom!").

Sukarno's use of the Spanish convention in naming Rizal is interesting, in part because the name, strictly speaking, is wrong. "Rizal Mercado" was the family name he carried, until the execution of the martyr-priests Mariano Gomez, Jose Burgos, and Jacinto Zamora in 1872 changed his family's fate. When the boy was enrolled at the Jesuit school in Manila later that year, it was under his father's second family name of Rizal; the precaution was to avoid the possibility of guilt by association with his much older brother Paciano Mercado, a Burgos acolyte. (Much later, after untold harassment and intimidation, his family quietly changed its name to Rizal too.)

Rizal was in fact baptized Jose Rizal Mercado; the standard accounts that became current in the first decade after his execution, especially the American ones, appropriated the Spanish convention, but mistakenly. Thus, for many years, the most famous man from the Philippines was referred to, wrongly, as Jose Rizal y Mercado. I estimate that these sources became the basis for many of the stories on Rizal that appeared in the Indonesian press in the first half of the twentieth century.

Sukarno, however, was nothing if not consistent. Two decades before the "trouble maker" speech, he had already paid tribute to "Jose Rizal y Mercado." It was the end of the holy month of Ramadan, known informally in Indonesia as *Lebaran*, in 1942; Sukarno had been returned to the political centre stage by the Japanese only a few months previously, and he was in the midst of a vigorous campaign to consolidate alliances, especially with the Islamic parties.

He had given a major radio address, reminding Indonesians that the war in the Pacific was still ongoing, and calling on the people to join the fight: "*Kita harus ikut berjuang.*" The speech was given extensive, even lavish coverage in *Pembangoen*, The Builder, a Muslim periodical published in Jakarta; it was the headline story of the day, and it took up two-thirds of the front page. Part of it read:

> Remember the nationalist movement in Egypt under the leadership of Arabi Pasha and Mustafa Kamil Pasha and Zaghlul Pasha, remember the movement in Turkey under the leadership of Kemal, the father of Turkey, remember the nationalist movement under the leaders Tilak, Gandhi and Nehru, remember the Chinese nationalist movement under the leadership of Sun Yat Sen, remember the nationalist movement in the Philippines under the leadership of Jose Rizal y Mercado and others.[4]

I can find only three mentions of "Jose Rizal y Mercado" in Indonesian newspapers between 1942 and 1945: a feature with that name as title on the front page of the 30 December 1943 issue of *Asia Raya*, a lengthy survey on the Philippines in the June 1943 issue of the monthly magazine *Minami* — and Sukarno's speech in the 10 October 1942 issue of *Pembangoen*.

Sukarno had another way of naming Rizal: by his doctor's title. In 1958 and 1959, in a series of lectures before students assembled at the presidential palace, at which time he was already laying the predicate for his Political Manifesto of 1959 and his proclamation of "the year of the rediscovery of the Revolution," Sukarno expanded on the *Panca Sila*, the five principles he had formulated in 1945, as the foundation of the state (and of his so-called Guided Democracy).

The old enemy, imperialism, lay wounded; but it was far from a dying beast. Part of the scandal of the 1955 Bandung summit of developing countries from Asia and Africa, which he hosted, was the background against which it was held: imperialism may have outgrown its orthodox, i.e. colonial, form, but it was growing into something else. In this history lesson[5] Sukarno found a place for Rizal:

> In the Philippines then, there was a powerful struggle of the people to fight against the orthodox Spanish imperialism. This Spanish imperialism was the same as the Portuguese imperialism in Timor today ... You know the history of the famous leaders of the Philippines. They were all leaders who opposed Spain. The name of Dr Rizal, for instance, who was executed by the Spaniards without due process of law, his name is sweet in our memory. He was the great leader of the Philippines, who fought against the orthodox Spanish imperialism. You've also heard about the name of Apolinario Mabini, Aguinaldo, they all fought against the orthodox Spanish imperialism. [Rosihan 1961: 299–300]

The following April, he had occasion to recruit "Dr Rizal" again, in another lecture[6] before students.

> Once I've said in one of my speech[es] that every nation has its own great leaders. But greater than these great men is the idea that dwells in the heart. Gandhi was great because his ideas were great. So were Sun Yat-sen, Thomas Jefferson, Dr Rizal from the Philippines was great because his ideas were great. Ideas, ideas, brother. Ideas that burst prison walls, said Gandhi.

My sense of Sukarno is that, like the most effective orators, his speeches were both universal and relentlessly topical. He rhapsodized on general themes — the war against imperialism, the making of a nation, the meaning of revolution, the virtues of the common man, "ideas that burst prison walls" — and these themes served him as well in 1927, when he first assumed prominence in the nationalist movement, as in 1955, when he assumed a leading role in the "neutral and independent" bloc of non-aligned nations. But he always had his ear to the ground, so to speak, and like the best rhetoricians tailored his phrases to what was then current: trends of the times, names and places in the news.

It explains in part why, for instance, in his autobiography as told to Cindy Adams (even his autobiography is essentially an epic series of speeches), he startles the contemporary Filipino reader with multiple mentions of Carlos Romulo, the prizewinning writer and long-time diplomat. In the mid-1960s, when the interviews for his autobiography were conducted, the man who had served as Philippine representative to the United States at the time of the proclamation of Indonesian independence in 1945 was at the height of his international celebrity; he was very much in the news.[7] (The "trouble maker" speech was made only a few months after the Philippines, and an international community of scholars, marked the centenary of Rizal's birth. Rizal, too, was again back in the news.)

Topicality also explains the changes in the "famous metaphor" (to use Sukarno's own description) that came to be associated with him. I have found three uses that Sukarno made of this metaphor, over a span of a little over three decades. The variations in the uses, and the fact that in Rosihan's 1961 paper this metaphor constitutes part of the proof of Rizal's influence in Indonesia, make a closer study necessary.

In the 1 January 1945 issue of *Asia Raya* (two days, that is, after Rosihan's *"Selamat tinggal, Tanah koepoedja"* saw print), Sukarno was among the dignitaries who had a New Year's message on the front page. Using his gift for animal symbolism, he sought to impress on his readers a strong image of a united front against "enemy forces," using a menagerie of national symbols:

> No power on earth can crush the strength of 1,000,000,000 united people of Asia. If the Liong Barongsai (Dragon) of China cooperates with the White Elephant of Thai, with the Buffalo of the Philippines, with the Peacock of Burma, with Nandi Cow of India, with the Sphinx of Egypt, with the Banteng of Indonesia, and this cooperation is illuminated by the radiant Sun of Dai Nippon, then all the enemy forces will crumble down. [Rosihan 1961: 299]

Twenty years later, in an interview with Adams, he recalled both context and text, albeit with some characteristic changes (Adams 1965: 179):

From my prewar writings my people knew I considered Japan the modern imperialist of Asia. So, during this period I coined my famous metaphor: "Under the blanket of the Rising Sun the Chinese dragon cooperates with the white elephant of Thailand, the caribou of the Philippines, the peacock of Burma, the Nandi cow of India, the hydra snake of Vietnam and, now, with the Banteng buffalo of Indonesia, in ridding our continent of Imperialism."

He quickly added a qualification:

To the Indonesian mind this was clear. It meant the occupied territories were united in the desire to exterminate aggression. I did not say we were cooperating with the Rising Sun. I said we were cooperating UNDER the Rising Sun [emphasis in the original].

In the 20 years between the two instances, the list of exemplary countries remains essentially the same, with one exception: the Sphinx of Egypt has been transformed into the hydra snake of Vietnam. It is possible that the transformation, in the mid-1960s, was prompted by the escalating American engagement in Vietnam — already very much in the news — and eased in part by the assertive positioning of Egypt under Sukarno's friend, Gamal Abdel Nasser.

To be sure, Vietnam's exclusion from the list in 1945, and Egypt's inclusion, is puzzling. Like large parts of China, in January 1945 Vietnam remained part of the (increasingly besieged) territory of conquest of the Japanese Imperial Army; in fact, Saigon served as the Japanese regional capital for Southeast Asia, which explains why Sukarno (and Hatta) had to undertake several risky flights to hold meetings there. And Egypt? The radiant Sun of the Japanese empire did not shine on the Sphinx. Could Sukarno's surprising choices be mere inattention, or code for something else, a hint to the alert Indonesian reader to, so to speak, read between the lines?

Another change: The grandiose terms used (perhaps ironically, perhaps in earnest) to refer to the conquering army — "illuminated by the radiant Sun" — have shape-shifted, to the more homely "blanket." In the 1960s there was no longer any need to humour the gods of Japan.

A third "improvement" involves the purpose of the inter-national cooperation: In 1945, precisely because many in Sukarno's audience knew that Japanese rule was merely another form of imperialism, Sukarno called only for the crushing of "enemy forces." Twenty years later, he could give full vent to his oldest ambition, and sound a call to arms to rid Asia of all forms of imperialism.

But Sukarno remembered wrong. He did not coin his famous metaphor in the depths of the Japanese occupation; he first strung the symbolic phrases together in 1933, a few months before he was arrested for the second time by Dutch colonial authorities.

In *Mentjapai Indonesia Merdeka* (Toward Indonesian Independence) — a pamphlet "considered so inflammatory that it was confiscated and banned immediately after publication," to use Sukarno's own admiring recollection (Adams 1965: 123) — the Indonesian leader deployed the following argument:

> If the Banteng [Bull] of Indonesia can work together with the Sphinx of Egypt, with Nandi Ox of the country of India, with the Dragon of the country of China, with the champions of independence from other countries – if the Banteng of Indonesia can work together with all the enemies of international capitalism and imperialism around the world — O, surely the end of international imperialism is coming fairly soon! [Sukarno 1963: 296–297]

We can immediately note the two main differences: The list of countries is much shorter, only extending to the most ancient in Asia; and the scope of the anti-imperialism campaign is not limited to the continent of Asia, but "around the world." (There is another, perhaps altogether minor difference which strikes me: In 1933, Sukarno preferred to speak of "countries," that is to say "states" — for instance, "negeri Tiongkok," the country or state of China — as though he was making a distinction between government and people. By 1945, there was no longer any deference to the official; he spoke directly, as though to the very national essence, of the countries in his list.)

What do we make of the evolution of this famous metaphor, this turn of thought?

The symbolism is not only effective, permitting Indonesian audiences to think in individual, almost personal terms of its neighbouring countries; it is also convenient, allowing Sukarno to add or subtract members of his symbolic menagerie as the situation requires.

And it does not privilege either Rizal or the Philippines — contrary to Rosihan's well-meaning assertion.

Other references to Rizal or the Philippines in Sukarno's speeches and writings abound. His autobiography refers to four Filipinos: Romulo, in a couple of quick anecdotes; Manuel L. Quezon, the flamboyant first president of the Philippine Commonwealth, with a (garbled) version of one of his most famous declarations;[8] Aguinaldo, in two passages offering a historical perspective; and Rizal, only briefly, even parenthetically. The first Aguinaldo passage has the Rizal mention in it:

> The inevitable reaction to this long-overdue resistance of oppressed elements led to our pioneer revolutionary period. Sun Yat-sen established China's National Movement in 1885. India's National Congress was born in 1887. Aguinaldo and Rizal roused the Philippines in the early 1900's. All Asia was growing up and in the glorious twentieth century, in which isolation could never occur again, even meek, timid Indonesia caught the feeling. [Sukarno 1965: 33–34]

As we have seen, this is a characteristic turn of thought. So far, so Sukarno. But the second Aguinaldo reference is of more than passing interest. One of the early milestones in Sukarno's cooperation with the Japanese military was his meeting in July 1942, a few days after being allowed to return from exile in Sumatra, with Lieutenant General Imamura, the *Saiko Sikikan* or commander-in-chief of the occupation army. The exact date remains undetermined, but both Sukarno and Imamura came away from the meeting, the first of many, with highly favourable impressions. A generation after the war, Sukarno recalled that first meeting, complete with remembered repartee.

He had thanked Imamura for driving the Dutch out of Indonesia.

> "With a torn, bedraggled remnant of an army," I said to the conqueror facing me, "you kicked out those who will always be considered the real tyrants of Indonesia. I am eternally grateful to you."
>
> This drama I was playing reminded me of the Philippines' hero, General Aguinaldo. He fought the Spaniards for years and when the Americans conquered the ex-conquerors, Aguinaldo first said to the Americans, "Thank you." Later, when the U.S. wanted to stay in the Philippines, he tried hard to kick them out.
>
> "How long do you estimate the military will function in an administrative capacity here?" I asked.
>
> "I do not honestly know. I have no plan as yet."
>
> Well, I had. And I made my first move. [Sukarno 1965: 176]

The retelling of that first meeting continues for three more paragraphs. Now the reference to Aguinaldo seems to me important; even if that detail is an improvement on the record, added only during the making of the autobiography (and I have no proof, either way), it is still a measure of Sukarno's instinct for utilizing historical figures in his own personal narrative. His decision to cooperate could have gone badly, as Aguinaldo's own faith in the good will of the Americans did, turning out to be catastrophically naive. Leaving the question of authenticity aside, *that* was the rhetorical point of the Aguinaldo reference: to suggest the scale of the risk of cooperation.

But the possibility that, in 1942, during a crucial meeting with the highest ranking official of the Japanese occupation, the parallel with Aguinaldo suggested itself to Sukarno is bracing. It is the only instance, in the many references Sukarno made to the Philippines, to

Filipino historical personalities or to Rizal himself in a high-profile public career that spanned five decades, when the appropriation is central, not peripheral, to the event.

If it was indeed true that in first meeting Imamura, Sukarno had Aguinaldo on his mind, then it is the only experience of Sukarno's in which a Filipino influence is active *during* the experience, and not merely in the retelling of it. I do not mean to suggest that Sukarno was insincere in his occasional but pointed use of Rizal and the Philippine struggle for independence; indeed, I think the opposite is the case: use, repeated use, is proof of sincerity.

But a look at the evidence shows that Sukarno had a frankly utilitarian attitude to the second rank of famous pioneers; if they were useful in a given context, he made use of them. There are many passages from Sukarno's speeches and writings narrating the decisive impact of, say, Sun Yat-sen, one of the statesmen and formative intellectuals who belonged to the first rank, which forced him to change his entire outlook. One example, out of many: In his most consequential speech, proposing the *Panca Sila* as the "philosophical basis" of "Indonesian Merdeka," in 1945, Sukarno defended the first principle of nationalism partly by confessing to a fundamental change of position. "... In 1918, thanks be to God, there was another man who recalled me, and that was Dr Sun Yat Sen. In his work *San Min Chu I*, or The Three People's Principles, I found a lesson which exposed the cosmopolitanism taught by A. Baars [an influential socialist who had had Sukarno under his sway]. Ever since then, nationalism has been implanted in my heart, through the influence of The Three People's Principles."

In contrast, and with the possible exception of the Aguinaldo passage, none of the references to Rizal or the Philippines show a change in his thinking or way of proceeding. They are used only to support his conclusions.

Paget (1975: lxiv–lxvi) has a telling example from Sukarno's famous defence oration of 1930, in his edition of *Indonesia Accuses!*

"Out of the more than one hundred quotations ... only once did Soekarno seriously distort content. When introducing the excerpt from Jaures [the French orator] he acknowledged that a 'few changes' had been made."

Some changes. As it turns out, the passage in *Indonesia Accuses!* that reads

> ... Have you never been struck by the universality of the nationalist movement? Everywhere simultaneously, in all the unfree countries of the earth, it bursts forth. For ten years you have not been able to write the history of Egypt, India, China, the Philippines and Indonesia without writing the history of the nationalist movement...

began as the following in Jaures' 1893 speech:

> ... Have you never been struck by the universality of the socialist movement? Everywhere simultaneously, in all the countries of the earth, it bursts forth. For ten years you have not been able to write the history of Belgium, Italy, Germany, Austria without writing the history of the socialist party...

Sukarno's appropriation of the nationalist movement in the Philippines, as well as in Egypt and the other "unfree" countries (as we have already seen, in other contexts the list can include still other countries), was merely to add more premises, to fill in the blanks in the syllogism, so to speak, in support of conclusions he had already reached. The use was utilitarian.

Interestingly, Sukarno's very many references to Jaures throughout his public life all issue from this one speech, made in 1893, when "the grandest orator in French history" was merely at the beginning of his legislative career. As we have noted: once read, never forgotten.

Jaures, as I mentioned in an earlier page, wrote a preface to the French journalist Henri Turot's eyewitness account of Aguinaldo, "who, after having fought Spanish tyranny, is fighting American disloyalty." (The book was published in 1900, when Aguinaldo was on the run from the American army.) The preface is notable for its condemnation of the "imperialist passion and power of capitalist interests in the United States," its level-headed estimate of Aguinaldo ("Perhaps [Turot's] elevated sympathy hides from him some of the errors committed by Aguinaldo ... But these reservations cannot diminish the admiration owed to courage. And they can in no way diminish the wrongs committed by the United States"), and above all for its recounting of the "drama" of Rizal:

> The life and death of Rizal are certainly one of the most touching episodes in human history. In Europe he fills himself with all of modern science; he returns to the Philippines not to raise it in revolt, but to attempt by a supreme effort to open their master's spirit to the new necessities. But he is seized, judged, and executed, and before dying, on the night preceding his final agony, while his fiancée cries as she kneels at his cell door, he writes an admirable poem where the love of freedom is mixed with a kind of pantheistic adoration for the earth and the heavens. Turot was right to give us the details of this drama: the life and death of Rizal sends a sacred shiver into our souls, and it is impossible that the people who aroused such devotion will not finally be free.[9]

Sukarno, who admired Jaures, could have never written a preface like this — it would have required a little more intimacy with the details of Rizal's life and death. That, as I see it, was what was missing from Sukarno's picture of the Philippine national hero. He never read Rizal; he must have only read about him.

It explains why Sukarno got the full name and even the dates wrong. (Having been executed in 1896, Rizal never made it to Sukarno's "glorious twentieth century.") It explains why, in almost every mention of Rizal, he has to provide a brief description, as though sensing that the audience needed it: "Dr Rizal from the Philippines." "He was the great leader of the Philippines, who fought against the orthodox Spanish imperialism." "Jose Rizal y Mercado, who was shot dead by the Spanish in 1903." And so on. (Nothing of the sort was ever necessary for Sun Yat-sen or Gandhi.)

Above all, it explains why, despite Rizal's two novels, a famous speech in Madrid, an even more famous farewell poem translated twice into Indonesian during Sukarno's lifetime, plus voluminous correspondence — in other words, despite Rizal being a writer — Sukarno never quoted from any of his writings.

Rizal, one of merdeka's avatars, was merely an idea — but an idea that bursts rhetoric's walls.

Notes

1. Pramoedya Ananta Toer insisted to Max Lane, the translator of his Buru Quartet into English and author of *Unfinished Nation*, a survey of post-Suharto Indonesia, that the true beginning of the Indonesian nation was the *Sumpah Pemuda* of 1928 — a full 20 years after the founding of Budi Utomo, or Noble Endeavour (Lane 2008: 302).
2. "Only a nation with self-reliance can be a great nation," 20 May 1962. The official version in English was published by Indonesia's Department of Information.
3. Other sources have been most useful too, including Anderson 2002, Anderson 2006, Djenar 1994, Ingleson 1979, Wejak 2000. Several of Sukarno's speeches are on YouTube.
4. As it happens, Rizal was navigating the Suez Canal on his first visit to Europe when Arabi Pasha rose in arms. He was also in Hong Kong at the same time his fellow doctor Sun Yat-sen was on the island; there is no record of their ever meeting, but Mariano Ponce became a good friend of the Chinese leader, and even wrote a biography of him.
5. The source is Rosihan Anwar's 1961 paper, but the quote is from "*Pantja Sila sebagai Dasar Negara*" (The *Panca Sila* as the Foundation of the State), the official version of the lectures (which included five in Jakarta and one in Yogyakarta) published in 1959.
6. Again, from Rosihan's paper. The lecture was "*Mahasiswa Indonesia Mendjawab Tantangan Zamannja*" — The Indonesian Student's Response to His Time," 3 April 1959.
7. Romulo's fame, if not his reputation, declined after prolonged service as foreign minister under Ferdinand Marcos. His identification with the American cause, including his service as wartime aide to General Douglas MacArthur and later his Cold War apotheosis (a leftist group, describing the epochal Bandung Afro-Asia conference of 1955, where he was head of the Philippine delegation, called him a "US stooge"), is also no longer to current Filipino taste. A pity; he was a man of many gifts.

8. "I prefer a government run like hell by Filipinos to a government run like heaven by Americans," said in 1909. Sukarno's version, which he offers when he explains his own famous declaration to the United States to "Go to hell with your aid," runs thus: "Manuel Quezon of the Philippines once said, 'It is better to go to hell without America than to go to heaven with her'" (Sukarno 1965, 296). But Quezon's quote actually has a second part, often ignored in the retelling: "Because, however bad a Filipino government might be, we can still change it."
9. The fine translation is by Mitchell Abidor; it is available on the most useful marxists.org website. The Jean Jaures Archive includes poignant sketches of the legislator from the diary of the writer Jules Renard.

9

The Myth Busters

At around the time Sukarno fell from political grace, the trailblazing Malaysian intellectual and one-time politician Syed Hussein Alatas lit on the area of study that would define his reputation. "Around 1966, I became interested in the theme of the lazy native," he wrote in a 2002 paper.[1] "The first question I posed was why were the natives of Indonesia, Malaysia and the Philippines judged as lazy, by hundreds of authors from the ruling colonial regime, in the course of some four centuries .... Such an inquiry had not been carried out before, in the sense of a research question requiring years of effort" (Alatas 2002: 152).

Rizal had carried out a pioneering exploration of the same theme, but limited to the Philippines; it was a reconnaissance mission, so to speak, into the area of study. Alatas' now-classic work, *The Myth of the Lazy Native*, reserves an entire chapter for a discussion of Rizal's "On the Indolence of the Filipinos," which first appeared in 1890. But Alatas' book was a full-scale assault on the theme, and deployed a disciplined army of arguments. Published in 1977 (after a tortuous path to publication), it has come to define Alatas' scholarly legacy. The affectionate portrait drawn by his youngest daughter Masturah, the first biography to appear after Alatas' death in 2007, recognizes the book's pride of place in her father's impressive library of original works. It carries the evocative, expansive title *The Life in the Writing: Syed Hussein Alatas: Author of The Myth of the Lazy Native*.

Alatas was born in Indonesia in 1928, but moved to Johor Bahru, Malaysia, when he was still a child. He was active in Malaysian opposition politics in 1968–71 (the year he served in the Malaysian Senate). With post-graduate degrees from the University of Amsterdam, he fashioned a sterling academic career, including two decades as the iconic head of Malay Studies at the National University of Singapore. And he was an inveterate writer.

Not even the lowly op-ed escaped his fierce attention. On 12 December 1981, for instance, *The Straits Times* of Singapore published a commentary of his on the errors of a history textbook. Some of the examples he found demonstrated a continuing interest in the history of Indonesia.

> There is also a serious error in connection with Sukarno. The author writes: "In August 1933, the Governor-General B. C. de Jonge re-arrested him and he was kept in prison until the Japanese released him in 1942." What did actually transpire? In August, 1933, Sukarno was detained for four months in Jakarta after which he was exiled to Endeh in Flores. Four years later, he was removed to Bengkulu in south Sumatra until the Japanese invasion in 1942. He was detained for four months and for the rest of the nine year period, he was in exile. To be placed in exile in a locality is not the same as to be kept in prison. [I accessed this passage from the Singapore Pages site, but saw the first reference in Masturah Alatas 2010: 59]

The sense of exacting attention to both detail in fact and nuance in meaning is pure Alatas. The fact that Sukarno was in prison for only four months may not be a detail that is important in its own right (at least I cannot imagine Alatas insisting that 14-year-old students surveying Southeast Asian history commit it to memory), but the difference between prison and exile is crucial and something schoolchildren must learn to distinguish. A textbook that could not appreciate the difference, or thought that the fudging could be justified by the necessary simplification a historical survey requires (as the textbook author did in fact argue in his reply, in a subsequent letter to the editor), was purveying an insidious form of nonsense.

The op-ed's title, "Sense and Nonsense," was not only apt but characteristic, because a war of attrition on nonsense, particularly those of colonial origins, might be one way to describe Alatas' life's work. His many meditations on the life of the public intellectual, precisely in the context of Malaysia or other Southeast Asian countries as developing societies, can be understood either as engagements in that war, or periods of recuperation from the long struggle.

"Despite the lack of awareness of the need for intellectual effort, the historical necessity for intellectual life is certainly there," he wrote. "In the intellectual history of mankind problems have often been ignored not because of objective circumstances but because of the limited vision of particular societies" (Alatas 1977a: 4). Many of his meditations centred on the absence of a thriving intellectual tradition in developing societies, and the consequences of this void. As it happens, part of his analysis of the causes closely parallels Rizal's own analysis of colonial indolence.

> ... If we take the nineteenth century as our cut-off point, we find that by that time there was not much intellectual activity under colonial domination. The traditional intellectuals in countries with intellectual traditions had declined in number and function. As the Western powers took over and created new educational elites, the break with the past became more pronounced. The colonially educated indigenous elites, while retaining cultural and religious continuity with their past, had entirely broken with their intellectual traditions. For those countries with hardly any intellectual tradition, it was more pronounced. What was retained of the traditional culture was what was daily observed at home. Apart from this little was retained and transmitted. [Alatas 1977a: 48]

It is of no small moment that the manuscript that first attracted the attention of the British academic publisher which ultimately decided to publish *Myth* was a sustained reflection on the role of *Intellectuals* in *Developing Societies* (the first book's eventual title). The correspondence Masturah Alatas reproduces in her biography suggests that the earlier book did not fit into the publishing house's usual categories. Alatas implied as much, in a letter to one of the manuscript's first readers. "In judging the manuscript please bear in mind that it is a reflective and analytic work by an Asian on Asian problems. It should not be judged from a conventional academic perspective" (Alatas 2010: 25–26). The Acknowledgements page of *Intellectuals in Developing Societies* pinpoints the book's nonconventional starting point: "The event which impelled me to reflect deeply on this theme was my withdrawal from active politics after four years of effort in Malaysia to promote an alternative to the present government. My experience ... brought me face to face with problems that were in many ways generated by the type of elites ruling the country and circumstances" (Alatas 1977a: xi).

Despite its title, then, *Intellectuals in Developing Societies* is not primarily intended for an academic audience; it is the work of an engaged public intellectual, with emphasis on public. ("I was writing more as a scholar thinking about the problems of his society than as a professional sociologist applying his craft" — Alatas 2010: 26.) The dust jacket copy quite accurately described the work as a "book of interest to social scientists, educators, planners and politicians."

Alatas had approached the Frank Cass publishing house to propose the publication of *Intellectuals*, on the advice of the eminent scholar Ernest Gellner. On 2 November 1972, at the first (if belated) sign of interest from Frank Cass, he let drop that he was also about to finish another book-length work.

> At the moment I am finishing a manuscript of about 100,000 words on the myth of the lazy native in the Philippines, Indonesia and Malaysia, during the sixteenth to the twentieth centuries. It is a study of the function and origin of this myth in the colonial ideology. Dutch, Malay and English sources are used. The discipline applied is the sociology of knowledge. This is a work which can be

properly described as academic in the conventional sense. I have not contacted a publisher for this work. I am writing my last two chapters. Thirteen chapters have been written. If you are interested in this work also please let me know. [Alatas 2010: 26]

The publishing house did signify its interest in the second book, but it took five years for both books to negotiate the road from initial query to actual publication. *Intellectuals in Developing Societies* and *The Myth of the Lazy Native* were finally published, on the same day, in 1977.

However, despite its title, which carries both commercial and literary appeal, *The Myth of the Lazy Native* was not primarily intended for a popular audience but for the academic reader. This explains two crucial differences in style between the two books. *Intellectuals* has a "lighter" tone — in the limited sense that light can be applied to Alatas' earnest prose. And *Myth* is much more restrained, more "academic," in its treatment of sources like Rizal.

Consider the abundance of adjectives in the following passage from *Intellectuals*:

> Jose Rizal (1861–96), the well-known Filipino patriot and martyr, was a leading intellectual of his time in addition to being a physician, poet and novelist. One of his most interesting works is his study of the indolence of the Filipinos …. Rizal was one of the few Asian intellectuals of the period who spent time and energy discussing his problems in a genuine and relevant manner." [Alatas 1977a: 11]

And the categorical judgment in this one:

> Rizal devoted two months in the summer of 1890 and about forty pages to analysing this problem and his work became the first scientific study of national character in modern Southeast Asia. [Alatas 1977a: 21]

Contrast these with the start of the opening paragraph of the chapter in *Myth* devoted to Rizal and his essay, *On the Indolence of the Filipinos*:

The title of this chapter is in honour of Rizal's work on the subject bearing a similar title. His work was probably the first historical sociological analysis of the subject, published in *La Solidaridad*, in Madrid in five instalments, from 15 July to 15 September 1890. He was reacting to the writing of a Filipino doctor of law, Sancianco, who discussed the subject of indolence and refuted it. Rizal pleaded for a dispassionate treatment of the subject. [Alatas 1977b: 98]

Dispassionate certainly describes Alatas' treatment of Rizal in *The Myth of the Lazy Native* (beginning with that careful qualifier "probably"). Of several dozen mentions, only the reference to honouring Rizal's five-part essay and a description of it as a "famous discourse" (Alatas 1997b: 71) may be said to constitute praise. In *Intellectuals in Developing Societies*, however, many of the references to Rizal (well-known patriot, leading intellectual) are as effusive as it gets in Alatas' scheme of things.

In either book, however, the same qualities that mark Alatas' scholarship are evident: the conscientious researcher's diversity of sources, the classroom teacher's willingness to repeat one's self, the practiced writer's pursuit of clarity above all else (Alatas, for instance, does not shrink from listing the six "characteristic problems and activities which only the intellectuals can undertake," the nine "traits" of ideology as "a system of belief," the 14 "features" of capitalism as "an economic system associated with a certain outlook").

Not least, there is also the pioneering thinker's gift for coining concepts. "The effort to construct new concepts for the study of Southeast Asian societies is in keeping with a genuine application of the social sciences," he explained his method in the lengthy introduction to *Myth*. With him, it was a never-ending effort. The result is a small but rich lexicon of powerfully explanatory terms, including colonial capitalism, psychological feudalism, the captive mind and the related concept of an autonomous intellectual tradition, and *bebalisma*.[2]

A prominent member of the younger generation of "Prof's" many students, the Malaysian political scientist and historian Farish A. Noor, summed up the impact of Alatas' boundary-busting *Myth* in a tribute in 2007. "Professor Syed Hussein Alatas will probably be best remembered for his path-breaking 'Myth of the Lazy Native', an analysis of the modalities involved in the construction of stereotypes of the 'native Other' seen from the point of view of the colonial metropole .... Never before had any Malaysian scholar attempted a work such a[s] this, which employed a range of analytical tools from sociology to history to discourse analysis and a critique of racialized capital; and never before with such deconstructive effect" (Noor 2007).

Much of the seventh chapter of *Myth*, titled "The Indolence of the Filipinos," consists of a recapitulation of Rizal's arguments, with extensive paraphrase and generous quotations. The following passage is representative of the manner in which Alatas discharged his primary task: presenting a nineteenth century Spanish text to a twentieth century English readership.

> The rulers gave the bad example of despising manual labour. "The pernicious influence of the rulers, that of surrounding themselves with servants and despising physical or manual labour as unworthy of the nobility and aristocratic pride of the heroes of so many centuries; those lordly manners that the Filipinos have translated into *Tila ka Kastila* (You're like a Spaniard); and the desire of the ruled to be the equal of the rulers, if not entirely, at least in manners — all these naturally produced aversion to activity and hatred or fear of work." This and all the factors previously cited caused any motivation to disappear. There was also the encouragement of gambling by the Spaniards. The cost of frequent religious functions; the curtailment of individual liberty; the fear of being accused as a rebel; the entire social system, with its corruption and iniquities, removed any motivation to excel, or to become rich. [Alatas 1977: 104]

Paraphrase, summary, and extensive direct quotation: these were the primary instruments by which Alatas extracted contemporary relevance from Rizal's post-*Noli*, pre-*Fili* reflections.

He begins, rightly, with Rizal's definition of indolence as "little love for work, lack of activity." (That definition — *el "poco amor al trabajo, falta de actividad, etc"* — is put to use even before the chapter on Rizal. Alatas, incidentally, is using the 1964 translation of Encarnacion Alzona, the chief translator of the Jose Rizal National Centennial Commission.)

Then follows an extended quote from a key paragraph where Rizal acknowledges that indolence does in fact exist in the islands. "We must confess that there [that is, the Philippines; he was writing in Brussels] indolence actually and positively exists: but instead of regarding it as the *cause* of the backwardness and disorder, we should regard it as the *effect* of disorder and backwardness, which fosters the growth of a *disastrous predisposition*" (the emphases[3] are Rizal's).

Essentially, Rizal's argument is from history. (He was primed to use this argument, since he had been researching old historical accounts on the Philippines at the British Museum for almost a year and painstakingly preparing his annotated edition of Morga's *Sucesos* over several months.) In Alatas' words: "As he considered the indolence of the Filipinos an effect rather than the root cause of their backwardness Rizal did not consider it to be hereditary. It was the social and historical experience of the Filipinos under Spanish domination which created the phenomenon of indolence. He recounted the illuminating past of the Filipinos" (Alatas 1977b: 100–101). And again: "How did the Filipinos abandon their former industry, their trade, their fishing, their enterprise, to the point of completely forgetting them? It was due to a combination of circumstances, some independent of the will and efforts of men, some due to ignorance and stupidity. The Spanish conquest and the resulting Spanish rule brought about the conditions leading to the decline of the Filipinos" (101).

While Rizal spoke of natural factors (the heat in the tropics, the human "tendency to indolence"), it was the destructiveness of the Spanish conquest that he identified as the real cause of Native laziness. A man who believed fervently in the power of example, he pointed to the demotivating effect of colonial exploitation: "The important thing to note," Alatas writes, "is his recourse to these methods of exploitation to explain the most important single factor generating what he called indolence, notably the lack of motivation to work"(103).

After all, why should the Indios till the soil "if their farms would be their graves, or if their crop would feed their executioner?" Why would the Native labour if "his work will be the cause of his trouble, that because of it he will be the object of vexations at home and the greed of the pirates from outside"? Why work with one's hands when the rulers themselves despise manual labour? If work equals exploitation, indolence is only to be expected.

It is precisely in this equation between work and exploitation, however, where Alatas parted company with Rizal.

> But we differ from Rizal on the extent of indolence in the Philippines and on whether the phenomenon which he alludes to can be called indolence. During the last war [that is, World War II] we had many prisoners of war held by the Japanese, British soldiers, who were not enthusiastic about working for the Japanese. Their reaction could hardly be called "indolence" .... it seems hardly appropriate to consider the larger section of Filipino society as indolent just because they were reacting to circumstances and conditions which suppressed motivation and enthusiasm for vigorous effort. [Alatas 1977b: 106]

Alatas here seems to be making a fundamental mistake, equating three years of Japanese occupation with three hundred years of Spanish rule. The difference is cultural — that is to say, the reaction to Japanese occupation was even then seen to be temporary, a response to immediate circumstances; the reaction to Spanish rule ingrained, a seemingly permanent adaptation to seemingly permanent conditions. To be sure, Rizal was not too clear on the aspect of cultural conditioning himself. But he did come close:

> "You can't do more than old So and So! Don't aspire to be greater than the curate! You belong to an inferior race! You haven't any

energy." They say this to the child; and as it is repeated so often, it has perforce become engraved in his mind and thence it seals and shapes all his actions. The child or the youth who tries to be anything else is charged [with] being vain and presumptuous; the curate ridicules him with cruel sarcasm, his relatives look upon him with fear, and strangers pity him greatly. No going forward! Get in line and follow the crowd!

His mind conditioned thus, the Filipino follows the most pernicious of all routines — a routine, not based on reason but imposed and forced. [Rizal 2007: 261]

Alatas is right to test Rizal's notion of imposition, but in my view he does not give enough weight to the accumulation of habit. In his critique of Rizal, he makes space for a diverting excerpt from an 1828 account by an unknown Englishman who had visited the Philippines, in order to give "a rare, clear, formulation of the capitalist concept of indolence, the mere provision for the needs of today" (Alatas 1977b: 107). But that same excerpt includes a passage which helps explain the qualitative difference between the effects of temporary circumstance and those of seemingly permanent conditions: "This apathy is perpetuated through numerous generations till it becomes national habit, and then we falsely call it nature" (107). The passage, however, does not elicit any comment from Alatas.

It must be said that Rizal himself was conflicted about the manner in which this "national habit" was perpetuated. In the second part of *Indolence*, we read:

Indolence in the Philippines is a chronic malady, but not a hereditary one. The Filipinos have not always been what they are now, witnesses being all the historians of the first years of the discovery of the Philippines. [Rizal 2007: 233]

He begins the third part by presenting a summary of "A fatal combination of circumstances" that "induced the decline of work" (239) and ends the third instalment with the following conclusion:

> It seems that these causes are sufficient to breed indolence even in the bosom of a beehive. Thus is explained why after thirty-two years of Spanish rule, the circumspect and prudent Morga said that the *Indios* "have forgotten much about farming, poultry and stock raising, cotton growing, and weaving of blankets as they did when they were Pagans and *long after the country had been conquered*." [244; emphasis supplied by Rizal]

Perhaps it is merely a matter of metaphors: In the second instalment he uses a figure from medicine, making a distinction between chronic and hereditary diseases. In the third he traces the roots of the forgotten trades to a kind of bred indolence; in other words, indolence has been inherited. It is important to remember, however, that despite the use of an incipient sociological approach, Rizal was principally writing a political tract. He was sufficiently scholarly enough to devote the fifth and last part of *Indolence* to those causes "emanating from the people."[4] But his primary purpose was to press the case for reform: first to recover a Native view of the problem of indolence (through his historical research), and then to argue for an end to the culture of indolence through a more enlightened administration of the Philippine colony.

> What we want is that no obstacles be placed in [the Indio's] way, not to increase the many that the climate and the situation of the islands already create for him, not to begrudge him educational opportunities for fear that when he becomes intelligent he will separate from the colonizing nation or demand rights to which he is entitled. Since some day or other he will become enlightened, whether the Government likes it or not, let his enlightenment be as a gift given to him and not as a spoil of war. [Rizal 2007: 264]

Alatas, a pioneer in what may be called the Asianization of the sociology of knowledge, is on much firmer ground when he critiques a second limitation of Rizal's views on Filipino indolence: "he neglected the Spanish contribution in exaggerating the significance of the theme. The fact that a conflict of interests conditioned the emergence of the theme escaped Rizal's notice" (Alatas 1977b: 106).

Alatas makes his case by appealing to the same authority Rizal invoked: history. He quotes (again generously) from the unknown Englishman and from the friar-chroniclers Gaspar de San Agustin and Sinibaldo de Mas, to sketch the confrontation between Spanish ecclesiastics and Native clergymen. "It was this underlying conflict between the Spanish and the Filipino clergy which had led to the arguments based on the theme of Filipino indolence," he writes.

This conflict led eventually to the emergence of the first nationalists, the generation of Filipino priests led by Father Jose Burgos whom the Propagandists and the revolutionaries would later trace their roots to. Rizal, the brother of one of Burgos' *protégés*, knew this only too well. But Alatas is right; Rizal did not dwell on this source of the ideological motivation behind the many, friar-written attacks on the character of the Native. Alatas quotes from John Leddy Phelan's landmark study, *The Hispanization of the Philippines*: "A numerous Filipino clergy obviously would have undermined the dominant position of the Spanish regulars" (Alatas 1977b: 109; quoting from Phelan 1959: 84–89). To forestall this, some of those opposed to so-called secularization launched attacks to degrade the Native and, by implication, the Native clergy.

> More than anything else the theme of the indolence of the Filipinos was brought into prominence as an outcome of the ideological conflict between the Spanish friars and native Filipino priests, preceded by a conflict of opinion between Spanish priests on the question of the Filipino priesthood. As the dominant group in the Philippines up to the time when Rizal wrote were the Spanish friars, their ideas became prevalent. [Alatas 1997b: 110]

Alatas, I think rightly, criticizes Rizal for failing to subject that very prevalence to closer scrutiny.

ALATAS MAY HAVE BEEN A TRAILBLAZER, but he was no prophet in the wilderness. He enjoyed what we may call the Socratic privilege, of leaving behind a living community, a lineage, so to speak, of independent scholars. We can trace the impact of Alatas' work as a scholar and a teacher on his students, who then went on to influence their own students. "For an entire generation of younger Malaysian academics and intellectuals who were born during the postcolonial era," Noor wrote, "Professor Syed Hussein Alatas was very much a mentor-figure, a model public intellectual and an example of what the academic world could do if and when academics applied their intellectual faculties to the pressing needs of the times" (Noor 2007).

It is possible to speak of a tradition of inquiry started by this mentor-figure. His personal example of rigorous research, hard work, and political engagement was the crucial foundation stone of that tradition, but certain themes were also taken up and looked into and passed on: the liberating influence of the sociology of knowledge, a relentless focus on the character of corruption, an examination of the distortions of the colonial experience, a search for the true face of progressive Islam, an insistence on the responsibilities of the public intellectual — and, perhaps not first but certainly not least, a recognition of Rizal as both kindred spirit and Asian pioneer.

Two students, in particular, are usually cited as following in the Alatas tradition. Clive Kessler's reference to the first and famous one is typical: "Alatas's student, the political scientist and internationally known civil society activist Chandra Muzaffar, wrote a brilliant study of the UMNO which argues that here the governing Malay political party has replaced the sultans and nobility. It epitomises the culture of patronage and self-interested deference; its modern dominance is now sustained by quasi-feudal attitudes" (Kessler 2008: 134).

A year before Kessler, Noor had already noted that by the publication of *The Myth of the Lazy Native*, "Professor Syed was no longer alone in his academic endeavours. Malaysian scholars like Chandra Muzaffar were also taking up his lead, questioning the logic of racialised patronage and the culture of neo-feudalism in Malaysia at the hands of UMNO in his work 'Protector?'" (Noor 2007).

Although Muzaffar's high, essentially political reputation is not without controversy, descriptions such as "Malaysia's best-known public intellectual" (from Countercurrents.org, 10 February 2010) are quite commonly used in articles about him. Attention is paid both to the work and his celebrity.

Shaharuddin bin Maaruf, Muzaffar's own student and an Alatas *protégé* too, toils in relative ordinariness in the groves of academe. But beginning with *Concept of a Hero in Malay Society*, he has fearlessly applied the lessons of the sociology of knowledge to Malaysian political culture; it is not an undertaking for the fainthearted.

Muzaffar began his remarks at the 1995 conference on Rizal and the Asian Renaissance hosted by the government of Malaysia by acknowledging that some information about Rizal was, one might say, stock knowledge. "Jose Rizal is a name that every student in Malaysia knows. In our secondary school history texts, Rizal is eulogized as an illustrious freedom fighter who struggled against Spanish colonial rule over the Philippines" (Muzaffar 1996: 198).

We can visualize the context: Rizal's name would be one of many mentioned, perhaps desultorily discussed, in a survey that would include Sukarno, Sun Yat-sen, Gandhi. Muzaffar learned about the "unique greatness of the man" only when he finally went to college. "It was only as a University undergraduate that I really discovered Rizal — and that too, not through any of the political science courses I took. Rizal in all his magnificent splendor was revealed to me in the countless conversations I used to have with Professor Syed Hussein Alatas, then Head of the Department of Malay Studies at my alma mater, the University of Singapore. Alatas recognized the importance of Rizal as a social reformer whose ideas and ideals transcended time and place" (198).

Rizal proved to be a significant influence on Muzaffar. "Rizal's life, his mission and his supreme sacrifice had such a profound impact upon me that when I founded a Malaysian social reform group, *Aliran Kesedaran Negara* (ALIRAN) or the National Consciousness

Movement in 1977, I chose 30 December, the day of his martyrdom, for the proclamation of the group's 'Basic Beliefs.' In fact, ALIRAN's basic beliefs revolved around 'justice, freedom and equality' — ideals that were so dear to Rizal" (198).

Muzaffar used the Asian Renaissance conference as an opportunity to bring Rizal into the heart of the great post-colonial debate.

> Do the writings of Rizal provide us with some hints, some clues as to how we could respond to the challenge of globalization? Though Rizal wrote in the nineteenth century, this is a pertinent question to ask since some of his concerns — as should be obvious by now — were not very different from some of the issues that trouble us today. How does one deal with the dominant power and influence of a hegemonic culture and civilization whose impact is all pervasive? What does one absorb and what does one reject from that dominant power? How does one decide what to absorb and what to reject? What criteria should be employed? What is the source of these criteria? [Muzaffar 1996: 200]

In the political sphere, Muzaffar highlights Rizal's religiously inspired sense of dignity as a standard: "In affirming his faith in a just religion as opposed to the unjust doctrine of the Spanish rulers and friars, Rizal had adopted a position that is not dissimilar to that of some dissidents in contemporary Southeast Asia who, while critical of Western manipulations of human rights, nevertheless remain devoted to the cause of human rights and human dignity itself" (201).

In the area of culture, he identifies "three major elements in Rizal's approach to his own native culture *vis-a-vis* Spanish culture — pride in one's own culture, a readiness to discard those aspects of one's culture which are inimical to progress, and an openness to healthy foreign cultural influences" (204).

It is in the field of economics, however, where we can hear the strongest echoes of Alatas in Muzaffar's voice. He quotes some of the same Morga-inflected passages from Rizal's *Indolence* which Alatas also used,[5] about the "active trade" in the islands before the Spanish conquest, the thriving traffic in exports, above all the testimony of "All the histories" about "the industry and agriculture of the natives."

The people of Southeast Asia, Muzaffar writes, can learn from Rizal's "accommodative attitude towards economic skills and practices associated with the colonial metropolises," because:

> Rizal had set a precedence for contemporary Southeast Asian elites who espouse active interaction with the prevailing centers of dominant economic power. Though some of them are also, at the same time, wary of Western economic domination through globalization, present-day Southeast Asian elites as a whole are far less appreciative of the virtues of the indigenous economy compared to Rizal. [203]

I am not too certain whether looking for confirmations in contemporary political or cultural or economic practice of specific themes in Rizal's writings is the best use of Rizal's work. Rizal may also be used as a critique: of miseducation, say, or of a too-materialistic vision of national progress. Or his story may be told as a cautionary tale. Rizal's deeply held conviction that change must come from above, something he expressed forthrightly in his controversial Manifesto of 15 December 1896, may resonate with businessmen and managers (it is an axiom that change in a corporate setting or a business enterprise must have the support of management for it to succeed) but it will get a difficult reception from change agents in politics or culture.

But the questions with which Muzaffar began his Southeast Asian survey are far-reaching; they are the right ones to ask. And they render both Rizal's achievement and continuing promise in helpful relief: He can tell us how to navigate the relationship between independent thought and dominant power.

Shaharuddin's unjustly neglected book, *Concept of A Hero in Malay Society*,[6] carries a foreword by Alatas which recognizes the pioneering nature of the work: "This is the first attempt made to study the conception of the hero in Malay society." Alatas situated Shaharuddin's analysis of the concept of the hero "as projected by the ruling class" within the category of leadership. In his straightforward scholarly prose, he writes: "The problem of leadership is indeed central to the progress of any community. As such its conception of what is heroic is significant in the sense that to some extent this conception moulds the motivational pattern of those involved" (Shaharuddin 1984: unnumbered).

Shaharuddin is quite aware of the stakes involved. In his introduction, he adopts a defensive pose. "The writer appreciates the fact that his attempt at diagnosis may be misinterpreted as an act of disloyalty to his people. The duty of revealing the unpleasant truth is too pressing to be waived aside for such a consideration. This is a paradox in life. Sometimes those who care most are attacked by the people they care for" (Shaharuddin 1984: unnumbered).

A not unsympathetic book review of the "provocative" title in the *Straits Times* on 12 October 1985 gives us an idea of the severity of the diagnosis. "He says the intention of his study is to invite Malays to cross-examine themselves, their values and their social philosophy so that they will be able to get to grips with the modern, rational world. To what extent he will succeed remains to be seen as, from the beginning, he alienates the entire Malay leadership regardless of their ideological leanings. He hasn't got a nice word for anyone."

To pre-empt the inevitable criticism his own critique of the traditional Malay heroes would meet, Shaharuddin makes his basis of evaluation clear and, for the most part, uncontroversial:

> "Since this study cover characters from feudal Malay history, the writer is aware that he needs relevant moral standards to judge them by, so as not to be guilty of judging the past using present-day standards. The standards used here are those derived mainly from Islam, which has been the religion of the Malays since the fifteenth and sixteenth century. The standards have been consciously selected in a way that they reflect the values of the Malays in the feudal past, as well as those of today. Some of these values are the love of learning, social justice, ethical integrity, good leadership, honesty, respect for the rule of law and the love of reforms. It is best that I illustrate my concept with concrete historical models such as Umar Ibn Khattab, the famous hero in Islamic history; Jose Rizal,

the Filipino patriot; and General Sudirman, the hero of Indonesian revolution, to represent the Islamic and modern democratic-humanitarian conception of the hero." [Shaharuddin 1984: 8]

Much of the book centres on "two feudal heroes, namely, Hang Tuah and Hang Jebat because they exercise great influence on the thinking of particular sections of Malay society." These central characters of the Malay epic *Hikayat Hang Tuah*, Shaharuddin writes, "represent the values of the warrior kingship group which emphasized martial prowess, aggressiveness, bravery, loyalty to the leader and pillage."

Official Malaysia champions these very values. In a survey of the writings of "four members of the Malay elite and intelligentsia," Shaharuddin unearths four themes or "certain distinctive features" running through their work (Shaharuddin 1984: 39). "One is that they would deny the people the right to judge their leaders in society" (39). "Another main feature in the romanticization of the Malay feudal period is the deterioration of moral standards" (40). "A third trait found in the writings of these feudal romanticists, perhaps the most glaring, is the glorification of unethical philosophy and deeds" (41). "The discussion about the intellectuals takes us to another trait of these feudal romanticists: they are often in praise of brawn and not brains" (46).

It is against this violent and licentious background[7] that Shaharuddin offers his three role models. Umar Ibn Khattab "has been chosen because he is generally accepted in the Muslim world as a hero and a great leader." That he lived during the seventh century AD is significant, as a counter-check on any tendency to judge the world of Hang Tuah by modern standards. "Jose Rizal and General Sudirman have been selected for their great struggles which reflect right sentiments and values as judged by Islamic and modern humanitarian standards. They are greatly admired in the Malay world of Southeast Asia. Their selection has an additional significance in that they are the heroes of that part of the Malay world which has broken off from the feudal tradition of the past by means of a social revolution. The fact that they pose a striking contrast to the feudal heroes, propagated by the Malay elite in Malaysia where there are many continuities with the feudal past, is by itself a significant point of cultural interest" (Shaharuddin 1984: 8–9).

Shaharuddin's sketch of Rizal is based almost entirely on the Guerrero biography. There are a couple of errors, possibly of transcription: "El Amor Patrio," which Guerrero translated not only as "Love of Country" but also as "Patriotism" (the title Shaharuddin uses), was written in 1882, not 1881. And the main character in the Fili is named Simoun, not Simon. The rest, however, is an insightful précis of Rizal's life.

There is the Alatas echo: a paragraph on Rizal's views on Filipino indolence.[8]

There is the detail that Wenceslao Retana noticed too, and deployed to such devastating effect: Rizal's 1879 poem, from which Shaharuddin extracts Rizal's "sense of patriotism [which] began early in his life" (and which Retana used in 1896 to make the separatist case against Rizal).

Then there are the many references which we do not find in Alatas' published writings on Rizal: to the two novels, to the "Letter to the Young Women of Malolos," to the founding of the Liga Filipina, to the "Ultimo Adios."

And there are the summaries of Rizal's life-work: "a conscious reformer who agitated his countrymen through his various writings" (Shahruddin 1984: 12); "a genuine patriot" (12); he "who provided the birth of the idea of nationhood for his country" (13).

Shaharuddin zeroes in on the task that Rizal set himself, the formation of a nation. "By nationhood, however, Rizal meant something more than just the attainment of formal political independence. He realized that what mattered was the emancipation in the thinking of the Filipinos" (13).

He ends with the passage from the *Fili* that contains the one line often used to summarize Rizal's mature political thought. "What is the use of independence if the slaves of today will be the tyrants of tomorrow?"

Like Muzaffar, Shaharuddin's deep interest in Rizal began when he went to university.

"When I was an undergraduate in Universiti Sains Malaysia, following the course in political science, I was exposed to the ideas of Jose Rizal. My course lecturer then, Chandra Muzaffar, was very much into the ideas of Jose Rizal. Of course Chandra and myself were then post-graduate students of Syed Hussein Alatas ... Once acquainted with some of his ideas, I tried then as an undergraduate and then as a post-graduate student to read as much as possible Rizal's writings ... materials were scanty and not readily available then. I had to combine my readings of biographies, autobiography, his literary works, correspondences in incomplete compilations, so as to acquaint myself with Rizal's ideas. Needless to say, the more you read, the more appreciative you become of his intellectual heritage."

"Personally I found his ideas on nationhood, notion of freedom and leadership, most appealing and relevant to our situation then. Being in a region newly independent, I found his ideas most relevant to the challenges of nation-building then. Take for instance, his insisten[ce] on how genuine freedom should not and could not be won by the sword, but by means of genuine emancipation of the spirit and the mind. Or take his idea on how mere political freedom in the sense of formal independence would be meaningless if it merely bring[s] a mechanical change of elite, the local or indigenous for the colonials. I remember how he posed us the perceptive question "what's the use if formal independen[ce] merely mean[s] the slave of today becoming the tyrant of tomorrow?" (Shaharuddin 2010).

(I note the use of "us," instead of the more usual phrasing: "how he posed *to his readers* the perceptive question.")

In his work, Shaharuddin has sought to use both Islamic and "modern democratic-humanitarian" standards by which to judge the dominant values in Malay culture. It is an academic project, a sustained experiment in the sociology of knowledge. But it is also very much political: it must, inevitably, take aim at the dominant class.

The critique of this class begins with its feudal hero-worship, its praise of folly. It ends with something of "wider significance and implication." In his concluding chapter, Shaharuddin focuses finally on "the central problem faced by Malay society and that is the problem of having an underdeveloped elite." Here, he is speaking truly as Alatas' heir. "The qualities necessary for development which the Malay elite lacks are ethical integrity and standards, intellectual capacity and stamina for productive and creative endeavours" (Shaharuddin 1984: 97).

So this is how a scholar alienates the "entire Malay leadership"!

In an interview published in the 11 April 1988 issue of the *Straits Times*, after his second book, *Malay Ideas on Development: From Feudal Lord to Capitalist*, came out, Shaharuddin explains himself. "What I am trying to say in both books is that there has been a crisis of evaluation — there must be when we promote less than noble characters as our heroes and we choose to keep promoting certain ideals." How can the crisis be resolved? He suggests a defining criterion: "The final test of a people's hero is whether what he stands for is able to raise the level of consciousness of the people."

Notes

1. Alatas said as much at the time. In *Intellectuals in Developing Societies*, the book he had written earlier but published at the same time as *The Myth of the Lazy Native*, he noted: "In 1966 I started studying this problem and spent more than two years of research on Dutch and Filipino sources, apart from the English and Malay sources" (Alatas 1977a: 21).
2. For the somewhat elusive concept of colonial capitalism, see, for instance, Alatas 1977b: 5–6 or 83–97. For a brisk introduction to psychological feudalism, the captive mind, and bebalisma, see Kessler 2008: 134–136. The extremely useful concept of bebalisma seems to be derived by analogy from the Russian novelist Goncharov's classic *Oblomov* (Alatas 2010: 104); based on the Malay word for stubbornly thick-headed, it refers to "a wilful stupidity that was not simply natural but had to be worked at, managed and socially

reproduced" (Kessler 2008: 135). "Oblomov the sublime sluggard and absentee," the peerless critic V. S. Pritchett wrote (1964: 396–397). "In a world of planners he plans himself to sleep. In a world of action he discovers the poetry of procrastination."

3. "*A disastrous predisposition*" seems to be Alzona's improvement on Rizal's "*una funesta predisposicion.*" Both the Charles Derbyshire and Guadalupe Fores-Ganzon translations locate the phrase somewhat lower on the direness scale, and render it as "a *lamentable predisposition.*"

4. "Now it behooves us to analyze those emanating from the people. Peoples and governments are correlated and complementary. A stupid government is an anomaly among a righteous people, just as a corrupt people cannot exist under rulers and wise laws. Like people, like government, we will say, paraphrasing a popular adage. All these causes can be reduced to two classes: Defects of education and lack of national sentiment" (Rizal 2007: 259).

5. Muzaffar, however, uses the 1913 Charles Derbyshire translation, not the Alzona of Alatas.

6. The title on the book's cover page is *Concept of A Hero in Malay Society*. The so-called running head on the verso (or left) page, however, renders the title as *The Conception of the Hero in Malay Society* — a sign, perhaps, that in the three years between completion of the manuscript and the writing of the author's preface, or in the two years between manuscript submission and first publication, there was an attempt to further refine the title. Just to keep things even more interesting, Kessler's 2008 tribute to Alatas cites Shaharuddin's work as *The Idea of a Hero in Malay Society*.

7. Farish A. Noor suggests another way of reading Hang Tuah. In "Hang Tuah the Pacifist: Deconstructing our National Hero" (Noor 2009: 233–277), he accepts the reality that "Hang Tuah, the fabled warrior of Melaka who was the admiral (*Laksamana*) in the service of his King, Sultan Mansur Shah," was "one of the most recognisable emblems of a particular mode of right-wing ethno-nationalist politics." He writes: "The reason for the unease that some of us harbour with regards to Tuah is simple and clear enough: more often than not, whenever Tuah's motto is sounded — "*Tak kan Melayu hilang di dunia*" [The Malays shall never perish from the earth] — the words are uttered by some right-wing politician who may be waving a keris in his hand" (237). But Noor reclaims the epic by a close reading of its second part, which presents a different, more humane, more cosmopolitan Tuah: "In the second part of the *Hikayat*, Tuah's character serves as a narrative vehicle for the exploration of selfhood and identity. Tuah's ease with others, his ability to stand outside his ethnic, religious and political

frontiers and his willingness to accept and understand cultural practices and norms that are not his own, stand in stark contrast to the warrior-figure who — in the first half of the *Hikayat* — stands perpetually on the frontier of his own national and ethnic identity in order to defend it" (274). In this light, Noor's reading is just as subversive, of current thinking about the epic hero, as Shaharuddin's. "By re-presenting Hang Tuah thus, the *Hikayat* takes a tentative step towards deconstructing the image of Tuah as the warrior-killing machine …. Tuah, having travelled, learns that he is at home *everywhere* — and that everywhere is *home*. The warrior begins to die, and the universal man within him begins to grow" (274–275).

8. The title Shaharuddin uses is borrowed from either Alzona or Derbyshire: *The Indolence of the Filipinos*. In fact, the original title of the five-part essay was "*Sobre la Indolencia de los Filipinos*" — which Fores-Ganzon translated, correctly, as "On the Indolence of the Filipinos."

10
"A Great Historical Experiment"

Crayonpedia has a touch of the Indonesian genius for acronyms. An online study resource based on the Indonesian educational curriculum, it stands for Create Your Open Education Encyclopaedia and manifests a becoming sense of history; it was launched on the centenary of the founding of the Budi Utomo movement, in 2008.

In two and a half years, Crayonpedia has grown to over 6,800 pages of material. "Page" is used here in its online context; it means a discrete topic, regardless of length. The single page on the "Rise and Development of the Indonesian National Movement" is in fact an entire chapter, and would require a printout of well over a dozen pages.

The chapter[1] begins with a schematic survey of the "internal" and "external" factors that led to the growth of nationalist consciousness in Indonesia. The section on the eight internal factors is followed by the section on the five external causes, those which in the words of the online module gave "*dorongan dan energi*" (encouragement and energy) to the nationalist movement: namely, the Japanese victory in the Russo-Japanese War in 1905, the growth of the Indian Congress Party, the Chinese nationalist movement, the rise of the Young Turks — and "*Filipina di bawah Jose Rizal*," that is, the Philippines under Jose Rizal.

This sounds, more or less, like Sukarno's roll call of awakened nations, which we have heard a few times in earlier pages. And it is a view reflected, more or less, in the standard references. "The first signs of an awakening national self-consciousness began to show themselves in Java early in the [twentieth] century," D. G. E. Hall writes in *A History of Southeast Asia*, his magisterial survey. "Such external influences as the Boxer Rising in China, the Filipino revolt against Spain, and the rise of Japan undoubtedly played their part" (Hall 1981: 790–791).

I say more or less, because other standard works appear to minimize the Philippine factor. For instance, the illuminating overview of "Nationalism and Modernist Reform" in the *Cambridge History of Southeast Asia*, by Paul Kratoska and Ben Batson, assumes a hierarchy of inspiration in assigning pride of place to Japan and China. "Japan, where the Meiji restoration was followed by a reformist movement which borrowed from abroad to defend indigenous traditions, inspired many political activists in Southeast Asia, notably in Vietnam and the Philippines. Japan's victory in the Russo-Japanese War of 1904–5 had an extraordinary impact in the region, since it represented the triumph of an Asian over a Western power. The nationalist struggle in China also served as a model" (Kratoska and Batson 1999: 248–249).

To this sweeping view, Rebecca Karl's adventurous expedition into Chinese intellectual history offers a tonic correction. In *Staging the World: Chinese Nationalism at the Turn of the Twentieth Century* (2002), Karl rediscovers the role the Philippine revolution played, even if only for a crucial few years, in the Chinese nationalist discourse.[2] It is a service that another intrepid scholar had performed decades before her, this time regarding Japanese expansionism. Josefa Saniel's work had already shown that while Filipino nationalists drew inspiration from the Asian historical experience, inspiration was very much a two-way street.[3]

Crayonpedia's list of external factors, then, restores the right balance; moreover, it corresponds closely to Pramoedya Ananta Toer's research-driven understanding of the origins of Indonesian nationalism. There is a paragraph in *Anak Semua Bangsa*, the second novel in the iconic Indonesian writer's magnificent Buru Quartet, that can serve as a summary of his attempt at historical exploration. That paragraph, in the widely available English translation, *Child of All Nations*, by the Australian ex-diplomat and reluctant academic Max Lane, reads as follows:

> I forced myself to think how all these things came together: the progress Japan was making, the restlessness among the Chinese Young Generation, the rebellion of the Filipino natives against Spain and then the United States, the jealousy of the colonial Netherlands Indies towards China, the colonial hatred of Japan. And why wasn't the Filipino rebellion reported in all the newspapers? [Pramoedya 1991: 92]

The "I" is the narrator of the first three novels and the (ostensible) subject of all four books, known by the nickname he got stuck with in school: Minke. (As the reader finds out in a cleverly executed sequence in the first volume, *Bumi Manusia* or *This Earth of Mankind*, the name is a corruption of "monkey," spat out as an insult). Minke is struggling to make sense of a recent series of events: his belated discovery of the story of the Philippine revolution through clandestine conversations with the illegal Chinese immigrant and activist Khouw Ah Soe; his temporary reconciliation with the Dutch editor who had butchered his interview on the Chinese militant, turning it into its exact opposite; not least, his hearing yet again the unforgiving counsel of his mother-in-law, the formidable Nyai Ontosoroh — "And there is one thing that stays the same, Child, that is eternal: The colonialist is always a devil."

"How all these things came together" — at this stage in the narrative Minke's political consciousness is as yet insufficiently evolved. He has not yet recovered from Nyai Ontosoroh's gentle chiding: "You have only one deficiency. You don't really know what the word *colonial* means" (Pramoedya 1991: 83). He has yet no answer to his Dutch editor's deft use of the false choice: "I think you would prefer to support your country than a truth that would hurt it" (92). He has heard the challenge in Khouw Ah Soe's words — "There is no power that can bring to a halt this passion to control, except greater science and learning, in the hands of more virtuous people" (90) — but he has yet no idea how to respond to them.

And he has not yet discovered Rizal.

The Buru Quartet (named after the island prison camp where Pramoedya was detained for 10 years, and where the stories began as oral narratives) privileges Rizal and the Philippine revolution; in particular, the second volume uses Minke's multi-stage discovery of Philippine history as crucial moments in the plot line and as milestones in his own awakening. But because the four novels together tell the story of nascent Indonesian nationalism (without ever using the word "Indonesia," as Lane has pointed out in an introduction), this appropriation of Philippine history may then be said to have played a role — as one of several midwives, perhaps — in the birth of Indonesia.

The fourth novel, *House of Glass*, also references Rizal (twice) and mentions the Philippines or Filipinos twenty-three times; there are two mentions of Andres Bonifacio and three of Emilio Aguinaldo — each as a point of comparison, when the possibility of Minke becoming the "third Asian president" after Aguinaldo and Sun Yat-sen is raised (and eventually dismissed). But these mentions merely form part of the background, the international context which frames the understanding of the Dutch colonial government (in the person of the Native police inspector who narrates the last volume) when it comes to the least stirring of nationalist consciousness. The government's aim, it is first suggested in a discussion in an elite club early in the last volume (Pramoedya 1992: 49), is to prevent the Dutch East Indies from becoming "a second Philippines."

In *Child of All Nations*, however, Rizal and the Philippine revolution are very much part of the foreground of action. There is only one reference each to Andres Bonifacio and Emilio Aguinaldo, but ten mentions of Rizal and sixty-one of Filipinos or the Philippine revolution. Beyond the sheer number, it is the role these historical markers play in the evolution of Minke's thinking that attracts our attention.

Or at least it attracts our attention now. One of the earliest and still among the most perceptive reviews of the first two volumes, Keith Foulcher's many-layered reading in 1981, manages to render the Philippine historical experience invisible.

> The first important influence in this process is the example of Japan, and then China, as alternative models of modernization. Minke comes into contact with a young Chinese man, an illegal immigrant in the Indies, who is risking his life to appeal to overseas Chinese communities to join the struggle for regeneration in their homeland. Khouw, the Chinese youth, presents Minke with a world he knows nothing about, full of examples of political activism, and imbued with the alien yet profoundly exciting notion of *kebangkitan suatu bangsa* (the rise of a nation). [Foulcher 1981: 10]

Granted, Foulcher was summarizing an entire book, but I think another reading of *Child of All Nations* will prove that yet another important influence "in this process" — that is, Minke's attempt to ground his "enthusiasm for the brightly dawning vision of modernity" in "the reality of life about him" (Foulcher 1981: 10) — was Philippine history at the turn of the twentieth century.

An alternative model of modernization, made possible through political activism, and understood as the emergence of a nation: This was precisely why Khouw Ah Soe involved Minke in a discussion on the Philippines. "You no doubt know what happened in the Philippines?" (Pramoedya 1991: 88ff). And why he justifies his "dangerous work" of political agitation by recalling the Philippine experience: "The Philippines cannot be forgotten, can they? Even if they were deceived by Spain and America? It is inevitable that other conquered peoples will follow in their footsteps. Yes, even in the Indies. If not now, then later, when people know how to handle their teachers" (89). These were Khouw Ah Soe's last words as Minke remembered them, before vanishing from sight.

"The figure of Khouw," Foulcher notes, "appears to be derived from the Chinese Reform Movement of 1898, which involved both conservative-reformist and radical views on the need for Western-influenced modernization in China" (Foulcher 1981: 10). But as becomes clear in the course of the novel, it isn't only Khouw Ah Soe's personal example or the glimpse he provided into the emerging Chinese nationalist movement that impressed Minke; it was also the tidings he brought of the Philippine revolution.

Foulcher's insightful retelling of Minke's evolving consciousness ends with "one more important discovery" (Foulcher 1981: 13), namely how a Native already alert to colonialism's depredations ought to appropriate the teachings of the colonials:

> *Rakus! Rakus! Bukan lagi kata, juga maknanya bertalu dengan otakku sebagai landasan. Rakus! Tapi itu masih lebih hoik daripada perang, pembunuhan, penghancuran. Apalagi perang tanpa harapan menang seperti di Aceh, seperti di Filipina, seperti Trunodongso. Tidak, Ter Haar sang pengusik, aku masih membutuhkan guru Eropa, termasuk kau. Hanya dengan kekuatanmu sendiri orang dapat hadapi kau.*
>
> (Greed! Greed! Not just the word, but the whole meaning of it pounded like a hammer on my brain. Greed! But better this awareness than war, murder, destruction. Let alone a war with no hope of victory, as in Aceh, in the Philippines, as with Trunodongso. No, Ter Haar, you meddler, I do still need European teachers, you included. Only with your own powers can you be successfully confronted.) [Foulcher 1981: 14]

The summing up that immediately follows this passage effectively reduces Razif Bahari's intricate interpretation of the Buru Quartet (published almost a generation after Foulcher's review, in the same indispensable journal; see below) to one resonant sentence: "Minke has attained a sense of himself as an historical being, and of the responsibility that accompanies it" (Foulcher 1981: 14).

But even here, despite the specific mention of the Philippines, the significance of the (ultimately unsuccessful) Philippine revolution in Minke's political awakening goes unremarked. It has once again become invisible. But consider its curious placement: it is sandwiched between a costly war in one part of the Netherlands Indies and a doomed uprising in another. I suggest that the sequence is deliberate, and follows Minke's personal logic. The ghastly 30-year war in Aceh is remotest to him; he knows of it only through the news and the experience of his friend, the transplanted French painter Jean Marais, who prefers not to talk about it. Trunodongso's little war is closest; he knew the peasant rebel, had not only befriended him but encouraged him, with what turned out to be the fatal, fleeting hope of publicity. The Philippine war "with no hope of victory" lies somewhere in the middle: Minke will never visit the neighbouring islands; his planned study tour of the Philippines is overtaken by events (foreshadowing E. F. E. Douwes Dekker's own aborted plan). But the connection with Khouw Ah Soe makes the Philippines familiar, even intimate; indeed, his struggle to understand the Philippine revolution helps him achieve precisely that sense of himself as an actor in history.

Two extended passages from *Child of All Nations* describe an evolution in Minke's perception of Rizal, and thus in his own awakening.

UNTIL HIS DEATH IN 2006 at the age of 81, Pramoedya was often mentioned as one of Southeast Asia's leading candidates for the Nobel Prize in Literature. (Today that curious distinction, essentially an index of frustration, belongs primarily to the Filipino F. Sionil Jose, another widely translated writer of historical novels on an epic scale.) He was a prolific writer, and already celebrated in Indonesia by the 1950s, but it was the four Buru novels, and the way they were composed in the 1970s, that sealed his worldwide reputation.

When the English translation of the fourth volume became available, in the 1990s, international critical acclaim for the entire Buru Quartet reached a crescendo. The exuberant review of *House of Glass* in the 11 August 1996 issue of the *Washington Post* may have hit the highest note, but I do not think it is unfair to say that its praise for Pramoedya's achievement was widely shared. "The Buru Tetralogy is one of the twentieth century's great artistic creations, a work of the richest variety, color, size and import, founded on a profound belief in mankind's potential for greatness and shaped by a huge compassion for mankind's weakness."

(The review included an extraordinary encomium for the translator: "The tetralogy has already been translated into 20 languages; translator Max Lane has devoted nearly two decades to this English version[4]....His work has been worth the time and effort. If there were a Nobel Prize for translations, he would deserve it.")

When Pramoedya died, the obituaries pointed to the four novels as the highlight of an extraordinary literary career. In the 3 May 2006 issue of *Asia Times*, to cite only one representative example, the former editor of the *Far Eastern Economic Review*, Michael Vatikiotis, wrote: "Pramoedya is best known overseas for his *Buru Quartet*, a majestic story spanning the dawn of Indonesian nationalism through to the dying days of colonial rule. Pramoedya composed the epic while exiled on a remote island in eastern Indonesia and recited it orally to his fellow inmates. Eventually published in the late 1970s, the books were banned in Indonesia. Alongside the great Filipino writer Jose Rizal's *Noli Me Tangere*, the *Buru Quartet* ranks as one of the most important works chronicling Southeast Asia's nationalist struggle against colonial rule."

Pramoedya himself acknowledged Rizal as an influence. During an interview he gave after receiving an honorary doctorate from the University of Michigan in May 1999, he spoke of the American writers John Steinbeck and William Saroyan as his main literary heroes, and then added: "I read a lot of Zola as a youth, and before my prison exile I translated Tolstoy into Indonesian. I was impressed by his liberation of his serfs but he didn't serve as a model for my writing. Gorky influenced me much more. He was a writer who portrayed the social fabric of his country and gives readers an insight into the distinctive character of the Russian people. The Philippine novelist Jose Rizal was also an inspiration for me" (Pramoedya 1999b).

It must be said that in the remarks he wrote upon accepting the Magsaysay Award in 1995 (in absentia, since he was effectively banned from leaving the country by the Suharto government), he did not mention Rizal at all — a conspicuous omission, given that the award, not infrequently referred to in wire news reports as "Asia's Nobel prize," is of Philippine provenance. The topic of his speech, on the danger novels posed to the state, was suggested by the Magsaysay Foundation (something Alex G. Bardsley noted in his translation); it seemed ready-made for referencing Rizal. Did the controversy surrounding his award, because of opposition led by other writers from Indonesia and the Philippines, vigorous opposition based on Pramoedya's own relationship to power in the last years of Sukarno's rule, narrow the scope of his remarks? "My apologies if I only discuss Indonesian literature," he wrote about two-thirds of the way through the speech, before reiterating his conviction — the very same set of beliefs that figured prominently in the cultural debates of those very years — that "literature is so closely tied to politics."

This ideal of an engaged literature led Pramoedya, as it led Rizal before him, to master his own nation's history. The official biography published by the Magsaysay Foundation noted this turning point midway through Pramoedya's career. "He was consumed with discovering the true roots of the Indonesian nation and worked tirelessly to unearth them in books, magazines, newspapers, and other primary documents from the late nineteenth and early twentieth centuries, amassing a huge private research library in the process" (Rush 1995).

Pramoedya as a historian: This is not yet the common view outside Indonesia of the man called "the most widely read Indonesian writer in history" (Rush 1995). The lack of familiarity helps account for Vatikiotis' necessary explanation that Pramoedya was "best known overseas" for the Buru novels. "Yet he was also a very conservative historian. He worried that too many Indonesians were ignorant of their history. Pramoedya compiled a detailed chronicle of the Indonesian revolution, revealing that it took several weeks for the declaration of independence in August 1945 to reach the extremities of the archipelago. When he died, he was working with his daughter on a new encyclopedia of Indonesia" (Vatikiotis 2006).

Lane, the novelist's devoted translator, reserves a higher superlative for Pramoedya's historical research. "Pramoedya is Indonesia's great novelist and, I also think, the country's greatest historian, although not fitting the conventional model" (Lane 2008: 6). In his introduction to *House of Glass*, Lane suggests just how unconventional Pramoedya's contribution is: "More than a great writer of historical fiction, he is a great writer of history in fiction" (Pramoedya 1992: xii).

Does the embedding of Rizal and the Philippine revolution in the fiction of *Child of All Nations* make for sound history? In the following extended excerpt, we find Minke on board the *Oosthoek*, on his way to study medicine in Batavia. It is the year 1903. As the ship leaves Surabaya, Ter Haar, a Dutch journalist of liberal convictions who recognizes Minke as the writer behind the pseudonym Max Tollenaar, introduces himself — and Jose Rizal.

> "The Filipinos have already carried out strikes," said Ter Haar. "But their rebellion is even more interesting; it rocked all of Europe, including Holland, Mr Minke." He hurriedly lit another cigarette. "They're all busy studying why it happened so they can make sure nothing similar occurs in their own colonies. A friend of mine knew one of the Native leaders there, someone called Dr Jose Rizal. My friend met him in Prague. Rizal was a poet, very brilliant, and a fiery lover also. The Spanish caught him in the end. A great pity — someone as outstanding as that. His faith wasn't strong enough. A pity." He smacked his lips. "Of course there can be no doubt now about his fate: The death sentence ended his life story. Someone as cultivated as that, writing poems in Spanish, just as you write in Dutch. A doctor, Mr Tollenaar, and you too intend to become a doctor. Perhaps that is no coincidence."
>
> "Somebody educated, a doctor, a poet ... rebelling ..."
>
> "Maybe the Dutch are cleverer than the Spanish. There has never been any rebellion by educated Natives against the Dutch here. Here the educated Natives always follow the Dutch. The Indies is not the Philippines, Holland isn't Spain."

"And he was sentenced to death?" I was reminded of Khouw Ah Soe.

"That's right. The Spanish military are famed for their viciousness."

An educated person had rebelled against his own teachers — indeed there had never been anything like that in the Indies.

"And then even when isolated from his comrades, Jose Rizal did not stand alone. So many, so very many people loved him, because with all his knowledge and learning, he loved his own people so much. Many prominent people, clever people in Europe pleaded with the Spanish government to pardon that brilliant, educated Filipino."

"What did he want to achieve with this rebellion?"

"You don't know? He wanted his people not to be ruled by the Spanish. He wanted them to rule themselves. A pity" — he made noises with his lips again — "that inexperienced people in the end became the victims of an alliance between Spain and America." [Pramoedya 1991: 264]

We can make an educated guess about some of Pramoedya's sources for his portrait of Rizal — the colours in his historiographical palette, so to speak — with some degree of confidence, based on the emphases he chose to make. The mention of prominent people in Europe seeking pardon for Rizal, for instance, seems to come straight from E. F. E. Douwes Dekker's main source on the Philippines, John Foreman's *The Philippine Islands*. Foreman spent an inordinate amount of space (one page out of a total of eight on Rizal) detailing the plans hatched "[i]n a house which I visit in London" to organise a European pressure group to free Rizal; Pramoedya's reference to "clever people" suggests Foreman's elaborate tale of a fake plot, with its storyline of conspiratorial hints "deftly thrown about" and insinuations of "ambassadorial intervention and foreign complications" if Madrid failed to grant the demand. (This particular colour demonstrates the watery weakness of some of Foreman's first-person accounts; he was partial to them because he was privy to them, even though, like the fake plot, they were entirely peripheral to history.)

Ter Haar's mention of Filipinos already carrying out labour strikes offers another telltale sign: That Pramoedya used at least one account written, a decade or so after Rizal's execution, from the Filipino working-class movement's perspective or, perhaps, as seems more likely to me, he consulted Tan Malaka's 1948 autobiography, *Dari Pendjara ke Pendjara*. The lengthy work carries several pages on the Philippines, where the pioneering Indonesian nationalist had found refuge in the 1920s. Tan Malaka's fascinating view of Rizal and the Philippine revolution, translated in *From Jail to Jail* by Helen Jarvis in 1991, offers an early Marxist perspective on what he calls "the revolution of 1898–1901;" he saw it as "a revolution of the workers and peasants under the leadership of a truly revolutionary section of the intelligentsia." (In this phrase we hear an echo of the scholar and labour organiser Isabelo de los Reyes' 1900 description[5] of the Katipunan revolutionary organization, as consisting of "the workmen and peasant classes." Indeed, it was De los Reyes who organised the first labour union in the Philippines and inspired the widespread but uncoordinated strikes of 1902, which Ter Haar had referred to.)

The reference to Rizal's "faith" in Ter Haar's exposition, as something not "strong enough," seems somewhat puzzling. Did the liberal Dutch journalist mean to point to Rizal's religious convictions? But in Tan Malaka's account of Rizal, there is a use of "faith" being put to the test that suggests Ter Haar's real meaning. Tan Malaka, to help his Indonesian readers judge the measure of Rizal, had compared him to the Indonesian nationalist pioneer Dr Sutomo, or Pak Tom, but he ends his account with a decisive contrast: "Pak Tom did not have his faith put to the test, but Dr Rizal passed the test and gave up his own life for his views with a calmness and a determination unsurpassed by anyone of any nation at any time. Dr Rizal can be criticized only for his excesses: he was too principled and too honest in confronting enemies who exhibited the morals and actions of snakes in the grass" (Tan Malaka 1991: 123). A great pity, Ter Haar says — because, I understand him to mean now, Rizal could have fought back but didn't. "His faith wasn't strong enough."

The consistent condemnation of the successor colonial regime is another striking colour Pramoedya uses often and to subtle but powerful effect. Filipinos as "victims of an alliance between Spain and America," the revolution as a continuum of struggle "of the Filipino natives against Spain and then the United States," the country itself as "deceived by Spain and America" — these are not the views of the standard references, or even of mainstream newspaper coverage, in the first years of the twentieth century, the time Ter Haar first met Minke. To be sure, there was articulate opposition from Apolinario Mabini within the Philippines and from the Anti-Imperialist League without, but the American rationalization machine was already in overdrive. Ter Haar's more consistently anti-colonial views, which do not excuse the American imperial project, seem to me to reflect later scholarship on the Philippines. (In contrast, the longer profiles on Rizal published in Indonesia during the Japanese occupation never failed to mention Henry Cooper's recitation of Rizal's farewell poem in the U.S. Congress in 1902, a high point in the saga of the Americanization of the Philippines. I believe this reflects the pro-American cast of the standard references available at the time.)

The question of Pramoedya's use of history arises, not so much because he wrote historical novels, but because he saw himself as a historian. It is possible to read his later work as a battle between history and myth. "In the Buru tetralogy," Bahari writes, "history does not stand outside individual consciousness as a form imposed, but rather, impinges on the consciousness of characters and forces its way into their considerations. History supervenes against the discourse of myth in these novels because it both shapes and is shaped by the private affairs of the self. In a practical sense, the most transparent manifestation of this reciprocity appears in the mechanisms of plot" (Bahari 2003: 75).

The discourse of myth: By this Bahari means both the unilateral assertions of the social realist novels that Pramoedya had outgrown and the official histories of Suharto's New Order. Against these two extremes, the Buru novels offer an alternative. "In contrast to the single-voiced discourse of myth that shapes social realism and New Order historiography and asserts authority over the real (i.e., truth) and the meaning of the real, the Buru tetralogy offers a different claim on history and historical truths. Propositional rather than assertive, this claim implies the recognition that to know the historical is to mediate and to narrate it with the voice of a subject in the present who is also positioned within history. If one of the proclaimed truths of our existence is that "being" means always being in time, it is a derivative but no less cogent conclusion that we are also in history — we belong to history" (Bahari 2003: 73).

This is a beguiling view of the novels; it certainly helps explain the critical acclaim the Quartet has received. But it is important to point out that Pramoedya had in fact very definite ideas about how his beloved Nusantara came to be today's Indonesia.

His contribution to the turn-of-the-millennium survey of the *New York Times Magazine*, in April 1999, retails an intriguing anecdote about an Indonesian diplomat — a tale that can be told from many points of view, a story that lends itself to "propositional" claims on history. But the historical truths Pramoedya draws from the anecdote are not only "assertive"; they are decisive.

> Is my tale about an Indonesian at the court of King James the greatest story of the millennium? Certainly not, though I must smile at the irreverence shown by my countryman. I include it here because it touches on what I would argue are the two most important "processes" of this millennium: the search for spices by Western countries, which brought alien nations and cultures into contact with one another for the first time; and the expansion of educational opportunities, which returned to the colonized peoples of the world a right they had been forced to forfeit under Western colonization — the right to determine their own futures. [Pramoedya 1999a]

Education as the antidote to colonialism: we have heard this before. It was the cure Dr Rizal himself prescribed.

PRAMOEDYA OWED RIZAL a debt of inspiration, but this did not prevent him from subordinating Rizal's image to the needs of his novel, understood as history. When Minke leaves Surabaya for Batavia, thus signalling a new, higher stage of consciousness, he is introduced to the martyred Rizal and the thrilling possibility of a revolt of the educated classes: "An educated person had rebelled against his teachers — indeed there had never been anything like that in the Indies." But on the same voyage, after reading magazine articles on the Philippine revolution provided by Ter Haar, Minke makes a dismaying discovery: In this second extended excerpt, Minke realizes that Rizal, for all his learning, was pitifully naive.

> I know these notes won't be of much interest to anyone, but I have no choice but to include them. Why? Because these thoughts are so much a real part of my environment, the world I inhabited. Ah, knowledge: Trunodongso would never know that there is a nearby country called the Philippines. And knowledge, the result of my reading this article, made the Philippines a part of my own world, even though only as an idea. The wonder of knowledge — without their eyes ever seeing the world, it makes people understand the breadth of the world: its richness, its depth, its height, and its womb, and all its pests and plagues as well.
>
> And Rizal still dreamed of the honor and nobility of Europe. But European power was a monster that became hungrier and hungrier the more it gobbled up. I found myself thinking of the greedy ogre in the wayang stories of my ancestors.
>
> But other groups of educated Filipino Natives had long lost their faith in Spanish colonial power. They took up arms and rebelled. Poor Trunodongso and his friends: They knew no geography; they thought that if they could rid Tulangan of the sugar mills they would win an eternal victory. But Rizal was even more pathetic than Trunodongso. When his comrades took up arms, he was still dreaming of the generosity of the Spanish governors of the

Philippines, even after he was arrested and exiled. And a few days before he was executed he was still urging his fellow Filipinos who had taken up arms to stop fighting. He was more pitiful than Trunodongso. Him — Rizal! Truno was defeated because of his lack of knowledge, Rizal because he did not believe in what he knew ... in his intellectual conscience. [Pramoedya 1991: 274–275]

Pramoedya's fateful detour into historical research took place in the early 1960s, and it shows. By then, the revisionist Philippine history championed by Teodoro Agoncillo was ascendant. The view, for instance, that Rizal was fatally naive pivots on the nationalist belief that he was irredeemably idealistic. As we have already seen, this is a complete misreading of the widely available evidence. The same thing can be said for the notion that Rizal "still dreamed of the honor and nobility of Europe." By 1892, at the time of his second return to the Philippines, the evidence shows that Rizal had clearly given up hope that Spanish colonial officials would act justly. He could still hold them to the code of the hidalgo; but justice was altogether out of reach. Not least, the idea that Rizal lacked the nerve to follow his conscience, "because he did not believe in what he knew," runs wholly against the evidence too.[6]

From Pramoedya's perspective, however, Rizal was an eminently useful historical character precisely because of his perceived shortcomings, because the accusations of impractical idealism or failure of nerve made him a necessary transitional figure. In fact, that is how Minke eventually came to understand the "meaning" of Khouw Ah Soe.

"And they [the Filipinos] built their own government on the French model! No wonder Khouw Ah Soe was so excited about the Philippines! He was still at the stage of crying out to his people like Rizal, at a time when his own country [that is, a cross-concessioned China] was suffering under the Americans, the English, the French, the Germans, and the Japanese, as well as being parched by drought, the whole country, north to south, east to west. He too died, just as Rizal did."

The Philippines as the key to understanding China; Rizal as the measure with which to gauge Khouw Ah Soe's life and death — at long last Minke has finally come around to appropriate Rizal for his own use, on his own terms.

Notes

1. The site's address is crayonpedia.org. The chapter on the Indonesian nationalist awakening is available at <http://www.crayonpedia.org/mw/BAB_5._MUNCUL_DAN_BERKEMBANGNYA_PERGERAKAN_NASIONAL_INDONESIA>.
2. See, for instance, Karl's fourth chapter, "Recognizing Colonialism: The Philippines and Revolution" (83–115). In this part of the narrative, special mention is made of Mariano Ponce, boon companion of Rizal and Marcelo del Pilar and a friend of Sun Yat-sen's. "Ponce's *History of the War for Philippine Independence*, written in Spanish in 1900, translated into Japanese in 1901 and into Chinese in 1902, was perhaps the single most influential text for post-1902 Chinese interpretations of the global and Chinese significance of the Philippine revolution. Moving beyond the American and Japanese geopolitical arguments, Ponce directed Chinese attention to an experience of colonialism that spoke directly to Chinese intellectuals" (102–103).
3. Aside from Saniel's *Japan and the Philippines: 1868–98* (see, for instance, pp. 222–268), her account of Rizal's influence on the Japanese political novelist Suehiro Tetcho is standard. After quoting from Tetcho's introduction to *Nanyo no Daiharan (The Great Wave in the South Seas)*, which reveals that the novel was based on his encounter with "a gentleman from Manila," Saniel notes, rather cautiously: "This quotation supports the contention that Rizal had influenced Suehiro Tetcho's *Nanyo no Daiharan* for the author, himself, who identified the 'gentleman from Manila' as Mr. Rizal in his *Memoirs of My Travels*, implies acknowledgment of Rizal's contribution to his novel" (Saniel 1968: 34). I think the acknowledgment is in fact direct, and not implied.
4. It may have taken two decades altogether, but the actual work was in stages. It took Lane "less than a year" to translate the first volume, for instance, and about the same amount of time to translate the second. Of particular interest, especially to those readers who must have noticed the glossary at the end of each book growing fatter by the volume, is Lane's attention to the various languages in play: "I couldn't imagine the novels translated in a way that eliminates the foreignness to the reader. You eliminate the sense of

foreignness, you eliminate Pramoedya and you will eliminate Indonesia" (Lane 2010).

5. The quote is from *The Religion of the Katipunan*, but my first source is that indispensable little book of my generation with its unmistakable green cover, *Roots of Dependency*, by Jonathan Fast and Jim Richardson (1979: 67). The source for De los Reyes' work in the labour movement is, among others, Resil Mojares' *Brains of the Nation* (2006: especially 278–279); but see also William Henry Scott's three essays on De los Reyes in *Cracks in the Parchment Curtain* (245–299 in the emended 1985 edition).

6. See the discussion in Chapters 1 to 3, above.

Epilogue

Every now and then it is said in the Philippines that national hero Jose Rizal influenced the course of the revolution in neighbouring Indonesia. A statement by former vice president Salvador Laurel, chairman of the Philippine Centennial Commission in the 1990s, may be taken as emblematic. Speaking at the Jakarta International Conference on the Centenary of the Philippine Revolution and the First Asian Republic in 1997, Laurel said: "Historians recount that Rizal's death and immortal poem, 'Mi Ultimo Adios,' translated into Bahasa Indonesia, inspired the Indonesian revolution."

It is a problematic statement, because certain terms demand an explanation. Which historians does Laurel mean? How does he define inspiration? It can be, strictly speaking, misleading. The Indonesian revolution, which began in 1945, did not depend on an acquaintance with Rizal or his poem. And yet it is truthful too. Journalist and occasional historian Rosihan Anwar argued the case as far back as 1961: Rizal's example and his exemplary poem were an inspiration for many in the revolutionary generation. The repeated experience of revolutionary pemuda claiming the translation as their own, in 1944 in Jakarta, in 1945 in Surabaya, in 1946 in Mojokerto, shows that, at least in Java, Indonesian nationalists at a moment of real peril had taken inspiration from a stirring poem that promised a useful, even glorious martyrdom.

It is in this last, nuanced sense that we can say that Rizal's influence in Southeast Asia outside the Philippines was real. It was both a part of the general background (in the exact same sense that Philippine "people power" was very much in the air in the late 1980s, seeping even through the cracks in the Iron Curtain), and specific to both time and place.

Rizal's impact was strongest in the Indonesian nationalist awakening. By the second decade of the twentieth century, a pioneer nationalist, the Eurasian E. F. E. Douwes Dekker, had embraced Rizal's work and example. It is a matter of debate whether Douwes Dekker's writings reached a broad public, but there is no doubt that, during a crisis in the emergence of Indonesian nationalism, he found Rizal congenial to his cause. He would eventually outgrow the notion of an independence movement led by mestizos like him, but it was Rizal who informed that transitional phase. The true leader of the Indonesian nationalist struggle assumed his role in the late 1920s; but there is no evidence (only mere assertion) that Sukarno already put Rizal to use in his speeches at the time. Sukarno would learn to appropriate the historical reputation of Rizal for his own nation-building purposes only from the beginning of the Japanese occupation. But Rosihan, in 1961 politically estranged from Sukarno, identified the Indonesian leader as a populariser of the Rizal name in Indonesia, and the evidence from Sukarno's speeches bear this out.

The impact on Malay nationalism is more vexing. A scholar like Ramlah Adam can assert (Ordoñez 1998) that "The influence of the Philippine revolution, Jose Rizal, and Philippine independence on Malay nationalism was very significant." But the available evidence seems scanty. True, there is a reference to Rizal as early as 1938, in a newspaper editorial written by Ibrahim Haji Yaacob; it is possibly the first mention of Rizal in a Malay-language publication. But perhaps it is only in the sense that Rizal was an inspiration for Indonesian nationalism, which in turn shaped Malay nationalist aspirations, that an argument for his influence can be claimed, and then only tangentially. Anwar Ibrahim's enthusiastic but belated discovery of Rizal has had a salutary effect on regional discourse, but it is difficult to escape the conclusion that his appropriation is not driven by nationalist objectives but by political concerns. It is in Rizal's impact on Malaysian intellectuals, however, where the true measure of his legacy was first plumbed in Southeast Asia. The work of Syed Hussein Alatas and the intellectual tradition he started, passing through Chandra Muzaffar and Shaharuddin bin Maaruf, now in the deft hands of Farish A. Noor and Syed Farid Alatas, among others, is a rich resource for both post-colonial studies and for regional polity-building.

The communist Tan Malaka had warm words for Rizal; his judgment of Rizal's lack of revolutionary sense was severe, but it was not harsh. The practised organiser, a sometime resident in American-era Manila, responded to the genuine admiration in which the politicising Philippine labour sector in the 1920s held the martyr of Bagumbayan. He did not attempt to appropriate Rizal for his own purposes, an act of generosity which allows the modern-day reader to compare their approaches to armed revolution, and to realize that Rizal was, in fact, animated by a genuine revolutionary spirit. He just thought the true revolution was the moral kind.

Unlike Tan Malaka, the great Indonesian novelist Pramoedya Ananta Toer did use the name of Rizal for his own purposes. In the second volume of the Buru Quartet, Rizal becomes the means through which the reader understands the depth of the colonial mindset that ruled the Dutch East Indies, and by which history's protagonist, Minke, politically comes of age. It is a richly satisfying device — that is to say, it works very well in the economy of the novels — but it has often been neglected or ignored outright in the scholarly or critical commentary. Pramoedya's use of Rizal is very specific to time and place, and yet, like the character of Rizal's influence on the Indonesian revolution, like the nature of inspiration itself, it is also and only as real as air.

Appendices

Appendix A

A Man of Letters

Rizal wrote several hundred letters, and received hundreds more. Many have since been lost, but perhaps the greater part has survived. They cannot all be found in one place, however.

The Jose Rizal National Centennial Commission tried to collate everything in 1961, but while its volumes of collected correspondence gathered most of the letters in the *Epistolario Rizalino*, the landmark volumes edited by Teodoro M. Kalaw in the 1930s, as well as the family letters compiled by the Lopez Museum in *One Hundred Letters* in 1959, errors and omissions marred the collection. A few more letters have since been discovered (see, for instance, Schumacher 1977). And there may be more new letters from the rediscovery (dating back to at least 1995) of the Blumentritt trove in Ceske Budejovice, in the Czech Republic.

But there is no one definitive edition of the correspondence. This is a great pity, because the letters, together, constitute a distinct body of work. They may almost be said to be Rizal's first novel.

The scholar Raul Bonoan SJ has written, persuasively, on Rizal's understanding of the novel form as influenced by a "peculiarly Spanish philosophical movement known as Krausism" (Bonoan 1996b: 223). In brief, Rizal understood the novel not merely as fiction but as "the conveyor of historical meaning" (224). The same thing can be said of his letter-writing.

The draft of a March 1887 letter in French, preserved in a notebook and written it seems likely to his older friend in Paris, the painter Felix Resurreccion Hidalgo, explains what he tried to do in the *Noli*, then just off the press. "I have told our compatriots our defects, our vices, our culpable and cowardly complacency with the miseries over there. Whenever I have found virtue I have proclaimed it and render homage to it; and I have not wept in speaking about our misfortunes, instead I have laughed, because no one would want to cry with me over the misery of our native land, and laughter is always good to conceal our sorrows. The incidents I relate are all true and they happened; I can give proofs of them" (Rizal 1963b: 84).

These lines come from a longer justification of the novelist's intent, but they can also serve as an explanation for Rizal's ambitions as letter-writer: the reporter's contract with reality (again and again we can hear him vouching for the truth of his news-by-correspondence), the proclamation of virtue whenever he found it (with Filipinos and foreigners alike he was not stingy with praise), the sorrow-concealing laughter he was so adept at provoking (in many of his letters we hear him strike the sardonic or the rueful note), not least the "telling off" that must be understood as self-criticism, of "our culpable and cowardly complacency."

The correspondence with his closest friend, the Austrian scholar Ferdinand Blumentritt, can be read as constituting a narrative in itself, a story within a story; the 211 surviving letters collected in the *Epistolario* form a substantial corpus — indeed, some of the most crucial insights into Rizal's life and character can be found in this decade-long correspondence — but they also trace a distinct narrative of their own.

The salutations they used, beginning with Rizal's first letter of 31 July 1886, sketch a quick outline of this narrative. "Esteemed Sir," the short letter, stiff with an elaborate formality, began. Unfortunately, the first letters from Blumentritt have been lost, although their contents are adverted to in Rizal's replies. The earliest of Blumentritt's letters to survive, dated 14 November 1886, greets Rizal most formally: "Very esteemed Sir." Within a month, however, the web of scholarly discussion having been strengthened by more and more filaments of a personal nature (mutual acquaintances, the exchange of photographs), Rizal was greeting Blumentritt more familiarly: "Esteemed Friend," his letter of 9 December 1886 began. This was the salutation the two letter-writers used for the next six months, until Rizal and his companion Maximo Viola visited Blumentritt and his family in Leitmeritz (present-day Litomerice, in the Czech Republic) in mid-May 1887. After that four-day visit, and for the next two and a half years, the letters became even more familiar, starting with just a simple "Dear Friend." It was around the time Rizal asked Blumentritt to write the prologue to his annotated version of Morga's history of the Philippines that the "intimate fraternity" reached its next level of intimacy. "My Dear Friend and Brother," a postcard of Blumentritt's, dated 10 November 1889 and addressed to Rizal in Paris, began. Rizal replied in kind. Within a couple of months, the two had shortened their salutation even further; now it was simply *"Mein Bruder"* (My Brother). This was the way they addressed each other for the next six years, until the eve of Rizal's execution. One of four letters he wrote in his prison cell on 29 December 1896, the day he received the death sentence, was for Blumentritt. "My dear brother," it began. "When you receive this letter I shall be dead by then."

If not a novel-in-all-but-name, or a series of stories-within-stories, then the letters may perhaps be understood as Rizal's own newspaper, published in instalments, and like a real one vulnerable to subscribers' moods or editorial limitations.

"As to news about myself," he writes his brother-in-law Manuel Hidalgo after a few months in Madrid (Rizal 1963a: 58), "I have little to give you, having already told them in my letter to our parents. Political news may be found in the *Diariong Tagalog* to which I sent a review." It was all of a piece. (He did relent, and related a tale about an Italian runner and Spanish bad manners.)

About two months later, he writes Hidalgo again with a variation on the theme (Rizal 1963a: 82). "The mine of my verbosity and news has been exhausted by the letters I have written to our parents and to my good sister Neneng. However, I believe I have something to your taste" — and proceeds to talk about international politics.

He could certainly fill up a page. For instance, a letter written from Berlin on 11 November 1886 and addressed to Hidalgo and his wife Saturnina (or Neneng, Rizal's eldest sister), begins with an improvement on the theme of exhaustion. "Although I have already told in my letters to our parents all the news I have, nevertheless this does not excuse me from writing to you," he begins. He then continues to write about Christmas customs and cultural traditions in Europe, contrasting those of Germany and of England (kissing under the mistletoe, for instance) with those of immature, indulgent Spain. He ends by saying: "This is how I have written you, filling four sheets of paper without saying anything, which shows that one can write even when one has no news to tell. Please write me" (Rizal 1963a: 246–247).

Most of his letters were not written for publication, but they were not exactly private. They were meant to be read in company, or to be copied, or to be passed from hand to hand. Sometimes he would say so himself. Writing to his friend and classmate Fernando Canon from on board the ship that was bringing him back to Asia (Rizal 1963b: 143), he said: "Tell our friends to consider this letter as addressed to them also. Tomorrow I buy paper at Port Said. Tell them [this] news of mine."

Such instructions litter the correspondence, but perhaps they were not even necessary. The habit of sharing each other's letters was ingrained, and in Rizal's case allowed even strangers to claim familiarity, or intimacy, with him.

On 21 November 1894, Rizal wrote Hidalgo about Governor-General Ramon Blanco's offer to transfer his place of exile to either Ilocos or La Union, and added somewhat optimistically, "I believe I shall leave this place in January" (Rizal 1963a: 388). A mere week later, Apolinario Mabini, who never met Rizal, whom Rizal did not know, was chatting up del Pilar in Madrid: "I have just read a letter of our Pepe [Rizal's diminutive] to his brother-in-law Hidalgo in which he writes that General Blanco … promised to transfer him, first to Iloilo [sic] or La Union and, later, to set him free. Pepe expects the transfer to be decreed this coming January" (Mabini 1999: 24).

It is no surprise then that when Spanish authorities raided the German-owned warehouse in Manila where Andres Bonifacio, the founder of the revolutionary organization Katipunan, was employed, in August 1896, they found several copies of letters to or from or about Rizal.

Rizal had the habit of writing several letters in one extended sitting, perhaps as a way of budgeting his time. "I have already written four very long letters and although I'm quite tired, I have the greatest pleasure and satisfaction of writing you and I feel that my pen is lighter and my ideas are freshened and quickened," he wrote his family on 29 January 1883.

On 30 December 1882, on the last weekend of his first year abroad, he sat down for an epic writing binge. He wrote at least 15 letters, of which at least four survive. To his younger sister Josefa (Pangoy to the family), he says, "Yesterday I received your letter together with that of Sra. [Señora] Maria. So that you may not say that I don't answer you, I'm now going to write you, although it seems I shall lack time. I have already finished fourteen letters and yours is the shortest, because I have run out of things to say" (Rizal 1963a: 71).

To his beloved brother Paciano, he talks about expenses in Madrid (double than in Barcelona, he says), invites his brother (as well as "the coming generation — the generation that will govern and lead Calamba by the beginning of the twentieth century") to travel to Europe, and adds a request that runs like a refrain through his correspondence: "Be informed of the contents of my other letters" (Rizal 1963a: 68).

And to Maria, slightly older but among his siblings the closest in age to him, he gives what would turn out to be fateful instructions (Rizal 1963a: 69). "I should like you to keep all my letters in Spanish beginning, *Mis queridos padres y hermanos*, because in them I relate all that have happened to me. When I get home, I shall collect them and clarify them." (Rizal himself kept many of the letters he received.

There is a celebrated and moving portrait of him, penned by Viola, carefully lugging the letters he had received from place to place.)

When Rizal made his request of Maria, he had written only three, perhaps four, such family letters. After the request, he wrote many more; at least 19 letters beginning "Dear Parents and Siblings" are extant. There are also eight letters addressed to the parents alone, but which were in all likelihood shared with the children and their relatives. All told, some 30 or so letters addressed to the entire family have survived, newsy digests of his travels abroad: his first passage through the Suez Canal, his love affair with the great city of Paris, his first impressions of London. Most of these omnibus letters, however, were written during his first European sojourn. After he took up residence in London in 1888, the "letters in Spanish beginning, *Mis queridos padres y hermanos*" became rare. In part this was because the volume of letters to individual members of the family had grown, and in part because he was no longer the eager tourist of the first voyage.

The last letter addressed to the entire family, using the same salutation he had flagged to Maria, was a short and earnest note written from his prison cell after he had been informed of his appointment with the firing squad (Rizal 1963a: 441). "My dear parents [and siblings]: I should like to see some of you before I die, though it may be very painful. Let the bravest come over. I have to say some important things."

APPENDIX B

Falling for the American Trap
Renato Constantino's "Veneration without Understanding" was the astounding Rizal Day Lecture of 1969. The courageous, cobweb-clearing exercise in provocation has since become the classic critique of Rizal and his pre-eminence in the Philippine pantheon of heroes.

What, exactly, did Constantino say? He said that Filipinos who hold Rizal up as the ideal hero do not understand that he was, in truth, a counter-revolutionary — and therefore insufficiently nationalistic. "Rizal repudiated the one act which really synthesized our nationalist aspiration, and yet we consider him a nationalist leader." That "one act" was the revolution of 1896.

"Veneration," however, is replete with false choices. Constantino's critique is based, not only on a Marxist reading of history and nationalism (for instance: "The exposure of his weaknesses and limitations will also mean our liberation, for he has, to a certain extent become part of the superstructure that supports present consciousness") but also, and tellingly, on a rhetoric of false dichotomies.

A Marxist reading of Rizal is not necessarily impossible; E. San Juan Jr. has written incisively on Rizal's writings from just such a perspective. For instance, in his post-2001 riposte to Constantino entitled "Understanding Rizal without Veneration," San Juan wrote: "As I have tried to argue in previous essays, Rizal displayed an astute dialectical materialist sensibility. One revealing example of concrete geopolitical analysis is the short piece on Madrid and its milieu excerpted in Palma's 'The Pride of the Malay Race' (pp. 60–62)." (Rizal's notes, originally written in French, in Heidelberg, show not only a sense of place but also some feel for demographic description and analysis.)

But an argument anchored on false choices is not only deceiving; it fosters a new misunderstanding. In 1969 (and again in 1979, when he published the lecture as one chapter in *Dissent and Counter-*

Consciousness), Constantino may have been moved by a genuine desire to offer a corrective to the prevailing hero worship of Rizal. But a corrective based on false logic can work only if it itself is based on false consciousness; in other words, if a reader or an auditor did not know any better.

Right at the start, "Veneration" offers a false choice between revolutionary leader and national hero. "In the histories of many nations, the national revolution represents a peak of achievement," Constantino writes. "It is not to be wondered at, therefore, that almost always the leader of that revolution becomes the principal hero of his people." He then offers mostly martial examples: Washington, Lenin, Bolivar, Sun Yat-sen, Mao, Ho Chi Minh. But if we take a closer look at his phrasing, we find that he has in fact qualified his sweeping statement: thus, "many nations," not all; "almost always," not always. If he admits exceptions, then his starting assumption that a country's "principal hero" is the leader that scaled the peak of that revolutionary achievement is not exceptional. In other words, if there are exceptions to this apparent rule, why take Rizal to task for being yet another exception?

It seems to me that the rhetorical objective of this first false choice is to imply that the Philippines, by choosing Rizal as its pre-eminent hero, is less of a nation. "In our case, our national hero was not the leader of our Revolution. In fact, he repudiated that Revolution."

Constantino's main proof for this repudiation is the famous Manifesto of 15 December 1896, which Rizal prepared as part of his legal defence. It is a controversial, still-disconcerting read, because as foremost Rizal biographer Leon Ma. Guerrero has noted, apropos of the Manifesto, "There can be no argument that he was against Bonifacio's Revolution." But again the nationalist historian offers us a false choice: Either Rizal was for the revolution, which broke out while Rizal was in Manila *en route* to Cuba; or his words "were treasonous in the light of the Filipinos' struggle against Spain."

But in fact there was a third alternative. The Judge Advocate General, Nicolas de la Peña, refused to publish the Manifesto, which would surely have been read by the revolutionaries, because Rizal "limits himself to condemning the present rebellious movement as premature and because he considers its success impossible at this time, but suggesting between the lines that the independence dreamed of can be achieved ... For Rizal it is a question of opportunity, not of principles or objectives. His manifesto can be condensed into these words: 'Faced with the proofs of defeat, lay down your arms, my countrymen; I shall lead you to the Promised Land on a later day' " (Guerrero 2007: 450–451).

This reading of Rizal's statement from the Spanish perspective, which Constantino did not acknowledge or advert to in his lecture, shows the fundamental flaw behind his historical approach. In using what he calls "historical forces unleashed by social development" to situate Rizal's "treason," he fails to reckon with the actual, life-or-death context in which Rizal wrote. Indeed, he fails to see Rizal the way the revolutionaries themselves, beginning with Andres Bonifacio, the founder of the Katipunan, saw him.

And how, exactly, did they see Rizal? Let one account, out of many, serve for the rest. Writing in April 1899, the revolutionary leader known as *Matatag* or Firm (his real name was Antonino Guevara) recalled a day at the Luneta in January 1898, when the people were celebrating the treaty, short-lived, as it turns out, of Biak-na-Bato. "At that time, while seated on one of the granite benches along the promenade at the Luneta, I pointed out the spot where our distinguished countryman, the hero and unfortunate Dr Jose Rizal, was executed by the firing squad. I told Pedro Guevara, Teodoro Arquiza, and others from the town of Magdalena, who were with me: 'There, my friends, is the place where our hero fell, irrigating that soil with his precious blood in defense of our beloved fatherland. May his life serve as a model for us. Let us pray for his eternal rest, and let us beseech God to give us many doctors such as Dr Jose Rizal whenever we find ourselves wanting, in order that we shall gain our coveted independence' " (Matatag 1988: 21–22).

Of the many false choices that are splayed throughout "Veneration without Understanding" like so much faulty electrical wiring, the most fraught, it seems to me, is Constantino's argument from Americanization. "Although Rizal was already a revered figure and became more so after his martyrdom, it cannot be denied that his pre-eminence among our heroes was partly the result of American sponsorship." And again: "History cannot deny his patriotism ... Still, we must accept the fact that his formal designation as our national hero, his elevation to his present eminence so far above all our other heroes was abetted and encouraged by the Americans." And yet again: "His choice was a master stroke by the Americans."

These passages imply that Rizal's pre-eminence is ultimately undeserved. His heroism is beyond question, but his place among our heroes is less secure because of American colonial intervention. To quote Constantino: "Rizal will still occupy a good position in our national pantheon even if we discard hagiolatry and subject him to a more mature historical evaluation."

But in his zeal to dissolve the Rizal mystique, Constantino fails to account for the views of the men and women who actually fought in the revolution. To that revolutionary generation, exemplified by Matatag but also reflected in the writings of Bonifacio and the official acts of Emilio Aguinaldo, Rizal's pre-eminence was undisputed. To minimize that honour, because the new colonial masters reinvented Rizal in their image, as the bearer of benevolence, is to accept the American view, that Rizal was a mere reformer.

There are other false choices in Constantino's lecture; perhaps the most consequential is the old reform-versus-revolution debate. Constantino quotes from a very early letter (I think it is the 15th in a correspondence that runs to 211 extant letters) that Rizal wrote to his great friend Ferdinand Blumentritt, in order to prove Rizal's mere "reformism."

"... under the present circumstances, we do not want separation from Spain. All that we ask is greater attention, better education, better government employees, one or two representatives and greater security for our persons and property. Spain could always win the appreciation of the Filipinos if she were only reasonable!"

Constantino, however, is guilty of a serious case of cut-and-paste. He left out the most telling passages. Here is the crucial paragraph from the letter dated 26 January 1887; the lines he removed are in boldface:

"**I agree with you concerning the independence of the Philippines. Only, such an event will never happen. A peaceful struggle shall always be a dream, for Spain will never learn the lesson of her former South American colonies. Spain cannot learn what England and the United States have learned. But,** under the present circumstances, we do not want separation from Spain. All that we ask is greater attention, better education, better government employees, one or two representatives and greater security for our persons and property. Spain could always win the appreciation of the Filipinos if she were only reasonable! **But,** *Quos vult perdere Jupiter, prius dementat!*" (Rizal 1963c: 44)

That Latin allusion, so characteristic of Rizal, is usually translated thus: Those whom Jupiter wishes to destroy, he first makes mad. In the context of Rizal's word and work, he obviously means Spain.

But Constantino did not only slight crucial passages; he slighted crucial letters. He does not show, for instance, that less than a month after Rizal wrote the Jupiter letter, he wrote to Blumentritt again, in these words: "The Filipinos had long wished for Hispanization and they were wrong in aspiring for it. It is Spain and not the Philippines who ought to wish for the assimilation of the country. Now we receive this lesson from the Spaniards [a rejection of a proposed reform] and we thank them for it" (Rizal 1963c: 51).

Five years after the Jupiter letter (to give another instance; we can easily multiply the examples), Rizal wrote to Blumentritt another explanation why he was bound to return to the Philippines: "Now I tell you: I have lost my hope in Spain. For that reason, I shall not write one more word for *La Solidaridad*. It seems to me it is in vain. All of us are *voces clamantis in deserto dum omnes rapiunt* [voices crying in the wilderness where all are lost]" (Rizal 1963b: 434).

Thus, Constantino's attempt to use Rizal's own letters to show a merely reformist rather than separatist or revolutionary outlook is fatally flawed: the letters, in their entirely, say otherwise. Rizal had realized at least as early as 1887 that the real battleground was back home. John Schumacher SJ dates the separatist tendency in the movement, and Rizal's leadership of it, to "after 1885, at least." In 1889, in a crucial letter to the staff of the *Soli*, Rizal responded to the news of more persecutions in the Philippines with a prophecy. "The day they lay their hands on us, the day they martyrize innocent families for our fault, goodbye, friar government, and perhaps, goodbye Spanish government!" (Rizal 1963b: 321). By 1892, Rizal was deep in plans to found a Filipino colony in northern Borneo, an idea fellow separatists like Antonio Luna welcomed as a political opportunity and a strategic advantage. And on 30 December 1896 Rizal walked calmly to his death, certain he was making his prophecy come true.

In using the reformer-versus-revolutionary box to classify Rizal, therefore, Constantino failed to reckon with another and truer alternative: radical.

A preliminary version of this essay first appeared in the Philippine Daily Inquirer in two parts, on 15 and 22 June 2010.

APPENDIX C

Colour and Scent, Light and Sound
In 1944, the 22-year-old journalist Rosihan Anwar was a frequent visitor to the Jakarta Museum. "My main interest at that time was not very specific. I just liked books, whatever I could lay my hands on at the time," he said in a lengthy interview (Rosihan 2010b). "[Because of] the situation, the Japanese occupation, there were no books [for sale] anymore."

So it was the library for him. One day, late in the year, he was browsing through a book on the Philippines — then very much in the news. "Surprisingly enough, as I read the book, I saw the poem [of Rizal's]. In Spanish. 'Adios Patria Adorada.' [the poem's famous opening line]. 'Mi Ultimo Pensamiento' or something [the poem's first title, meaning My Last Thoughts]. I don't understand Spanish .... [But] as I read further, I saw the translation [in English]."

He had found the most famous poem in Philippine history. It is pleasing to imagine the scene: a newspaper reporter and occasional poet, active in the pemuda or militant youth networks of the time, stopped in his tracks by a martyr's poem. He decided, then and there, to translate it into Indonesian.

"The situation was favourable to promote nationalism. In that context, I thought it would be good that I could disseminate this story about Jose Rizal among our younger people at that time. It was quite natural. I thought it would be good to tell the story of Jose Rizal, this rebel against the Spanish. And of course the climax, when he was already sentenced to death and then hauled off to face the firing squad, and he wrote that [poem] …"

Three sources of Rosihan's translation of "Mi Ultimo Adios" may be considered to carry some authority — the 30 December 1944 issue of *Asia Raya*, published in Jakarta, in which the translation first appeared; the paper "Rizal's Name in Indonesia," which Rosihan contributed to the International Congress on Rizal, in Manila, and from which he read excerpts on 7 December 1961; and the proceedings of the International Conference on the Philippine Revolution and the First Asian Republic, held in Jakarta in August 1997. Many of the conference papers were included in *Toward the First Asian Republic*, edited by Elmer A. Ordoñez and published by the Philippine Centennial Commission; the compilation included the Rosihan translation on pages xvi–xvii.

As may be expected, differences exist between the versions.

The translation in the 1997 volume is clearly based on the 1961 paper. Characteristics of the 1961 version are repeated in 1997: among them, one missing line, two added words, and four word substitutions. The line breaks in the 1997 version, as well as the choices in punctuation, also follow those of 1961. Even then, the 1997 translation carries two new if minor differences: a missing period (to punctuate the first stanza), and a newly spelled word (*masa* has become *massa*).

Some of the differences between Rosihan's two versions, however, between that of 1944 and that of 1961, cannot be classified as minor. The missing line in the 1961 poem is the third in the following sequence:

Sebab beta akan mendjadi:
oedara diatas djalanan
tanah didalam padangmoe

This is a rendering of the second line of Rizal's twelfth stanza, after he accepts the possibility of being forgotten by his own people — the fate of "oblivion," to appropriate the word used in the two most popular English translations, those of Charles Derbyshire (1911) and Nick Joaquin (1944). It doesn't matter if you forget me, he says,

Because I myself will become:
air above the street
the soil in your field

The same idea of an encompassing presence, in both earth and sky, is current in Rizal's second line. The missing words, in all likelihood an inadvertence, thus reduce the scope of Rizal's promise.

The 1961 version also makes two additions; these do not change the meaning of the poem, but all the same they subtract some nuance from the affected lines.

In the 1944 original, Rizal's coming to terms with the possibility of oblivion is phrased thus:

> *Apakah artinja lagi, Tanah Airkoe,*
> *djikalaupoen dikau loepakan akoe*

> What does it matter, my homeland,
> even if you forget me

In 1961, the translation becomes

> *Apatah artinja lagi tanah airku,*
> *djikalau pula dikau lupakan aku*

> So what does it matter, my homeland,
> if you also forget me

The second word addition adds everything — literally.

> *Selamat tinggal, sekali lagi:*
> *Koetinggalkan bagimoe segala*
> *handai-taulan, kasih sajangkoe*

> Goodbye, once again:
> I leave all to you,
> my friends, my love

becomes, in the 1961 version:

> *Selamat tinggal sekali lagi*
> *Kutinggalkan bagimu segala-galanja*
> *handai tolan, kasih sajang*

Goodbye, once again
I leave with you everything
friends, love

There are three more word substitutions. The act of prayer, from *Berdo'alah* to *Berdo'a*; the action of repeating, from *mengoelang* to *pengulang*; and degrees of causation, in the sense of reason, from *lantaran* to *karena*.

To the first-time reader, however, the 1961 version differs most from the 1944 translation in spelling; the first of the major changes to standardize Indonesian orthography, rendering *oe* as *u*, was already in effect when Rosihan took the floor of the Philamlife Auditorium on Isaac Peral street in Manila, on the afternoon of the fourth day of the Rizal centennial congress.

There is a fourth source for Rosihan's translation: In July 1946, *Bakti*, a nationalist magazine published by the youth of Mojokerto, in East Java, ran Rosihan's version, uncredited, in its issue marking Philippine independence. (The transfer of sovereignty from an over-extended, war-weary America to a devastated Philippines took place on 4 July 1946.) Except for one crucial change — *Daerah pilihan*, chosen region, had morphed into *Daerah Pilipina*, the Philippine region, in the second line — the Bakti version is an accurate copy of the *Asia Raya* original. No missing line, no additions or substitutions.

To the reader familiar with Rizal's farewell poem in the Spanish original or in the many English translations or in the lengthy Tagalog version (double the number of stanzas of the original) that is popularly attributed to the revolutionary leader Andres Bonifacio, it should be clear that the Anwar translation is not only a free verse rendition of a 14-stanza poem written to a strict meter, but an incomplete version. The reason, Anwar says, is it was based on an incomplete English translation.

But it has its merits. Its simplicity of language speaks directly to the heart, as well as to the time in which it was written. And it introduced Rizal to a wider Indonesian audience, at that exact point in Indonesian history when Rizal's articulate spirit of self-sacrifice, his readiness to die for his country, found a response in the Indonesian *pemuda*.

It is for these reasons that I propose that the 1944 translation be considered the definitive source. (It is available online, as it appears in the 30 December 1944 issue, through the wonderful Indonesian Newspaper Project of the Netherlands Institute for War Documentation. Many of the newspapers published during the Japanese occupation of what is now Indonesia, including most of the issues of *Asia Raya*, are included, accessible at <http://niod.x-cago.com/maleise_kranten/index.do>.

The 1944 translation used part of the first line of Rizal's originally untitled poem, rightly in my view, as the title. What follows is a faithful copy of that first translation in Bahasa Indonesia, down to the extended ellipses. The English translation that comes after is based primarily on consultation, on 21 May 2010, with Rosihan Anwar.

Adios, Patria Adorada ...
Selamat tinggal, Tanah koepoedja
Daerah pilihan, soerja Selatan......
Alangkah nikmatnja tidoer abadi
dalam pangkoean dikau, o Tanah merawan hati
Pabila ditengah roempoet hidjau melambai
jang menjelimoeti mesra perhentian beta,
Engkau melihat soeatoe masa
merekah-mekar boenga setangkai
alit-djelita tersipoe-sipoe
ketjoeplah dia dengan bibirmoe,
sebab itoelah soekmakoe......
Dan bila dimalam hari
seorang insan jang soenji
mohonkan restoe, semoga damailah tidoerkoe,

berdo'alah poela, Engkau, Toempah Darahkoe.
Do'akan mereka jang meninggal doenia
dengan doeka-nestapa tiada terperikan,
Do'akan mereka jang masih hidoep
merintih-derita dalam teroengkoe,
Do'akan agar ringanlah beban
perasaian Iboe serta djanda
anak jatim piatoe kita,
Do'akan djoega dirimoe sendiri
Engkau jang tengah menoedjoe Merdeka...
Djika koeboerankoe bertanda tiada
Tiada bersalib diloepakan soedah,
Biarlah petani meloekoe tanahnja
dan aboekoe achirnja berbaoer-satoe
dengan boekit serta lembahmoe.
Apakah artinja lagi, Tanah Airkoe,
djikalaupoen dikau loepakan akoe,
Sebab beta akan mendjadi:
oedara diatas djalanan
tanah didalam padangmoe,
mendjadilah beta
kata bergetar pada telingamoe
rona dan wangi, sinar dan boenji
njanjian tertjinta, mengoelang abadi
Amanatkoe......
Tanah Airkoe koedjoendjoeng tinggi
poentja dan alas djiwa larakoe
Goegoesan Filipina nan indah djoewita
Selamat tinggal, sekali lagi:
Koetinggalkan bagimoe segala
handai-taulan, kasih sajangkoe.
Akoe berangkat pergi ketempat,
dimana tiada boedak-belian

*haroes bertekoek toendoekkan kepala
dibawah tjerpoe kaoem penindas,
dimana insan tiada tiwas
lantaran menganoet Kejakinannja
dimana Toehanlah kekal bertachta......*

Goodbye, land I adore
Region chosen in the Southern sun......
How wonderful to sleep forever
In your bosom, O blessed land.
When in the waving green grass
that shrouds my grave
the time comes when you see
a sprig of flower bloom from a crack
smiling, blushing,
touch it with your lips
because that is my soul.
And when in the still evening
a lone man
asks for the blessing of peaceful sleep,
Pray for me, O my country.
Pray for those who left our world
with indescribable grief, sorrow,
Pray for those who are still alive
groaning in pain in prison,
Pray to lighten the load
of the suffering mother and widow
and the orphan,
Pray also for yourself
You who are headed Freedom's way...
If there is no longer a cross to mark my grave
and I have already been forgotten,
Let the farmers plough the land

so my ashes will merge in time
with the hills and valleys.
What does it matter, my homeland,
even if you forget me,
Because I myself will become:
air above the street
the soil in your field,
a pure note
vibrating in your ears
colour and scent, light and sound
a beloved song, endlessly repeating
My faith ......
My homeland I hold up high
the very basis of my being
The beautiful isles of the Philippines
Good-bye, once again:
I leave all to you,
my friends, my love.
I leave to go to that place,
where there are no slaves
who bow their head
under the oppressor's sole
where no one dies
because of what he believes
where God reigns eternal ......

References

Abidor, Mitchell. "Preface to 'Aguinaldo and the Philippines'." Jean Jaures Archive, available at <http://marxists.org> (accessed 2010).

Abinales, Patricio and Donna Amoroso. *State and Society in the Philippines.* Pasig City: Anvil, 2005.

Adams, Cindy. *Sukarno: An Autobiography, As Told to Cindy Adams.* The Bobbs-Merrill Company, 1965.

Agoncillo, Teodoro. *Malolos: The Crisis of the Republic.* Quezon City: University of the Philippines Press, 1997.

———. *The Revolt of the Masses: The Story of Bonifacio and the Katipunan.* Quezon City: University of the Philippines Press, 2002.

Aguinaldo, Emilio. *My Memoirs.* Vol. 1. Translated by Luz Colendrino-Bucu. Manila: Cristina Aguinaldo Suntay, 1967.

———. *Reseña Veridica de la Revolucion Filipina: True Version of the Philippine Revolution.* Manila: National Historical Institute, 2002.

Alatas, Syed Hussein. *Intellectuals in Developing Societies.* London: Frank Cass, 1977a.

———. *The Myth of the Lazy Native. A Study of the Image of the Malays, Filipinos and Javanese from the Sixteenth to the Twentieth Century and its Function in the Ideology of Colonial Capitalism.* London: Frank Cass, 1977b.

———. "The Development of an Autonomous Social Science Tradition in Asia: Problems and Prospects." *Asian Journal of Social Science* 30, no. 1 (2002).

Alatas, Syed Farid. "Ideology and Utopia In the Thought of Syed Shaykh Al-Hady." Singapore, 2005.

———. *Alternative Discourses in Asian Social Science: Responses to Eurocentrism.* New Delhi: Sage, 2006.

———. "Religion and Reform: Two Exemplars for Autonomous Sociology in the Non-Western Context." In Patel, Sujata. *The ISA Handbook of Diverse Sociological Traditions.* Singapore: Sage, 2010.

———. "Rizal and the Sociology of Colonial Society." Unpublished paper.

Alatas, Masturah. *The Life in the Writing: Syed Hussein Alatas: Author of The Myth of the Lazy Native.* Marshall Cavendish, 2010.

Alejandrino, Jose. *The Price of Freedom: Episodes and Anecdotes of our Struggles for Freedom.* Translated by Jose M. Alejandrino. Manila: Jose Alejandrino, 1949.

Alvarez, Santiago. *The Katipunan and the Revolution: Memoirs of a General, With the Original Tagalog Text.* Translated into English by Paula Carolina Malay. Quezon City: Ateneo de Manila University Press, 1992.

Anderson, Benedict. *Java in a Time of Revolution: Occupation and Resistance, 1944–1946.* Ithaca and London: Cornell University Press, 1972.

———. *Imagined Communities: Reflections on the Origin and Spread of Nationalism.* Pasig City: Anvil, 1991.

———. "The First Filipino." *London Review of Books* 19 (October 16): 20ff. Reprinted in Anderson, Benedict. 2004. *The Spectre of Comparisons: Nationalism, Southeast Asia, and the World.* Quezon City: Ateneo de Manila University Press, 1997.

———. "Bung Karno and the Fossilization of Soekarno's Thought." *Indonesia* 74, 2002.

———. *The Spectre of Comparisons: Nationalism, Southeast Asia, and the World.* Quezon City: Ateneo de Manila University Press, 2004.

———. *Under Three Flags: Anarchism and the Anti-Colonial Imagination.* Pasig City: Anvil, 2005.

———. *Language and Power: Exploring Political Cultures in Indonesia.* Jakarta: Equinox, 2006.

———. "A Talk on Pramoedya Ananta Toer" available at <http://www.bangkokpost.com/280408_Outlook/28Apr2008_out50.php> (accessed 2008).

An Eagle Flight: A Filipino Novel: Adapted from "Noli Me Tangere" by Dr Jose Rizal. New York: McClure, Phillips & Co. (Translator unknown), 1990.

Aspillera, Paraluman, ed. *Talambuhay ni Lope K. Santos.* Capitol Publishing, 1972.

Ataviado, Elias. *The Philippine Revolution in the Bicol Region. Vol. 1: From August 1896 to January 1899.* Translated by Juan Ataviado. Quezon City: New Day, 1999.

Bahari, Razif. "Remembering History, W/Righting History: Piecing the Past in Pramoedya Ananta Toer's Buru Tetralogy," *Indonesia* 75. Cornell Southeast Asia Programme, 2003.

Bantug, Asuncion Lopez. *Lolo Jose: An Intimate and Illustrated Portrait of Jose Rizal,* 2nd edition. Quezon City: Vibal Foundation and Intramuros Administration.

Barrows, David. *A History of the Philippines.* New York, Cincinnati, Chicago: American Book Company, 1905.

———. *A History of the Philippines.* New York: World Book Company, 1914.

———. *History of the Philippines*. New York: World Book Company, 1924.
Bonoan, Raul. *The Rizal-Pastells Correspondence: The Hitherto Unpublished Letters of Jose Rizal and Portions of Fr. Pablo Pastell's Fourth Letter and Translation of the Correspondence, together with a Historical Background and Theological Critique*. Quezon City: Ateneo de Manila University Press, 1994.
———. "Rizal's First Published Essay: El Amor Patrio." *Philippine Studies* 44, no. 3 (1996). Ateneo de Manila University.
———. "Rizal's Asia [sic] Enlightenment Philosophe in the Age of Colonialism." In Rajaretnam, M., ed., 1996. *Jose Rizal and the Asian Renaissance*. Kuala Lumpur: Institut Kajian Dasar, 1996b.
Bootsma, N. *Buren in de koloniale tijd: De Philippijnen onder Amerikaans bewind en de Nederlandse, Indische en Indonesische reacties daarop, 1898–1942*. Dordrecht: Foris, 1986.
———. "The discovery of Indonesia: Western (non-Dutch) historiography on the decolonization of Indonesia." Bijdragen tot de Taal-, Land- en Volkenkunde 151, no. 1. Available at <http://www.kitlv-journals.nl> (accessed 1995).
Borromeo-Buehler, Soledad. *The Cry of Balintawak: A Contrived Controversy: A Textual Analysis with Appended Documents*. Quezon City: Ateneo de Manila University Press, 1998.
Bosma, Ulbe and Remco Raben. *Being "Dutch" in the Indies: A History of Creolisation and Empire: 1500–1920*. Translated by Wendie Shaffer. Singapore: NUS Press, 2008.
Chong, Alan. "Asian Contributions on Democratic Dignity and Responsibility: Rizal, Sukarno and Lee on Guided Democracy," *East Asia* 25 no. 3 (2008).
Churchill, Bernardita Reyes, ed. *Resistance and Revolution: Philippine Archipelago in Arms*. Manila: National Commission for Culture and the Arts, 2002.
Coates, Austin. *Rizal: Philippine Nationalist and Martyr*. Hong Kong: Oxford University Press, 1968.
Craig, Austin. *Lineage, Life and Labours of Jose Rizal, Philippine Patriot: A Study of the Growth of Free Ideas in the Trans-Pacific American Territory*. Manila, 1913.
Cruz, Hermenegildo. *Kartilyang Makabayan: Mga Tanong at Sagot Ukol kay Andres Bonifacio at sa Kataastaasan, Kagalanggalang Katipunan ng mga Anak ng Bayan na Nagturo at Nagakay sa Bayang Pilipino sa Paghihimagsik Laban sa Kapangyarihang Dayo*. Manila: Lupong Tagaganap ng Araw ng Bonifacio, 1922.
Dahm, Bernhard. *Sukarno and the Struggle for Indonesian Independence*. Translated by Mary F. Somers Heidhues. Ithaca and London: Cornell University Press, 1969.

———. "Rizal and the European Influence." *Solidaridad* April 1991. An English translation of Dahm, Bernhard. 1988. *Jose Rizal: Der Nationalheld der Filipinos*. Zurich: Muster-Schmidt Verlag, 1991.

Daroy, Petronila and Dolores Feria. (eds), *Rizal: Contrary Essays*. Quezon City: Guro Books, 1968.

De Jesus, Alejandro. *Talambuhay ni Hermenegildo Cruz*. Manila: Bureau of Printing, 1955.

De la Costa, Horacio. *The Trial of Rizal: W. E. Retana's Transcription of the Official Spanish Documents*. Quezon City: Ateneo de Manila University Press, 1996.

De los Reyes, Isabelo. "The Religion of the Katipunan, or The Old Beliefs of the Filipinos." Translated by Joseph Martin Yap. In Alcantara, Teresita, ed., 2002. *Views on Philippine Revolution*, Vol. 1. Quezon City: Teresita Antonio Alcantara, 2002.

De los Santos, Epifanio. *The Revolutionists: Aguinaldo, Bonifacio, Jacinto*. Manila: National Historical Commission. Reprinted 1993 by the National Historical Institute, 1973.

Del Pilar, Marcelo. *Epistolario de Marcelo H. del Pilar*. Tomo 1. Manila: Imprenta del Gobierno, 1955.

———. *Epistolario de Marcelo H. del Pilar*. Tomo 2. Manila. Imprenta del Gobierno, 1958.

———. *A Collection of Letters of Marcelo H. del Pilar*. Vol. 1. Translated by Maria Luisa Garcia. Manila: National Historical Institute, 2006.

De Veyra, Jaime. *"El Ultimo Adios" de Rizal: Estudio Critico-Expositivo En Dos Partes*." Manila: Bureau of Printing, 1946.

De Viana, Augusto. *The I-Stories: The Philippine Revolution and the Filipino-American War as Told by its Eyewitnesses and Participants*. Manila: University of Santo Tomas Publishing House, 2006.

Dwi Noverini Djenar. "Sukarno's Fire: Metaphor in Political Oration." La Strobe Asian Studies Papers, 1994.

Douwes Dekker, Ernest Francois Eugene "Rizal." *Het Tijdschrift*. 15 May 1913.

Fast, Jonathan and Jim Richardson. *Roots of Dependency: Political and Economic Revolution in Nineteenth Century Philippines*. Quezon City: Foundation for Nationalist Studies, 1979.

Foreman, John. *The Philippine Islands: A Political, Geographical, Ethnographical, Social and Commercial History of the Philippine Archipelago Embracing the Whole Period of Spanish Rule with an Account of the Succeeding American Insular Government*. Third edition (1906). Reprinted Manila: Cacho Hermanos, 1985.

Foulcher, Keith. "*Bumi Manusia* and *Anak Semua Bangsa*: Pramoedya Ananta Toer Enters the 1980s." *Indonesia* 32. Cornell University, 1981.

Gannett, Frank Ernest. *Friars and Filipinos: An Abridged Translation of Dr Jose Rizal's Tagalog Novel, "Noli Me Tangere."* New York: The St. James Press, 1900.
Goenawan. *Sidelines: Thought Pieces from Tempo Magazine*, Goenawan Mohamad. Translated by Jennifer Lindsay. PT Equinox Publishing Indonesia, 2005.
Guerrero, Leon Ma. *The First Filipino*. Manila: Guerrero Publishing, 2007.
Hall, D. G. E. *A History of Southeast Asia*. Fourth edition. Palgrave MacMillan, 1981.
Idrus. "Surabaja." Idrus; translated by S. U. Nababan and Ben Anderson. *Indonesia* 5. Cornell Southeast Asia Programme, 1968.
Ileto, Reynaldo. *Pasyon and Revolution: Popular Movements in the Philippines, 1840–1910*. Quezon City: Ateneo de Manila University Press, 1979.
———. "The Revolution of 1896 and the Mythology of the Nation State." In Ordoñez, Elmer, 1998. *The Philippine Revolution and Beyond*, Vol. 1. Manila: Philippine Centennial Commission and National Commission for Culture and the Arts, 1997.
———. *Filipinos and their Revolution: Event, Discourse, and Historiography*. Quezon City: Ateneo de Manila University Press, 1998.
———. "Superfluous Men: Syed Hussein Alatas in the Company of Southeast Asian Scholars", 2007.
———. "On the Historiography of Southeast Asia and the Philippines: The 'Golden Age' of Southeast Asian Studies — Experiences and Reflections." Undated.
Ingleson, John. *The Road to Exile: The Indonesian Nationalist Movement 1927–1934*. Asian Studies Association of Australia, 1979.
Kahin, George McTurnan. *Nationalism and Revolution in Indonesia*. Ithaca, New York: Cornell University Press, 1952.
———. "Some Recollections from and Reflections on the Indonesian Revolution." In Taufik Abdullah, ed. *The Heartbeat of Indonesian Revolution*. Jakarta: PT Gramedia Pustaka Utama, 1997.
Kahin, Audrey. "The 1927 Communist Uprising in Sumatra: A Reappraisal. *Indonesia* 62. Cornell Southeast Asia Programme, 1996.
Kalaw, Teodoro. *Aide-de-Camp to Freedom*. Translated by Maria Kalaw Katigbak. Manila: Teodoro M. Kalaw Society, 1965.
———. *The Philippine Revolution*. Mandaluyong: Jorge B. Vargas Filipiniana Foundation, 1969.
Karl, Rebecca. *Staging the World: Chinese Nationalism at the Turn of the Twentieth Century*. Durham and London: Duke University Press, 2002.
Kerkvliet, Melinda Tria. *Manila Workers' Unions, 1900-1950*. Quezon City: New Day, 1992.

Kessler, Clive. "Wise Muslim Rationalist, Culturally Grounded Cosmopolitan". *Akademika* 73, 2008.
Kramer, Paul. "Empires, Exceptions, and Anglo-Saxons: Race and Rule between the British and U.S. Empires, 1880–1910". In Go, Julian and Anne Foster, eds. 2005. *The American Colonial State in the Philippines: Global Perspectives.* Manila: Anvil, 2005.
Kratoska, Paul and Ben Batson. "Nationalism and Modernist Reform". In Tarling, Nicholas. 1999. *The Cambridge History of Southeast Asia,* Vol. 3: From c. 1800 to the 1930s. Cambridge University Press, 1999.
Kingsbury, Damien. *The Politics of Indonesia.* Melbourne: Oxford University Press, 1998.
Lane, Max. *Unfinished Nation: Indonesia Before and After Suharto.* London, New York: Verso, 2008.
———. Interview on 3 June 2010. Singapore, 2010.
Lapian, Adrian. "Indonesian and Dutch Reactions to the Philippine Struggle for Independence." In Ordoñez, Elmer, ed., 1998. *Toward the First Asian Republic.* Manila: Philippine Centennial Commission, 1998.
Legge, J. D. *Indonesia.* New Jersey: Prentice-Hall, 1964.
Levesque, Rodrigue. "A Filipino Separatist—Jose Rizal. A translation of Retana, Wenceslao. "Un Separatista Filipino: Jose Rizal. *La Politica de España en Filipinas,* 30 September 1896. In Besa, Luzvisminda, ed. *Filipiniana Series in Ultramar* No. 2.
Lopez-Rizal. "R.D.L.M. and Jose Rizal", *Historical Bulletin,* Vol. IV, June 1960.
Lucas, Henri and Ramon Sempau. *Au Pays des Moines.* Paris: Ancienne Librairie Tresse & Stock, 1899.
Lumbera, Bienvenido. *Tagalog Poetry 1570–1898: Tradition and Influences in its Development.* Quezon City: Ateneo de Manila University Press, 1986.
Mabini, Apolinario. *The Letters of Apolinario Mabini.* Manila: National Heroes Commission, 1965.
———. *The Philippine Revolution.* In Majul, Cesar Adib. 1998. *Apolinario Mabini, Revolutionary: The Great Role He Played in the Malolos Congress, the Birth of the Philippine Republic and the Filipino-American War.* Manila: Trademark Publishing, 1998.
———. *The Philippine Revolution (With Other Documents of the Period).* Vol 2. Manila: National Historical Institute. Undated.
Macaraig, Serafin. *Social Problems.* Manila: The Educational Supply Co., 1929.
Majul, Cesar Adib. *Apolinario Mabini, Revolutionary: The Great Role He Played in the Malolos Congress, the Birth of the Philippine Republic and the Filipino-American War.* Manila: Trademark Publishing, 1998.

Marias, Julian. *Miguel de Unamuno*. Translated by Frances Lopez-Morillas. Cambridge: Harvard University Press, 1966.

Matatag [Antonino Guevara y Mendoza]. *History of One of the Initiators of the Filipino Revolution*. Translated by O. D. Corpuz. Manila: National Historical Institute, 1988.

McCoy, Alfred and Ed de Jesus. *Philippine Social History: Global Trade and Local Transformations*. Quezon City: Ateneo de Manila University Press, 1982.

McInerney, Andy. "Tan Malaka and Indonesia's Freedom Struggle." Available at <http://PSLweb.org> (published on 1 January 2007).

Medina, Isagani. *Ang Kabite sa Gunita: Essays on Cavite and the Philippine Revolution*. Quezon City: University of the Philippines Press, 2001.

Medina, Elizabeth. *Rizal According to Retana: Portrait of a Hero and a Revolution: An Annotated Selective Translation*. Santiago; Manila, 2001.

Mendez, Paz Policarpio. *Adventures in Rizaliana*. Manila: National Historical Institute, 1978.

Mojares, Resil. *Brains of the Nation: Pedro Paterno, T.H. Pardo de Tavera, Isabelo de los Reyes and the Production of Modern Knowledge*. Quezon City: Ateneo de Manila University Press, 2006.

———. "Early 'Asianism' in the Philippines." *IDEYA: Journal of the Humanities* 11, no. 1 (2009). De La Salle University.

Mrazek, Rudolf. "Just as Artisans, When Gathered Together." *Indonesia* 53. Cornell Southeast Asia Programme, 1992.

Multatuli [Eduard Douwes Dekker]. *Max Havelaar, Or the Coffee Auctions of A Dutch Trading Company*. Translated with Notes by Roy Edwards. Penguin Books, 1987.

Muijzenberg, Otto van den. "The Philippine Revolution in the Netherlands and the Indies Press, 1896/97: A Study in 'Localization'." In Ordoñez, Elmer. 1998. *The Philippine Revolution and Beyond*, Vol. 1. Manila: Philippine Centennial Commission and National Commission for Culture and the Arts, 1998.

Muzaffar, Chandra. "The Relevance of Rizal to Contemporary Southeast Asia." In Rajaretnam, M. ed., 1996. *Jose Rizal and the Asian Renaissance*. Kuala Lumpur: Institut Kajian Dasar, 1996.

Noor, Farish. "In Memoriam: Professor Syed Hussein Alatas, Myth-breaker." Available at <http://Ummaonline.com> (published on 27 January 2007).

———. *What Your Teacher Didn't Tell You: The Annexe Lectures Vol. 1*. Petaling Jaya: Matahari Books, 2009.

Ocampo, Nilo. *May Gawa na Kaming Natapus Dini: Si Rizal at and Wikang Tagalog*. Quezon City: University of the Philippines, 2002.

Ordoñez, Elmer. *The Philippine Revolution and Beyond*, Vol. 1. Manila: Philippine

Centennial Commission and National Commission for Culture and the Arts, 1998.
Ordoñez, Elmer, ed. *Toward the First Asian Republic*. Manila: Philippine Centennial Commission, 1998.
Ortega y Gasset, Jose. *The Origin of Philosophy*. Translated by TobyTalbot. New York, London: W. W. Norton & Company, 1967.
Owen, Norman, ed. *The Emergence of Modern Southeast Asia: A New History*. Honolulu: University of Hawai'i Press, 2005.
Paget, Roger. *Indonesia Accuses! Soekarno's Defence Oration in the Political Trial of 1930*. Kuala Lumpur: Oxford University Press, 1975.
Pardo de Tavera, Trinidad H. "The Character of Rizal." *The Philippine Review (Revista Filipina)*. June 1917. Published originally as "El Caracter de Rizal." *The Philippine Review (Revista Filipina)*. May 1917.
Paular, Regino. *Dr Jose Rizal's Mi Ultimo Adios in Foreign and Local Translations*. Vol. 1. Manila: National Historical Institute, 1989.
———. *Dr Jose Rizal's Mi Ultimo Adios in Foreign and Local Translations*. Vol. 2. Manila: National Historical Institute, 1990.
Phelan, John Leddy. *The Hispanization of the Philippines: Spanish Aims and Filipino Responses 1565–1700*. Madison: University of Wisconsin Press, 1959.
Pramoedya Ananta Toer. *Child of All Nations*. Translated by Max Lane. Penguin Books. (Original published as *Anak Semua Bangsa*, 1980. Jakarta: Hasta Mitra.), 1991.
———. *House of Glass*. Translated by Max Lane. Penguin Books. (Original published as *Rumah Kaca*. 1988. Jakarta: Hasta Mitra.), 1992.
———. "Literature, Censorship and the State: To What Extent is a Novel Dangerous?" (1995 Ramon Magsaysay Award acceptance speech). Translated by Alex Bardsley. Available at <http://sites.google.com/site/pramoedyasite/>, 1995.
———. "The Book that Killed Colonialism." *New York Times Magazine*. 18 April 1999.
———. "A Chat with Pramoedya Ananta Toer." *Michigan Today*. Summer 1999. University of Michigan, 1999b.
Pritchett, V. S. *The Living Novel and Later Appreciations*. New York: Vintage Books, 1964.
Quibuyen, Floro. *A Nation Aborted: Rizal, American Hegemony, and Philippine Nationalism*. Quezon City: Ateneo de Manila University Press, 2008.
Quirino, Carlos. *The Great Malayan*. Manila: Tahanan Books, 1997.
Rajaretnam, M., ed. *Jose Rizal and the Asian Renaissance*. Kuala Lumpur: Institut Kajian Dasar, 1996.
Reid, Anthony. *The Indonesian National Revolution*. Melbourne: Longman, 1974.

———. "Understanding Melayu (Malay) as a Source of Diverse Modern Identities." *Journal of Southeast Asian Studies* 32 (October 2001): 295-313.
———. *Imperial Alchemy: Nationalism and Political Identity in Southeast Asia.* Cambridge University Press, 2010.
Retana, Wenceslao. *Vida y Escritos del Dr Jose Rizal.* Madrid: Libreria General de Victoriano Suarez, 1907.
Ricarte, Artemio. *Himagsikan Nang Manga Pilipino Laban sa Kastila: Salaysay na Sinulat ni Artemio Ricrate [sic] Vivora.* Yokohama: Karihan Cafe, 1927.
———. *Memoirs of General Artemio Ricarte.* Translated by Armando Malay. Manila: National Historical Institute, 1992.
Richardson, Jim. "Notes on the Katipunan in Manila, 1892–1896." In *Katipunan: Documents and Studies*, available at <http://kasaysayan-kkk.info>. 2007.
Rizal, Jose. *Epistolario Rizalino*, Tomo Primero: 1877–1887. Edited by Teodoro M. Kalaw. Manila: Bureau of Printing, 1930.
———. *Epistolario Rizalino*, Tomo Segundo: 1887–1890. Edited by Teodoro M. Kalaw. Manila: Bureau of Printing, 1931.
———. *Epistolario Rizalino*, Tomo Tercero: 1890–1892. Edited by Teodoro M. Kalaw. Manila: Bureau of Printing, 1933.
———. *Epistolario Rizalino*, Tomo Cuarto: 1892–1896. Edited by Teodoro M. Kalaw. Manila: Bureau of Printing, 1936.
———. *Epistolario Rizalino*, Tomo Quinto, Primera Parte: 1886–1888. Edited by Teodoro M. Kalaw. Manila: Bureau of Printing, 1938a.
———. *Epistolario Rizalino*, Tomo Quinto, Segunda Parte: 1888–1896. Edited by Teodoro M. Kalaw. Manila: Bureau of Printing, 1938b.
———. *Documentos Rizalinos.* Manila: Bureau of Public Libraries, 1953.
———. A translation of the diary published in *Unitas*, October–December 1953, available at <http://joserizal.info>. 1953a.
———. *Noli Me Tangere.* Manila: Comision Nacional del Centenario de Jose Rizal. Reprinted 1995 by the National Historical Institute, 1961a.
———. *El Filibusterismo.* Manila: Comision Nacional del Centenario de Jose Rizal. Reprinted 1996 by the National Historical Institute, 1961b.
———. *Letters Between Rizal and Family Members.* Translated by Encarnacion Alzona. Manila: National Heroes Commission. Reprinted 1993 by the National Historical Institute, 1963a.
———. *Rizal's Correspondence with Fellow Reformists.* Translated by Encarnacion Alzona. Manila: National Heroes Commission. Reprinted 1992 by the National Historical Institute, 1963b.
———. *The Rizal-Blumentritt Correspondence*, Vol. 1: 1886–1889. Translated by Encarnacion Alzona. Manila: Jose Rizal National Centennial Commission. Reprinted 1992 by the National Historical Institute, 1963c.

———. *The Rizal-Blumentritt Correspondence*, Vol. 2: 1890–1896. Translated by Encarnacion Alzona. Manila: Jose Rizal National Centennial Commission. Reprinted 1992 by the National Historical Institute, 1963d.

———. *Miscellaneous Correspondence of Dr Jose Rizal*. Translated by Encarnacion Alzona. Manila: National Heroes Commission. Reprinted 1992 by the National Historical Institute, 1963e.

———. *Sucesos de las Islas Filipinas por el Doctor Antonio de Morga*. Offset impression of the 1890 edition. Manila: National Historical Institute, 1991.

———. *Political and Historical Writings*. Manila: National Historical Institute, 2007.

Rodriguez, Jose. "CAIÑGAT CAYO! Sa mañga masasamang libro,t, casulatan." Project Gutenberg, 1888.

Rosihan Anwar. "Rizal's Name in Indonesia." In *Proceedings of the International Congress on Rizal, 4–8 December 1961*. Manila: Jose Rizal National Centennial Commission, 1961.

———. "Reminiscences of the Indonesian Press During the Revolution 1945–1949." In Taufik Abdullah, ed., 1997. *The Heartbeat of Indonesian Revolution*. Jakarta: PT Gramedia Pustaka Utama, 1997.

———. *Sutan Sjahrir: Demokrat Sejati, Pejuang Kemanusiaan/True Democrat, Fighter for Humanity, 1909–1966*. KITLV Press, 2010a.

———. Interview on 21 May 2010. Jakarta.

———. Interview on 16 July 2010. Jakarta.

Rush, James. "Biography of Pramoedya Ananta Toer." Ramon Magsaysay Awards Foundation, available at <http://www.rmaf.org.ph/Awardees/Biography/BiographyPramoedyaAna.htm>. 1995.

Russell, Charles Edward and E. B. Rodriguez. *The Hero of the Filipinos: The Story of Jose Rizal, Poet, Patriot and Martyr*. New York and London: The Century Co., 1923.

Sabam Siagian. "An Indonesian Appreciation of Rizal," in Rajaretnam, M. 1996. *Jose Rizal and the Asian Renaissance*. Kuala Lumpur: Institut Kajian Dasar, 1996.

Salazar, Zeus. *The Malayan Connection: Ang Pilipinas sa Dunia Melayu*. Quezon City: Palimbagan ng Lahi, 1998.

Saniel, Josefa. *Japan and the Philippines 1868–1898*. Quezon City: University of the Philippines, 1963.

———. "Rizal and Suehiro Tetcho." In Daroy, Petronila and Dolores Feria, eds., 1968. *Rizal: Contrary Essays*. Quezon City: Guro Books, 1968.

Saulo, Alfredo. *Communism in the Philippines: An Introduction*, enlarged edition. Quezon City: Ateneo de Manila University Press, 1990.

Schmidt-Nowara, Christopher. *The Conquest of History: Spanish Colonialism and National Histories in the Nineteenth Century.* Pittsburgh: University of Pittsburgh Press, 2006.

Schumacher, John. "Rizal and Blumentritt." *Philippine Studies* 2, no. 2 (1954).

———. "Some Notes on Rizal in Dapitan." *Philippine Studies* 11, no. 2 (1963).

———. "On the Greatness of Rizal: The First Filipino." [A review of Leon Ma. Guerrero's *The First Filipino.*] *Philippine Studies* 12, no. 3 (1964).

———. "The Religious Thought of Rizal." *Philippine Studies* 13, no. 3 (1965).

———. "Due Process and the Rule of Law: Three Unpublished Letters of Rizal." *Philippine Studies* 25, no. 2 (1977).

———. *Revolutionary Clergy: The Filipino Clergy and the Nationalist Movement, 1850–1903.* Quezon City: Ateneo de Manila University Press, 1981.

———. *The Making of a Nation: Essays on Nineteenth-Century Filipino Nationalism.* Quezon City: Ateneo de Manila University Press, 1991.

———. *The Propaganda Movement: 1880-1895: The Creation of a Filipino Consciousness, The Making of the Revolution.* Quezon City: Ateneo de Manila University Press, 1997.

Scott, William Henry. *Cracks in the Parchment Curtain, and Other Essays in Philippine History,* amended edition. Quezon City: New Day, 1985.

Shaharuddin b. Maaruf. *Concept of a Hero in Malay Society.* Singapore: Eastern Universities Press, 1984.

———. Personal communication. 18 May 2010.

Shiraishi, Takashi. *An Age in Motion: Popular Radicalism in Java, 1912–1926.* Ithaca and London: Cornell University Press, 1990.

Sibal, J. V. "A Century of the Philippine Labor Movement." *Illawarra Unity* 4, no. 1 (2004).

Sison, Jose Ma. "Impact of the Communist International on the Founding and Development of the Communist Party of the Philippines." Contribution to the 15th International Communist Seminar "Present and Past Experiences in the International Communist Movement", <http://archivesolidaire.org>. 2006.

Sjahrir, Soetan. *Out of Exile.* Translated by Charles Wolf, Jr. New York: The John Day Company, 1949.

Sukarno. *Toward Freedom and the Dignity of Man.* Djakarta: Department of Foreign Affairs, Republic of Indonesia, 1961.

———. "Only a Nation with Self-Reliance can Become a Great Nation." Speech by H. E. President Sukarno at a Commemoration of National Reawakening Day, 20 May 1962, at Negara Palace, Djakarta. Department of Information, Republic of Indonesia, 1962.

———. *Dibawah Bendera Revolusi,* Vol. 1. Panitya Penerbit, 1963.

Sulistomo, Bambang. Personal communication, 2010.

Tan Malaka. *From Jail to Jail*, Vol. 1. Translated by Helen Jarvis. Ohio University Press, 1991.

Taufik Abdullah, ed. *The Heartbeat of Indonesian Revolution*. Jakarta: PT Gramedia Pustaka Utama. 1997.

Teeuw, A. "The ideology of nationalism in Pramoedya Ananta Toer's fiction," *Indonesia and the Malay World* 25, no. 73 (1997).

Tjetje Jusuf. *Noli Me Tangere (Jangan Sentuh Aku)*, translated by Tjetje Jusuf. Pustaka Jaya: Jakarta, 1975.

Turot, Henri. *Les Hommes de Revolution: Aguinaldo et les Philippins*. Paris: Librairie Leopold Cerf, 1900.

Unamuno, Miguel de. "Rizal." Epilogo. In Retana, Wenceslao. 1907. *Vida y Escritos del Dr Jose Rizal*. Madrid: Libreria General de Victoriano Suarez, 1907.

———. *Tragic Sense of Life*. Translated by J. E. Crawford Flitch. Introduction by Salvador de Madariaga. New York: Dover, 1921.

———. "Rizal: The Tagalog Hamlet." Antolina Antonio's translation of the first three parts of Unamuno's Epilogue. In Daroy, Petronila and Dolores Feria, eds. 1968. *Rizal: Contrary Essays*. Quezon City: Guro Books, 1968.

———. *The Private World: Selections from the Diario Intimo and Selected Letters 1890–1936*. Translated by Anthony Kerrigan, Allen Lacy, and Martin Nozick; annotated by Martin Nozick with Allen Lacy, with an introduction by Allen Lacy. Princeton University Press, 1984.

Valdez, Maria Stella Sibal. *Dr Jose Rizal and the Writing of His Story*. Quezon City: Rex Book Store, 2007.

Van der Veur, Paul. "E.F.E. Douwes Dekker: Evangelist for Indonesian Political Nationalism." *Journal of Asian Studies*, 1958.

———. *The Lion and the Gadfly: Dutch Colonialism and the Spirit of E.F.E. Douwes Dekker*. Leiden: KITLV Press, 2006.

Van Nieuwenhuijze, C.A.O. "Taking Stock in Indonesia." *Pacific Affairs* 25, no. 1 (1952).

———. "Broadening Indonesian Horizons." *Pacific Affairs* 25, no. 4 (1952).

Vatikiotis, Michael. 2006. *Asia Times*. 3 May 2006.

Ventura Castro, Jovita. *Anthology of Asean Literatures: Noli Me Tangere by Jose Rizal*. Manila: Nalandangan, Inc., 1989.

———. *Anthology of Asean Literatures: The Revolution by Jose Rizal*. (A translation of *El Filibusterismo*.) Manila: Nalandangan, Inc., 1992.

Villa, Simeon. *The Flight and Wanderings of General Emilio Aguinaldo from Bayambang to Palanan 1899–1901; a diary*. Translated by J. C. Hixson. Manila: Philippine Historical Association, 1969.

Wehl, David. *The Birth of Indonesia*. London: George Allen & Unwin, 1948.

Wezak, Justin. "Soekarno: His Mannerism and Method of Communication." Jurusan Sasta Inggris, Fakultas Sastra, Universitas Kristen Petra, 2000.
Wildman, Edwin. *Aguinaldo: A Narrative of Filipino Ambitions*. Boston: Lothrop Publishing, 1901.
Zaide, Gregorio and Zaide, Sonia. *Jose Rizal: Life, Works and Writings of a Genius, Writer, Scientist and National Hero*, second edition. Quezon City: All Nations Publishing, 2008.

Periodicals

Ang Manggagawa. Various issues. Accessed through the University of Michigan: The United States and its Territories 1870–1925: The Age of Imperialism, at <http://quod.lib.umich.edu/p/philamer/>.
Asia Raya. Various issues. Perpustakaan Nasional Republik Indonesia. Also accessed through the Nederlands Instituut voor Oorlogsdocumentatie: Indonesian Newspaper Project, at <http://niod.x-cago.com/maleise_kranten/index.do>.
Asia Times, 3 May 2006.
Bakti. Various Issues. Perpustakaan Nasional Republik Indonesia.
Blackwood's Magazine, November 1902 (620–638). ("The Story of Jose Rizal the Filipino: A Fragment of Recent Asiatic History." By Hugh Clifford.) Available at <http://archive.org>.
Boston Evening Transcript. "A Filipino Tolstoi: The Patriotic Novelist and Poet, Rizal." Accessed through the Google News Archive, 25 March 1899.
British Medical Journal (829). ("St. Joseph Rizal, M.D."), 6 April 1907.
China Mail. Accessed through Hong Kong Public Libraries, available at <http://hkpl.gov.hk>, 6 January 1897.
El Imparcial. Accessed through Biblioteca Nacional de España, available at <http://www.bne.es/es/Catalogos/HemerotecaDigital/>, 26 June 1884; 19 January 1897.
Het Nieuws van den Dag. Various issues. Accessed through the Royal Library of the Netherlands, available at <http://kranten.kb.nl/>.
Het Tijdschrift. Various Issues. Perpustakaan Nasional Republik Indonesia.
Hong Kong Telegraph. Accessed through Hong Kong Public Libraries, avilable at <http://hkpl.gov.hk>.
La Ilustracion: Revista Hispano-Americana. Barcelona. Accessed through Biblioteca Nacional de España, available at <http://www.bne.es/es/Catalogos/HemerotecaDigital/>, 28 February 1886.
La Ilustracion Española y Americana. Madrid. Accessed through Biblioteca Nacional de España, available at <http://www.bne.es/es/Catalogos/HemerotecaDigital/>, 15 February 1897.

La Solidaridad. Vol 2. Translated by Guadalupe Fores-Ganzon. Pasig City: Fundacion Santiago, 1890.

Nieuwe Tilsburgsche Courant. Accessed through the Royal Library of the Netherlands, available at <http://kranten.kb.nl/>.

Popular Science Monthly (222–229). ("Views of Dr Rizal, the Filipino Scholar, upon Race Differences." Translated by R. L. Packard.), July 1902

Singapore Free Press and Mercantile Advertiser. Accessed through NewspaperSG, available at <http://newspapers.nl.sg/>, 31 December 1896.

Straits Telegraph and Daily Advertiser. Accessed through NewspaperSG, available at <http://newspapers.nl.sg/>, 11 and 12 April 1899.

The Filipino magazine. Accessed through the University of Michigan: The United States and its Territories 1870–1925: The Age of Imperialism, available at <http://quod.lib.umich.edu/p/philamer/>, March 1906.

The Philippine Republic. Accessed through the University of Michigan: The United States and its Territories 1870–1925: The Age of Imperialism, available at <http://quod.lib.umich.edu/p/philamer/>, July 1925.

The Philippine Review (Revista Filipina). Accessed through the University of Michigan: The United States and its Territories 1870–1925: The Age of Imperialism, available at <http://quod.lib.umich.edu/p/philamer/>. 1917.

The Straits Times, issues of 12 December 1981; 12 October 1985; 11 April 1988. Accessed through NewspaperSG, available at <http://newspapers.nl.sg/>.

Tilburgsche Courant. Accessed through the Royal Library of the Netherlands, available at <http://kranten.kb.nl/>, 18 August 1898.

Index

A

Abella, Enrique, 78
Abidor, Mitchell, 11–12
Adams, Cindy, 179–80
Adriano, Numeriano, 11
Agoncillo, Teodoro, 6, 20, 30, 43, 67, 93–94, 96, 101–02, 128, 141, 228
Aguinaldo: A Narrative of Filipino Ambitions, 113
Aguinaldo, Emilio, 11, 38–39, 80, 91–92, 94–95, 98–100, 110, 113, 120–21, 129, 131, 137, 164, 172, 183–87, 216, 246
Aguilera, Gregorio, 57–58
Aguirre, Evaristo, 15, 46–47
"A la Juventud Filipina", 32
Alejandrino, Jose, 50, 83
ALIRAN (Nationalist Consciousness Movement), 44, 203–04
Almayer's Folly, 1
Alvarez, Santiago, 41, 94–95, 97–102, 128
Alzona, Encarnacion, 197
Amal Hamzah, 43
American imperialism, 131
Amir Sharifuddin, 158
Andersen, Hans Christian, 47, 60
Anderson, Benedict, 1–2, 5, 18–20, 44, 106
Andriesse, George Albertus, 114

Angkatan 45 (1945 generation of writers), 157
Ang Manggagawa (The Worker), 139
Anthropology of Primitive Peoples, 47
Anti-Imperialist League, 225
Antonio, Antolina, 23
Anwar Ibrahim, 45, 232
Arellano, Deodato, 11
Arek Suroboyo (youth of Surabaya), 157
Asociacion Hispano-Filipina, 9–10
Association Internationale des Philippinistes, 106–07
Asia Magazine, 29
Asia Raya, 41–42, 143–45, 151–54, 156, 159, 166–70, 178, 180, 249, 252
Asia Times, 220
Asia Timoer Raja (Greater East Asia), 144
Asrama Indonesia Merdeka (Free Indonesia Asrama), 152
Astray, Jose Millan, 30
Ataviado, Elias, 93

B

Bakti, magazine, 42, 161–63, 165, 167–70, 252
Balagtas, Masonic lodge, 7
Bambang Sulistomo, 160

Bantug, Asuncion Lopez, 6, 13, 16–17
Bardsley, Alex G., 221
Barrows, David P., 6, 18–19, 29
Basa, Jose Ma., 50–51, 53, 57
Bataviaasch Nieuwsblad, 109, 115
Batson, Ben, 214
Battle of Surabaya, 42, 171
bebalisma, 195, 210
Belgic, ship, 34
Benitez, Conrado, 19
Biak-na-bato, treaty of, 92
Bilibid, prison, 15
Blanco, Ramon, 37, 49, 240
Blumenbach, Johann, 55
Blumentritt, Ferdinand, 2, 5, 13, 33–35, 47–51, 53, 55, 60, 105–08, 110, 120, 237–39, 246–47
Boer War, 115
Bonifacio, Andres, 36, 40, 43, 64, 73, 80, 84, 88, 95–98, 100, 122–33, 135–36, 140–41, 216, 241, 244, 246, 252
Bonifacio Day, 138
Bonoan SJ, Raul, 237
Boston Evening Transcript, 113
Bracken, Josephine, 37, 99–100, 108, 112–13
Brains of the Nation, 30, 67, 230
British Museum, 35
Budi Utomo, 115, 118, 134, 172, 188, 213
Bung Tomo, 157, 159–60
Burgos, Jose, 32, 53, 177, 201
Buru Quartet, 104, 109, 120, 159, 214–15, 218–21, 225–26, 233

C
Calderon, Felipe, 121
Cambridge History of Southeast Asia, 214

Canon, Fernando, 240
Castilla, cruiser, 37, 49, 87–89, 97
Castro, Jovita Ventura, 60
Cavite Mutiny, 32, 50
Chanco, Father Jose, 64
Chandra Muzaffar, 44, 202–05, 209, 233
"Character of Rizal, The", 22
China, nationalist movement, 213–14
Chinese Reform Movement, 217
Coates, Austin, 17, 52, 67–68
Colon, 87
colonial capitalism, 195, 210
Cold War, 165, 188
Columnas Volantes de la Federacion Malaya, 57
Comite de Propaganda, 11, 50
Communist International, 40
Communist Party of the Philippines, 138
communist uprising, 41
Concept of a Hero in Malay Society, 28, 44, 203, 205, 211
review of, 206
Congreso Obrero de Filipinas (Workers' Congress), 134, 138
Constantino, Renato, 43, 93, 243–48
Cooper, Henry, 148, 154, 225
Cordero, Francisco, 84
Cortezo, Daniel, 15
Council of War, 98
Cracks in the Parchment Curtain, 230
Craig, Austin, 6, 20, 52–53
Crayonpedia, 213–14
Cruz, Hermenegildo, 40, 122–27, 133–34, 141
Cry of Balintawak, 101
cultural conditioning, 198

INDEX 273

D
Dahm, Bernhard, 149, 151, 159, 170
Danu Dirdjo Setiabuddhi, 119
Dari Pendjara ke Pendjara, 129, 224
Daroy, Petronilo Bn., 23
de Alcocer, Enrique, 78
de Andrade, Luis Taviel, 6, 78–79, 88
De Express, 40, 117–18
Dekker, E.F.E. Douwes, 40, 104, 111–19, 130, 219, 223, 232
de la Costa SJ, Horacio, 5–6
de la Croix, Miriam, 104
de la Pena, Nicolas, 81–82, 96, 245
de Leon, Ceferino, 46
de los Reyes, Isabelo, 24, 67, 90, 127, 141, 224, 230
del Pilar, Marcelo, 2–4, 7–11, 33, 35, 48, 50, 52, 56, 58, 61–64, 66, 68, 70, 91, 240
del Rosario, Aguedo, 84
Del Sentimiento Tragico de la Vida en los Hombres y en los Pueblos, 21
de Madariaga, Salvador, 30
de Morga, Antonio, 2, 6, 9, 33, 35, 48, 52, 77, 239
de Ora, Antonino, 138
Derbyshire, Charles, 44, 250
de Mas, Sinibaldo, 201
de Rivera, Primo, 27
de San Agustin, Gaspar, 201
Despujol, Eulogio, 50, 76, 87, 90
de Tavera, Joaquin Pardo, 51, 53
de Tavera, Trinidad Pardo, 22–27, 30, 50–51, 53, 67
de Unamuno, Miguel, 6, 20–28, 30
de Veyra, Jaime, 100
de Viana, Augusto, 29
Diah, B.M., 152, 167
Diariong Tagalog, 33, 63, 239

Djajabaja prophecy, 149–50
Djemnah, steamship, 103–04
Dominguez, Rafael, 77
Dominican University of Santo Thomas, 32
Don Quixote, 21, 120
Dutch East Indies, 39–40, 104, 107, 115, 132, 147, 171, 216
Dutch Labour Party, 115

E
Eagle Flight, An, 7, 148
El Amor Patrio, 29, 33, 63
El Filibusterismo, 2, 19, 35, 43–44, 48, 50, 76, 78–79, 89, 101, 106, 120, 133, 196, 208
Epistolario Rizalino, 237, 238
errors, types of, 6
Espana en Filipinas, 8, 9, 47
Evangelista, Crisanto, 134
Evangelista, Edilberto, 91, 138–39

F
Far Eastern Economic Review, 220
Farish A. Noor, 196, 202, 211–12, 233
Fast, Jonathan, 230
Feria, Dolores, 23
"field of battle", letter, 9, 13, 35
Filipino colony, 48, 84
Filipino Malay identity, 55, 59
  see also Malay
Fili, see *El Filibusterismo*
"First Filipino, The", essay, 1, 47
Flitch, J.E. Crawford, 30
Flores, Ambrosio, 84
Font, Salvador, 85
Foreman, John, 111–13, 132, 223
Fort Santiago, prison, 15–16, 36, 38, 87–88

Foulcher, Keith, 217–18
Francesco, Irineo, 84
Francia, Benito, 83
Franco, Domingo, 84
Frank Cass publishing house, 193
Free Indonesia Asrama (Asrama Indonesia Merdeka), 152
Freemasonry, 64
"Friendly Estimate of the Filipinos, A", essay, 29

G
Gaceta de Manila, 36
Gamal Abdel Nasser, 181
Gasset, Jose Ortega y, 30
Gellner, Ernest, 193
Generation of '98, 20
"German doctor, the", 34
Gil, Mariano, 112
Gom-Bur,Za, execution, 32, 53
Gomez, Mariano, 32, 53, 177
Greater East Asia (*Asia Timoer Raja*), 144
Guerrero, Leon Ma., 47, 52, 74, 167, 208, 244
Guevara, Antonino, 245
Guided Democracy, 178
Gunseikanbu, Japanese military administration, 143, 147

H
"*halfbloed*", 114
Hall, D.G.E., 214
Heartbeat of Indonesian Revolution, The, 159
Hero of the Filipinos, The, 148
Het Nieuws van den Dag, 108
Het Tijdschrift, 40, 111–12
Hidalgo, Felix Resurreccion, 33, 120, 237

Hidalgo, Manuel, 47, 239
Hikayat Hang Tuah, 207, 211–12
Hispanization of the Philippines, The, 201
History of One of the Initiators of the Filipino Revolution, 39, 90
History of Southeast Asia, A, 214
History of the Philippines, A, 18–19, 29
Huk rebellion, 25
History of the *War for Philippine Independence*, 39

I
Ibn Batuta, 107
Ibrahim Haji Yaacob, 41, 232
Idrus, 157–58
Ileto, Reynaldo, 19, 129
Imagined Communities, 44
Indian Congress Party, 213
Indian National Congress, 109
Indios Bravos, 35, 56, 65, 68
Indische Bond, 39, 114–15
Indische Partij, 114, 116, 119
Indolence of the Filipinos, see On the Indolence of the Filipinos
Indonesia
  independence, 169
  Japanese occupation, 144–51, 225, 232
  nationalism, 114, 119, 150, 216, 220, 232
  see also Sukarno
Indonesia Accuses, 174, 176, 185–86
Indonesian Revolution, 156–57, 221, 231, 233
Indonesia Raya, anthem, 150
instructive error, 6, 18
Intellectuals in Developing Societies, 44, 190, 192–95, 210

INDEX 275

International Conference on Jose Rizal and the Asian Renaissance, 45
Iron Curtain, 232
Isla de Panay, 87
I-Stories, The, 29

J
Jacinto, Emilio, 125
Jaena, Graciano Lopez, 8–9, 35, 91
Jagor, Feodor, 47
Jakarta Museum, 146, 249
Japanese expansionism, 110
Japanese military administration, Gunseikanbu, 143, 147
Japanese occupation
  Indonesia, 144–51, 225, 232
  Philippines, 144
Jarvis, Helen, 42, 129, 132, 224
Jaures, Jean, 6, 11–12, 186–87
Java Bode, 38, 109
Joaquin, Nick, 86, 250
Jones, Howard, 176
Jose Protasio Rizal: Pelopor Kemerdekaan Bangsa Pilipina (Pioneer of Philippine Independence), 42
Jose Rizal National Centennial Commission, 67, 197, 237

K
Kahin, George, 146
Kalayaan, 8, 89, 102
Kalaw, Teodoro M., 125, 237
Katipunan and the Revolution, The, 102
Katipunan, revolutionary organization, 9, 36–37, 43, 83–84, 87–91, 94–98, 100–02, 122–25, 130–31, 137, 224, 241
  membership grades, 126, 141

Karl, Rebecca, 214
Kartilyang Makabayan, 40, 122–23, 134
Kerkvliet, Melinda Tria, 138–39
Kessler, Clive, 202
Kidlat Club, 35–56
Kleden, Ignas, 153
Kobayashi, Ichizo, 149–50
Koiso Declaration, 41, 145, 151
Koiso, Kuniaki, 151
Kratoska, Paul, 214

L
labour movement, 123, 127
labour sector divisions, 139
Lacy, Allen, 30
La Liga Filipina, 7–8, 36, 48, 78, 83–84, 90, 124, 133–34, 208
La Masonizacion de Filipinas – Rizal y su obra, 26
Lane, Max, 188, 215–16, 220, 222, 229–30
Laong Laan, pseudonym, 3
La Politica de Espana en Filipinas, 37, 73–74
La Revolucion Filipina, 7–8, 11, 13
La Solidaridad, 1–3, 7–11, 18–19, 35, 46, 59, 64–66, 73, 76–77, 90–91, 195, 248
Lapian, Adrian, 109–10
La Publicidad, 62
Laurel, Jose P., 42, 145, 164
Laurel, Salvador, 231
La Vida de Don Quijote y Sancho, 21
Legge, John, 147
LeRoy, James, 113
Life, Lineage and Labours of Jose Rizal, 52
Liga Filipina *see La Liga Filipina*
Linggajati Agreement, 171

Liukkonen, Petri, 30
Llorente, Julio, 46, 64
Locomotief, 115
Lolo Jose, 13, 17
London Review of Books, 1
Lopez-Morillas, Frances, 30
Lopez Museum, 237
Lopez-Rizal, Leoncio, 57–58
Lozano, Martin Constantino, 84
Lucas, Henri, 12
Lumbera, Bienvenido, 127–28
Luna, Antonio, 13, 80, 83, 248
Luna, Juan, 33

M
Mabini, Apolinario, 6–11, 18, 38, 50, 66, 80, 84, 90, 131, 225, 240
Macaraig, Serafin E., 29
MacArthur, Douglas, 144, 165, 188
Madiun rebellion, 171
Maeda, Tadashi, 152
Magsaysay Award, 220
Majlis, newspaper, 41
Malay
  feudal period, 207
  identity, 54–56
  nationalism, 232
  of the Philippines, 54
  see also Filipino Malay identity; Malay *under* Rizal, Jose
Malay, Armando, 101
Malay Ideas on Development: From Feudal Lord to Capitalist, 210
Malay, Paula Carolina, 102
Maloles, Eustacio, 93
Malolos Congress, 92, 100
Manahan, Jacinto, 139–40
Manifestation of 1888, 34
Manifesto to Certain Filipinos, 80–81
Marcos, Ferdinand, 188

Marias, Julian, 30
Marques, Lourenco Pereira, 4
Marxism, 25, 224
"Masjoemi" Muslim association, 144
Masturah Alatas, 190–91, 193
Max Havelaar, 31, 35, 68, 105–07, 120
M. Balfas, 157
Medina, Elizabeth, 86
Meiji restoration, 214
Mendez, Paz Policarpio, 120
Mendoza, Antonio Guevara y, 39, 90
Mercado, Jose Rizal, *see* Rizal, Jose
Merdeka, weekly, 152, 158, 167
"mestizo", 130–31, 232
Meyer, A.B., 107
Mojare, Resil, 230
Mojica, Diego, 128
Montjuich prison, 38, 87
Michels, F.W., 43
"Mi Ultimo Adios", poem, 38, 42–43, 45, 99–100, 127–28, 145, 208, 231
  translation, 147–48, 156, 164, 169, 249–53
Mohammad Hatta, 143, 158, 171, 181
Mrazek, Rudolf, 132, 142
Muhammad Iqbal, 45
Muijzenberg, Otto van den, 108–10
Multatuli, 31, 35, 56, 68, 104–07, 110
"My Plan to Save Rizal", 98
Myth of the Lazy Native, The, 44, 190, 192, 194–96, 202, 210

N
Nacionalista Party, 138–39
Nationalist Consciousness Movement, *see* ALIRAN
"National Reawakening Day", 173
National University of Singapore, 191

Nahuijs, Baron Alphonse, 31, 105
Natividad, Mamerto, 83
"new Kalamba", 84
New Order, 226
New York Times, 113
New York Times Magazine, 226
Nieva, Gregorio, 22
Nieuwe Rotterdamsche Courant, 108
Noli Me Tangere, 1, 3–5, 7–8, 12–14, 17–20, 29–30, 33–34, 43–44, 47–48, 51, 53, 65, 70–71, 75, 78–79, 89, 101, 104–05, 120, 133, 148, 196, 220, 237

O
Ocampo, Nilo S., 60–62, 68
Ongjunco, Doroteo, 36
On the Indolence of the Filipinos, 194, 199–201, 204, 212
Ordonez, Elmer A., 250
Out of Exile, 146

P
Paget, Roger, 176, 185
Panca Sila, 178, 185
Panganiban, Jose Ma., 91
Paris Exposition, 35, 56
Partai Komunis Indonesia, 136
Partido Komunista sa Pilipinas (PKP), 139
Partido Obrero (Workers' Party), 138
Pastells, Pablo, 14, 26, 72, 82, 168
Paterno, Pedro, 24, 67
Pembangoen (The Builder), periodical, 178
pernicious error, 6, 20
"people power", 231
Phelan, John Leddy, 201

Philippine-American War, 57, 91–92
Philippine Centennial Commission, 231
Philippine Islands, The, 111, 113, 223
Philippine republic, 42
Philippine Republic, The, 19
Philippine Review, 22
Philippine Revolution, 101, 117, 232
Philippine Revolution, The, 125
Philippines Free Press, 29
Philippines
   ceded to the United States, 92
   independence, 165–66
   Japanese occupation, 144
PKP (Partido Komunista sa Pilipinas), 139
Plata, Teodoro, 84
"Poetry and the Revolution (1882–1898)", 127
Ponce, Mariano, 4, 9, 39, 48, 52–53, 58, 60–63, 65–66, 85
Portillo, Luis, 30
Pramoedya Anantar Toer, 45, 61, 104, 109, 119–20, 188, 214–15, 219–28, 230, 233
Private World: Selections from the Diario Intimo and Selected Letters, The, 21, 30
Proletarian Labor Congress of the Philippines, 139
Propaganda, campaign, 2, 7–8, 11, 13, 29, 35, 46–47, 50, 61, 90–91, 93
Propaganda Movement, The, 47

Q
Quezon, Manuel L., 129, 183
Quibuyen, Floro, 93, 102

R

Radio Pemberontakkan (Radio of Revolt), 157
Ramirez Printing Press, 15
Ramlah Adam, 232
Razif Bahari, 218, 226
"Rd. L. M.", secret society, 35, 50, 53, 56–58, 64–65, 68, 108
"Redemption of the Malay Race", 58
"*Redencion de los Malayos*", 58, 68
Regidor, Antonio Ma., 49–53, 67–68, 107
Reid, Anthony, 55
Religion of the Katipunan, The, 230
Renville Agreement, 171
Retana, Wenceslao, 6, 20–25, 27, 37, 52, 72–76, 83, 85–86, 108, 121, 208
Revista Filipina, 22
Revolt of the Masses, The, 20, 30, 43, 141
Revolution of the Filipinos Against the Spanish, 88
Revolution, The, 60
Rhodes, Sir Cecil, 109
Ricarte, Artemio, 40–41, 87–90, 99–102
Richardson, Jim, 138, 230
Riego, Perfecto Rufino, 29
"Rights of Man, The", 60
Rizal: Contrary Essays, 23
"Rizal Day", 38, 43, 92–93, 243
"Rizaline Republic", 40, 101
Rizal, Jose
 biography, 5, 16–17, 34
 born, 31
 chronology, 31–45
 diaries, 28, 80, 103
 Europe, in, 2–5, 18, 36, 47, 62, 65, 75–76, 86, 103, 107
 execution, 90–92, 97–100, 108–09, 112, 116, 120–21, 125, 133
 exile, 8–9, 11, 49, 87, 112, 125
 family, 115
 Hong Kong, in, 9–10, 12–13
 leadership, 11
 letters, 17, 29, 72, 105, 107, 167–68, 237–41, 247–48
 Malay, and, 54–59, 153–55, *see also* Malay
 martyrdom, 92–94, 204
 projects, and, 46–48
 prosecution, 75–78
 pseudonym, 3
 Spain, in, 32–33
 Tagalog, and, 60–67
Rizal Monument, 39
Rizal, Paciano, 32, 53, 69, 90, 97–99, 112, 177, 241
Rizal, Saturnina, 52
Rizal's Life and Minor Writings, 53
"Rizal: The Tagalog Hamlet", 24
Robledo, Francisco Romero, 86
Rodriguez, E.B., 148
Rodriguez, Jose, 70–71, 85
Romulo, Carlos P., 165, 180, 183, 188
Roots of Dependency, 230
Rosihan Anwar, 7, 42–43, 45, 143, 145–48, 151–54, 156, 158–60, 164, 166–67, 169–70, 173, 180, 183, 188, 231–32, 249–53
Roxas, Baldomero, 56, 58
Roxas, Francisco, 86
Roxas, Manuel, 164
Royal Netherlands Academy of Sciences, 110
Russell, Charles Edward, 148
Russo-Japanese War, 39, 213–14

S

Sabam Siagian, 156, 159–60
Salazar, Zeus, 6, 54

Salvador, Moises, 83
Sandiko, Teodoro, 29
Santos, Lope K., 40, 85, 141
Sarekat Islam, 118–19
Saroyan, William, 220
Schumacher SJ, John, 8, 47, 86, 248
Scott, William Henry, 230
Second World War, 165, 170, 198
Shaharuddin bin Maaruf, 28, 44, 203, 205–10, 212, 233
Shiraishi, Takashi, 118
Sison, Jose Ma., 138
Social Problems, 29
Soerabaiaasch Handelsblad, 115
Soerjo, 161
Soewardi Soerjaningrat, 117
Soli, see La Solidaridad
Spain
   ceded Philippines to the United States, 92
   enemies of, 96
Spanish Civil War, 27
Spanish colonialism, 27
   effect of, 197–98
"Spanish doctor", 9
Staging the World: Chinese Nationalism at the Turn of the Twentieth Century, 214
Steinbeck, John, 220
Straits Times, 191, 206, 210
Sucesos de las Islas Filipinas, 48
Sudirman, General, 207
Suez Canal, 31, 242
Suharto, 221, 226
Sukarno, 11, 28, 41–42, 119, 134, 145, 147, 149–50, 158–59, 162, 171, 181–82, 184–87, 190–91, 203–04, 213, 232
   speech, 172–80, 183, 188
   see also Indonesia

Sukarno and the Struggle for Indonesian Independence, 170
Sun Yat Sen, 185, 203, 216
Surabaja, story, 157
Sutan Ibrahim, 129
Sutan Sjahrir, 146, 149, 152, 159
Sutomo, 134, 224
Syed Farid Alatas, 233
Syed Hussein Alatas, 44, 190, 192–205, 208–10, 212, 233
   born, 191

T
"Tagalog Malay", 55
Tagalog orthography, 77
Tagore, Rabindranath, 45
Tan Malaka, 40, 42, 128–38, 142, 224, 233
Tetcho, Suehiro, 34, 229
The Filipino, 18
Tjahaja Sijang, 120
Tjetje Jusuf, 44
Tjipto Mangoenkoesomo, 117
Tjokroaminoto, 118
Tojo, Hideki, 147, 151
Tolentino, Jose Reyes, 84
Toward the First Asian Republic, 250
Tragic Sense of Life, The, 21, 30
treaty of Biak-na-bato, 92
True Version of the Philippine Revolution, 91
Turot, Henri, 11–12, 186–87

U
Ullmer, Karl, 14, 17
"Ultimo Adios", *see* "Mi Ultimo Adios"
Umar Ibn Khattab, 206–07
UMNO (United Malay National Organisation), 202
Under Three Flags, 19

unfortunate error, 6, 18
United States, Philippines ceded to, 92
Universiti Sains Malaysia, 209
University Central de Madrid, 33
University of Amsterdam, 191
University of California, 18
University of Michigan, 45, 220
University of Salamanca, 20, 30
University of the Philippines, 19
"Un Separatista Filipino – Jose Rizal", 37, 73
U.S. Philippine Commission, 67

V
Valenzuela, Pio, 37, 80, 83, 94, 96–97, 101–02, 125, 136
Vatikiotis, Michael, 220–21
"Veneration without Understanding", 243–44, 246
Veterano, revolutionary fighters, 131
Vida y Escritos, 20
Viola, Maximo, 15, 34, 238, 242
Villa, Simeon, 94
Vincent, Paul, 106

"Viva Espana", 26
von Humbolt, Wilhelm, 55

W
Wallace, Alfred Russel, 55
Waitz, Theodor, 47
Washington Post, 219
Wehl, David, 146
Wildman, Edwin, 113
Wilhemsfeld, vicarage, 14, 17
Wilhelm Tell, 29, 47, 60
Workers' Congress (Congreso Obrero de Filipinas), 134, 138
Workers' Party (Partido Obrero), 138
World War II, *see* Second World War

Y
Yamamoto, Moichiro, 147, 151
Young Turks, 213

Z
Zaide, Gregorio, 60
Zamora, Jacinto, 32, 53, 177

www.ingramcontent.com/pod-product-compliance
Lightning Source LLC
Chambersburg PA
CBHW021355290426
44108CB00010B/253